KAKURO

CROSS SUMS

300 Easy Puzzles

Volume 1

Christian Demarco

COPYRIGHT NOTICE

A big thank you for buying this book, and a personal favor to ask.

If you enjoy this book, would you please spare just a couple of minutes of your time to leave a review on Amazon. It would be greatly appreciated.

Thanks in advance

Christian

CONTENTS

INTRODUCTION

Kakuro puzzles are number puzzles solved in a crossword style grid.

A number above the diagonal line in a black square represents the total of the numbers in the white squares to the right of it; similarly, a number below the diagonal line is the total sum of the digits in the white squares below it.

The white squares can contain any of the digits 1 to 9, however, these digits cannot be repeated more than once in any connected vertical column or horizontal line. For example, if the total number in the black square is 4 and there are 2 white squares, the digits must be 1 and 3, they cannot be 2 and 2.

All puzzles have unique solutions and can be solved using logical methods without guessing.

For your convenience, located at the back of this book is a handy reference which lists target numbers, number of cells and all the possible combinations.

Printable Number combinations can be downloaded from:

http://www.christian-demarco.com/kakuro/

1

2

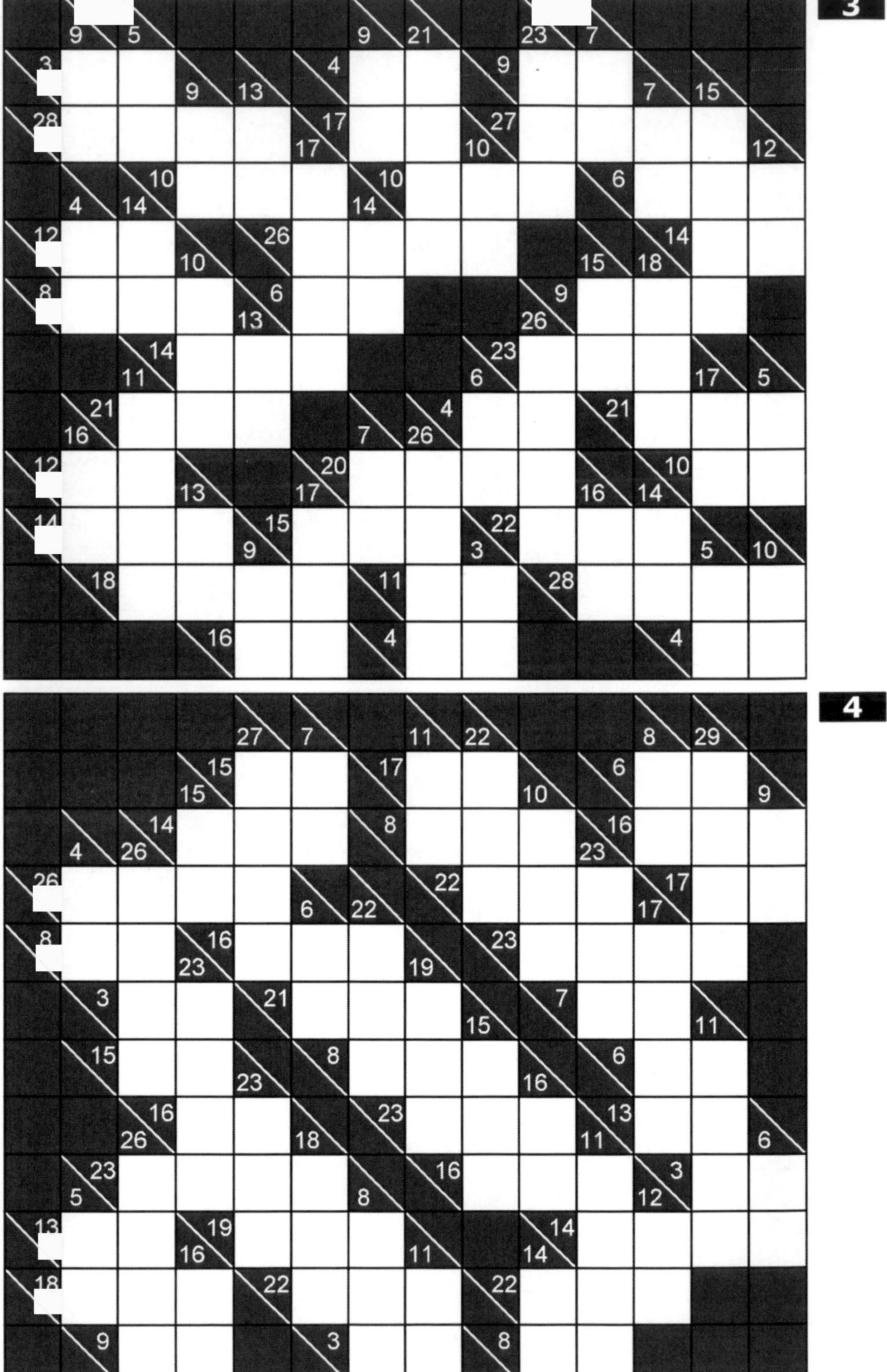
3
4

5

6

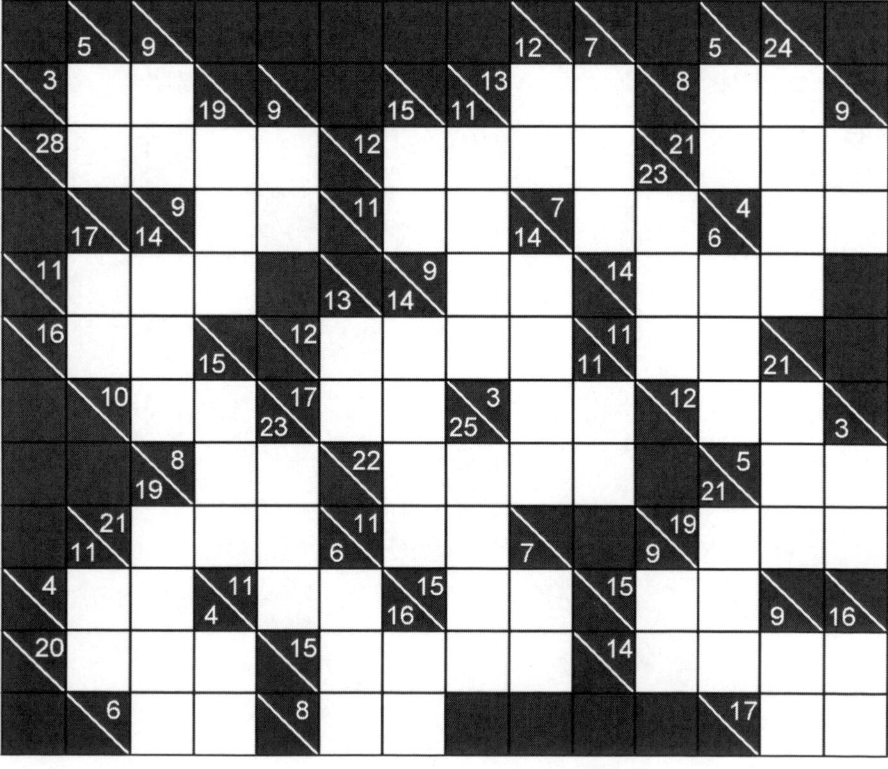

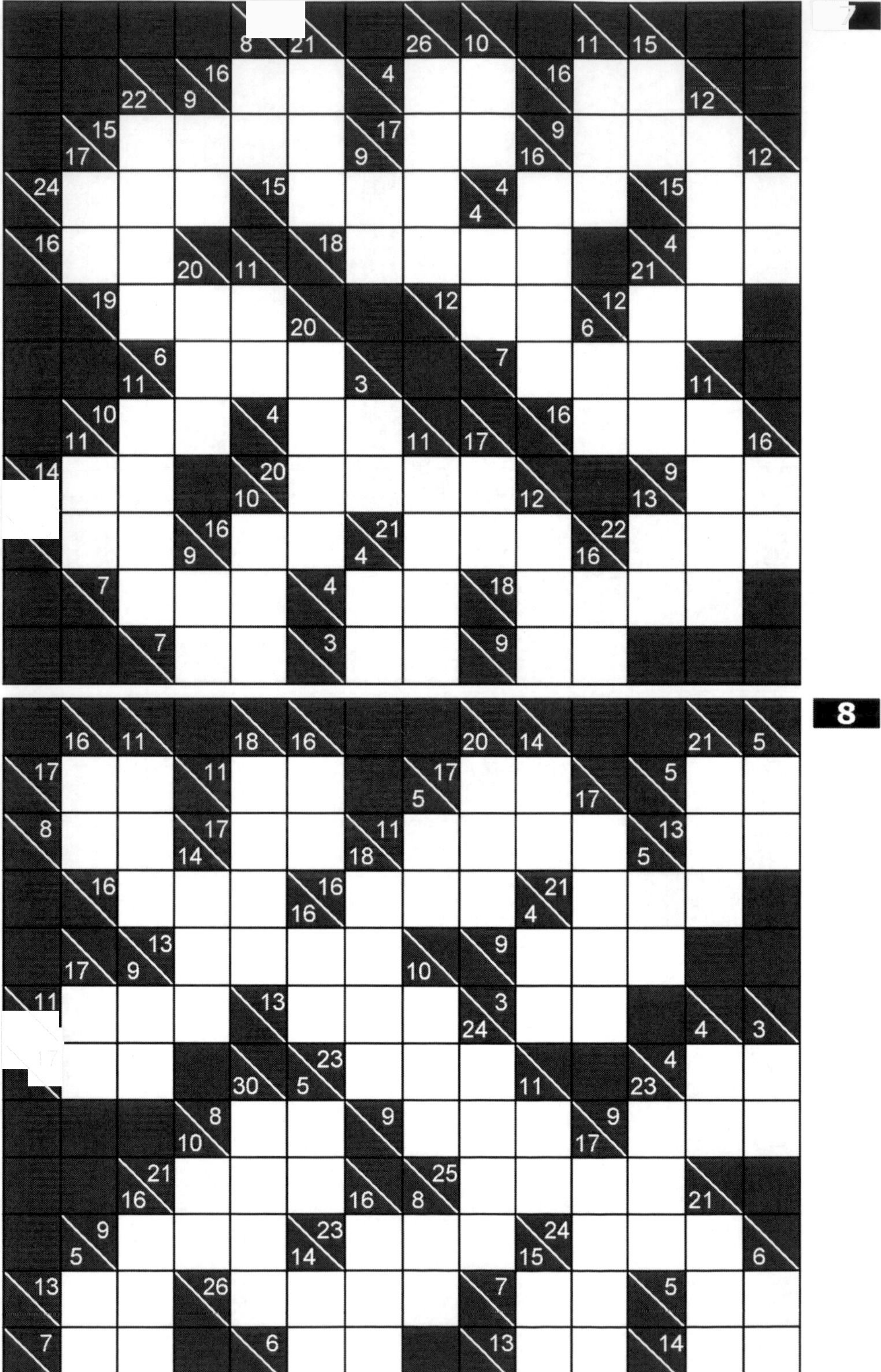

9

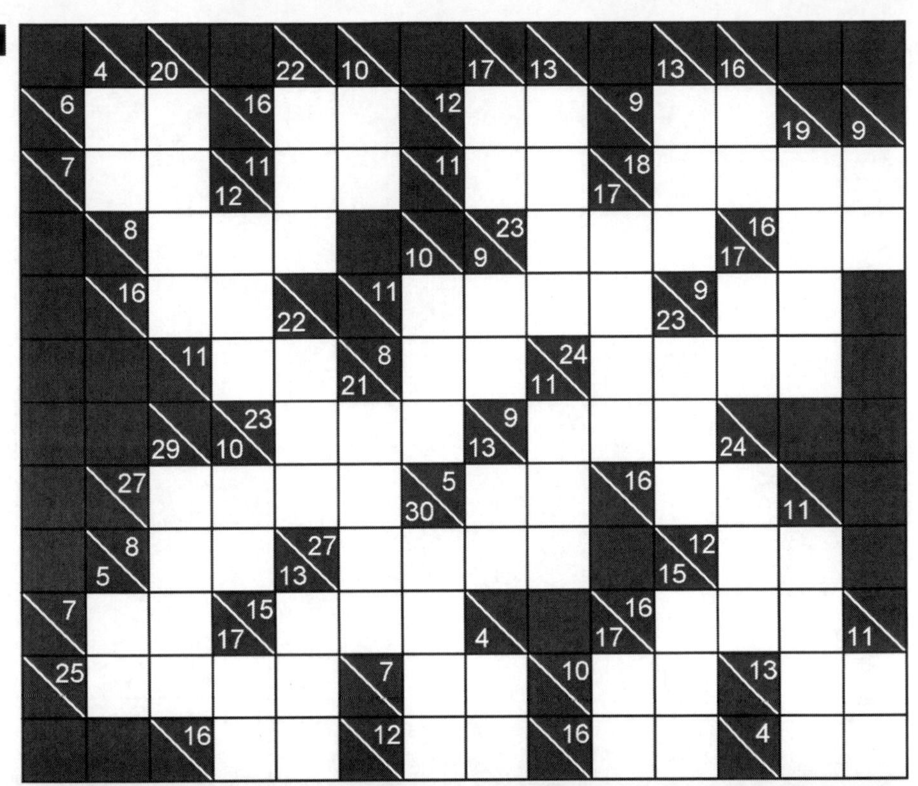

10

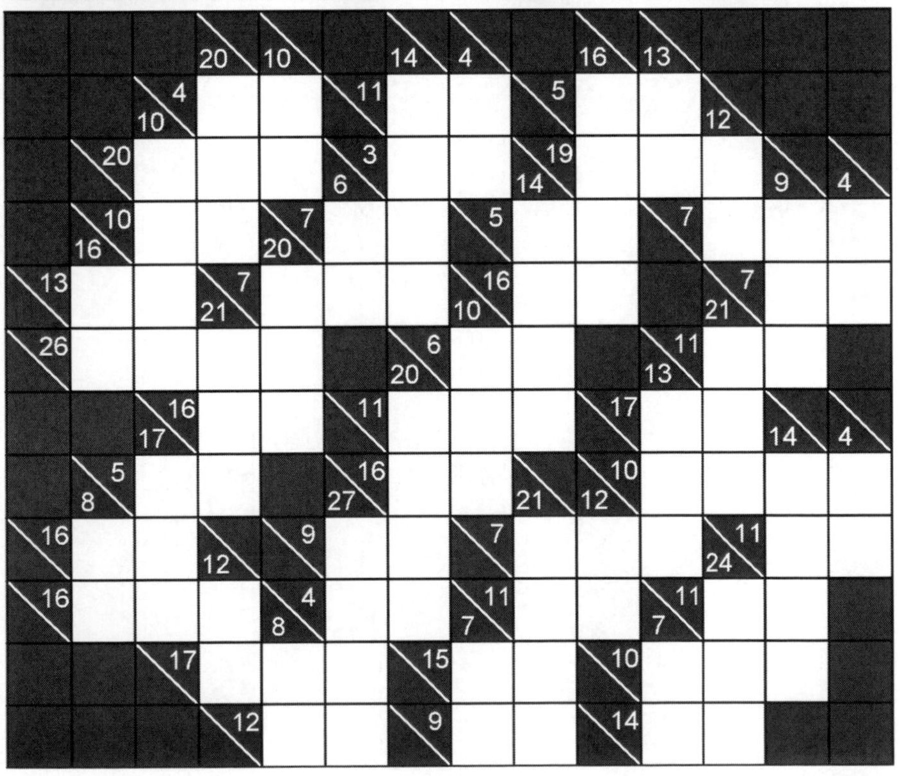

11

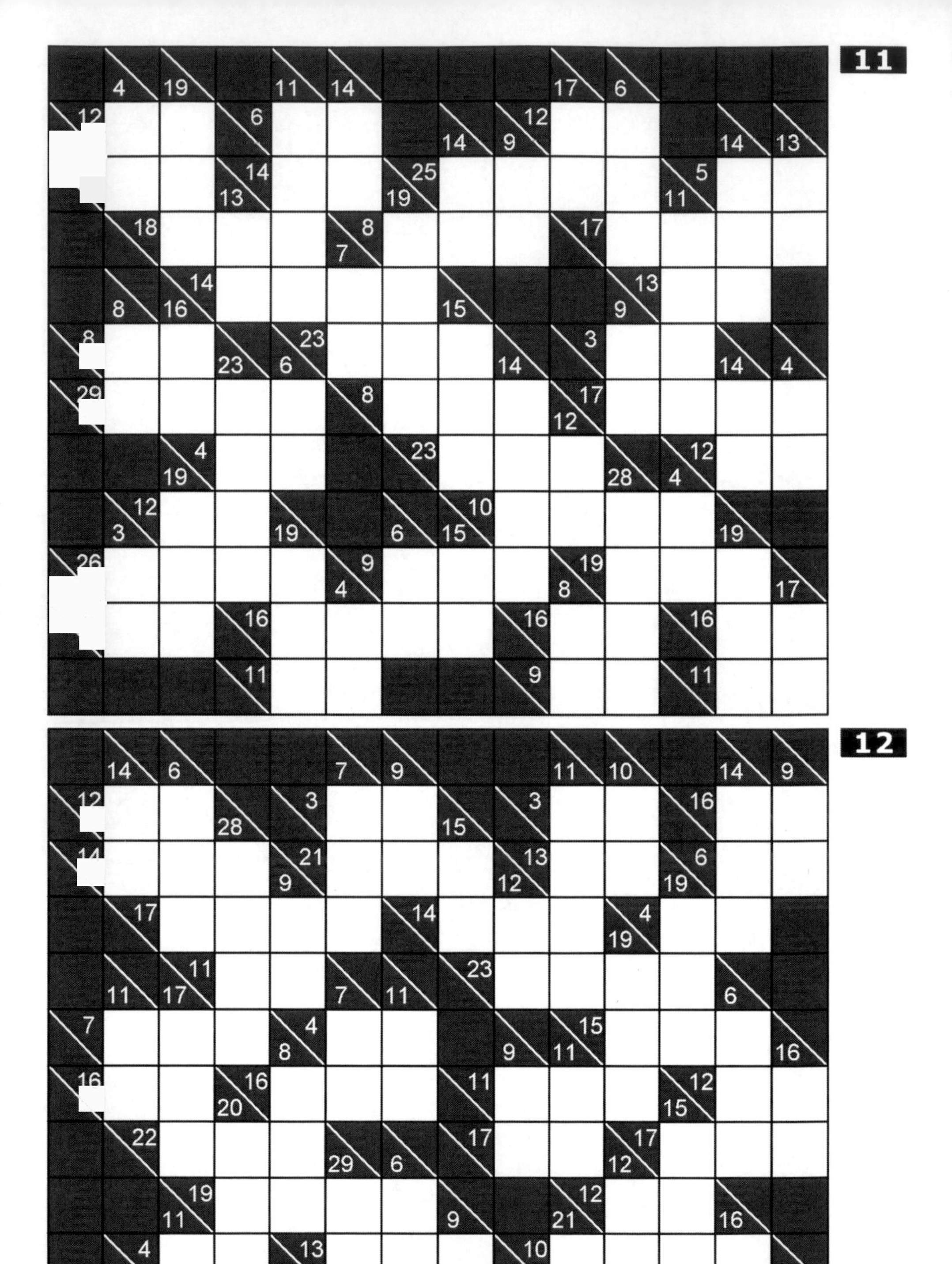

12

13

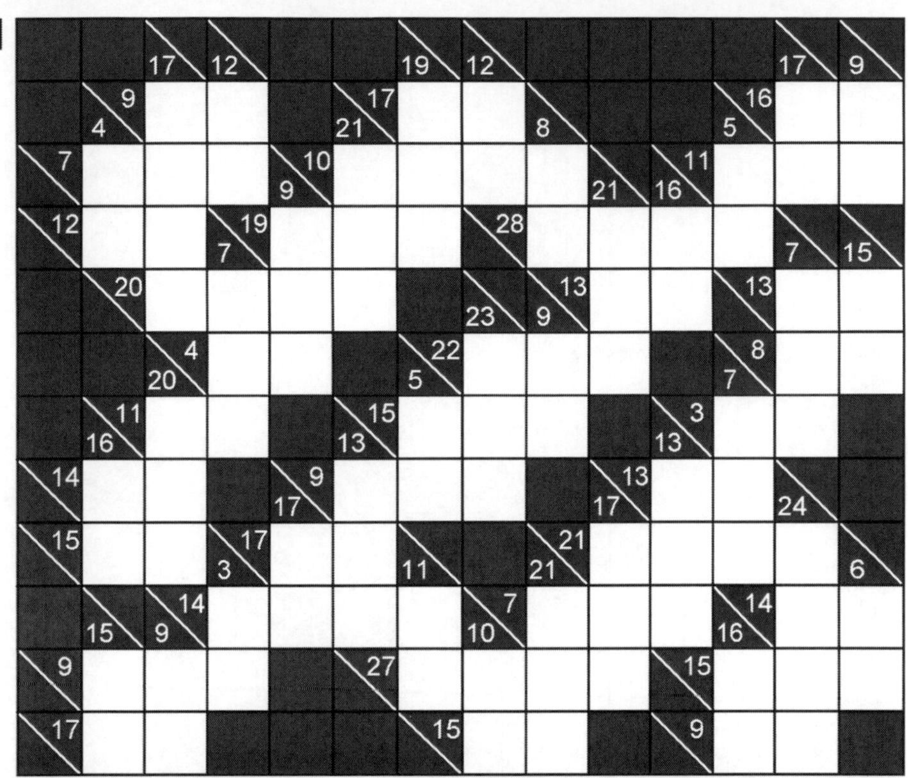

14

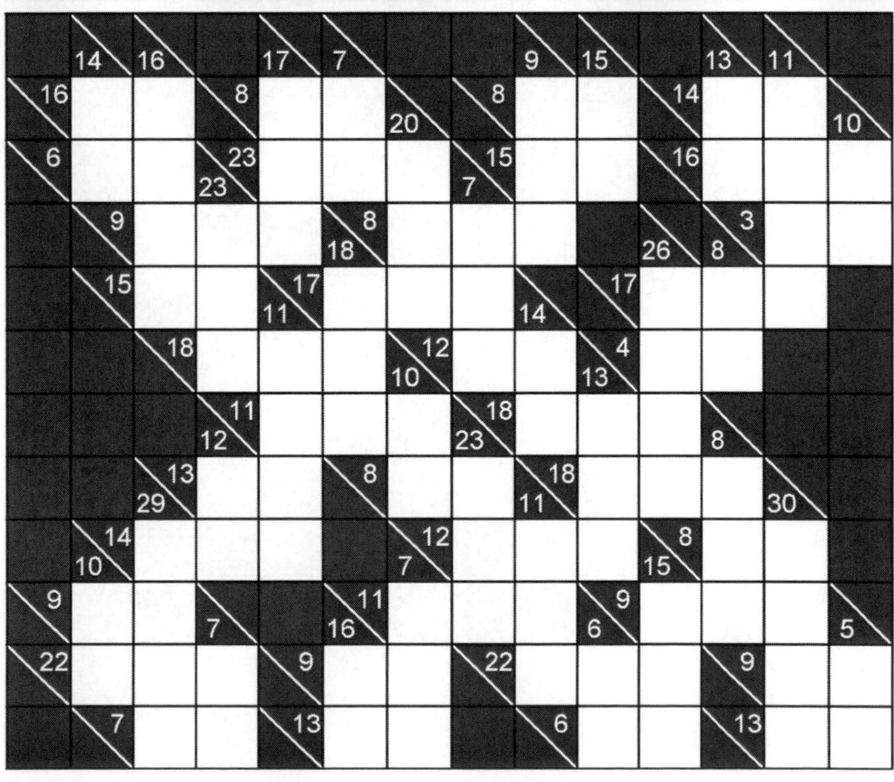

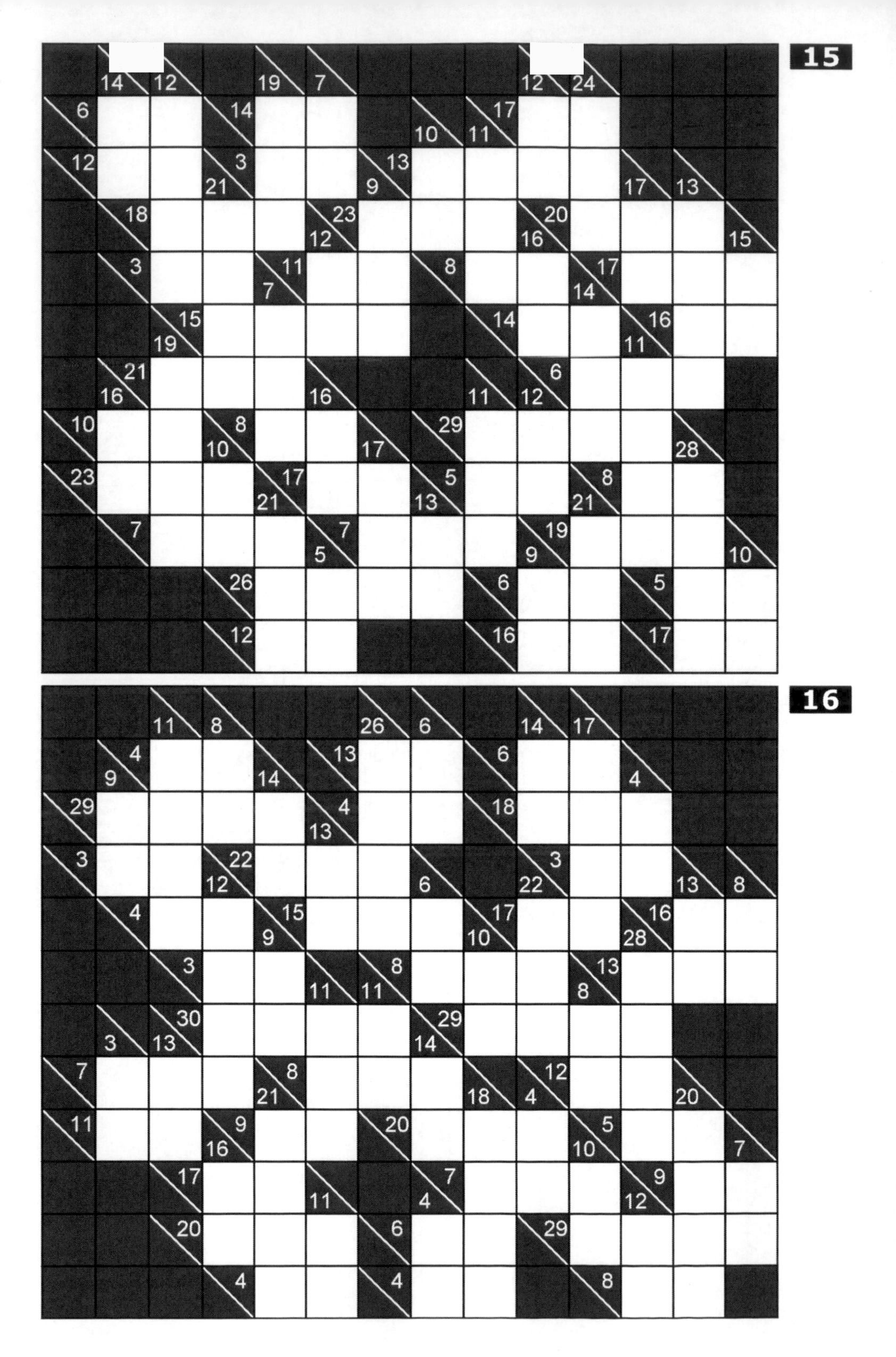
15
16

17

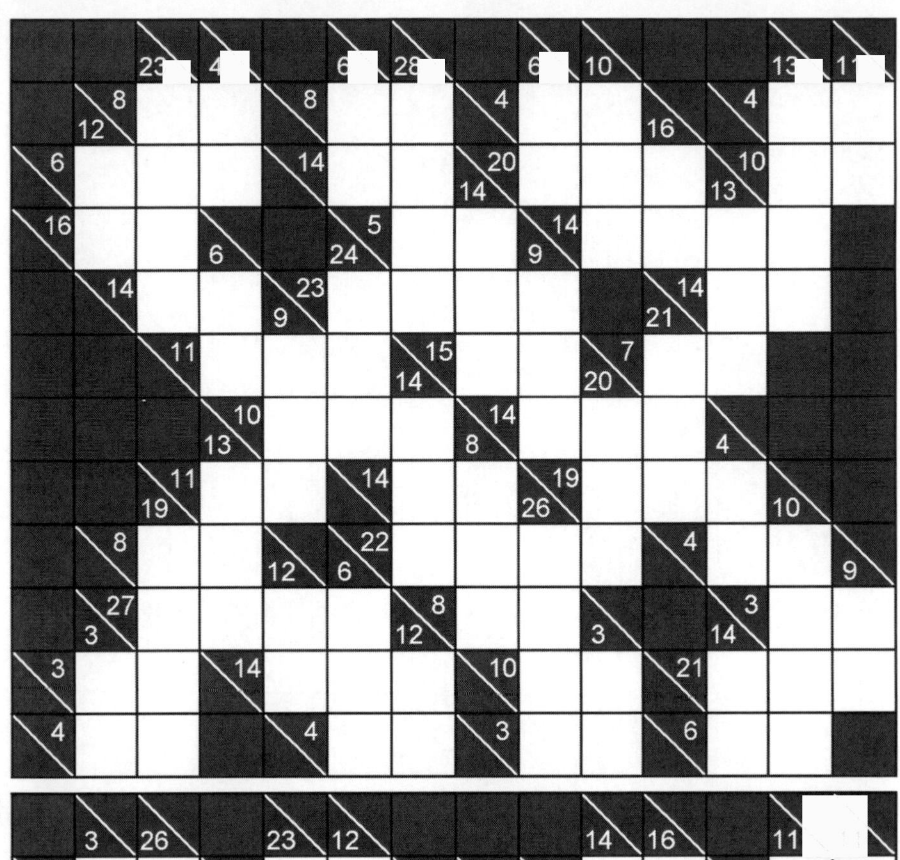

18

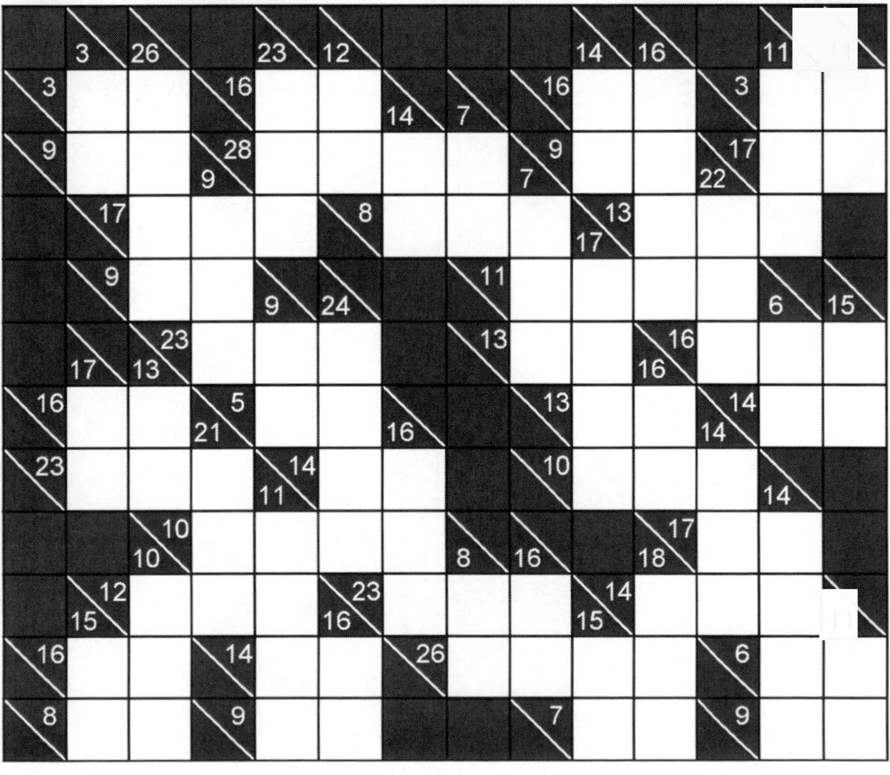

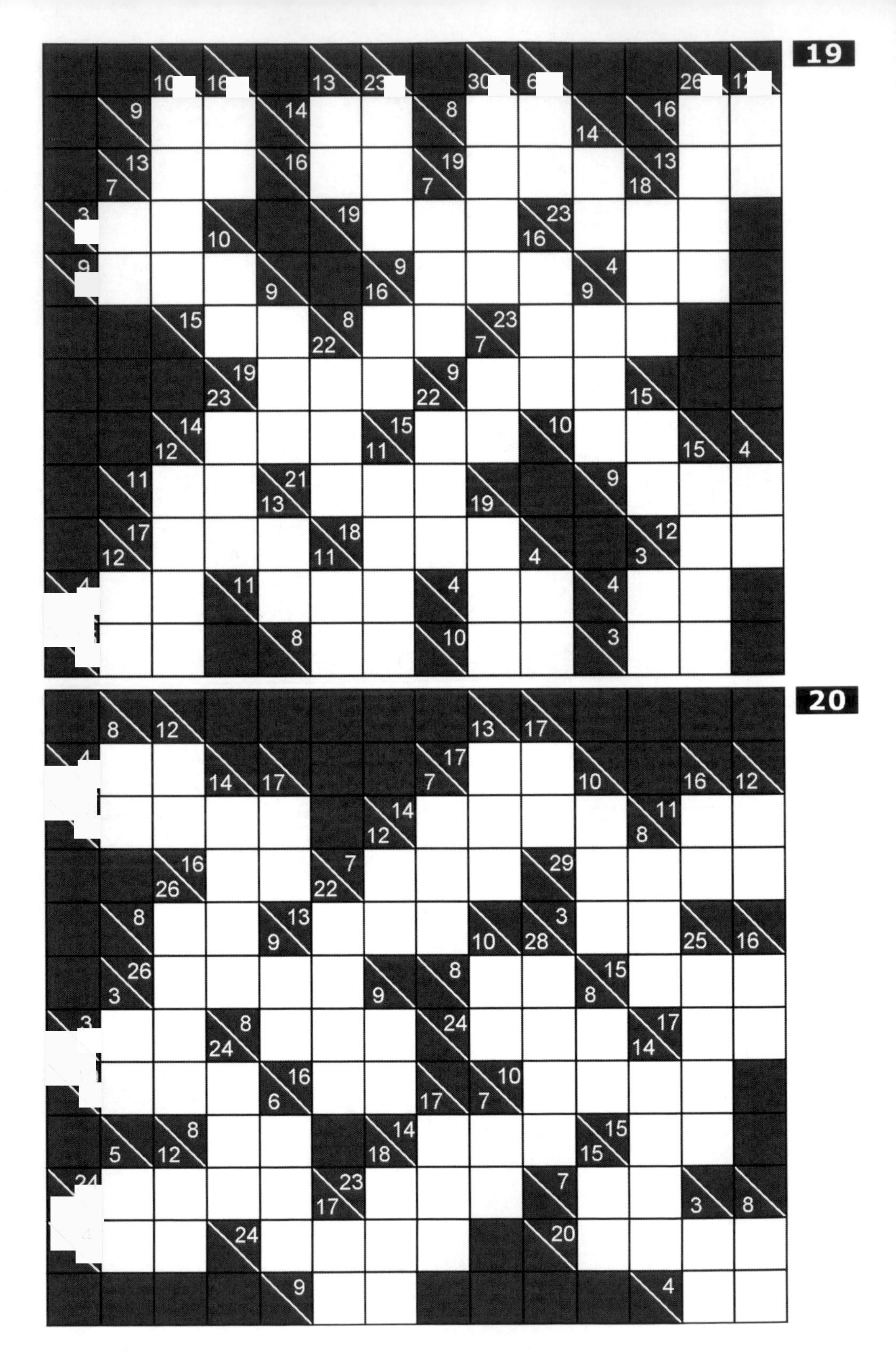

21

22

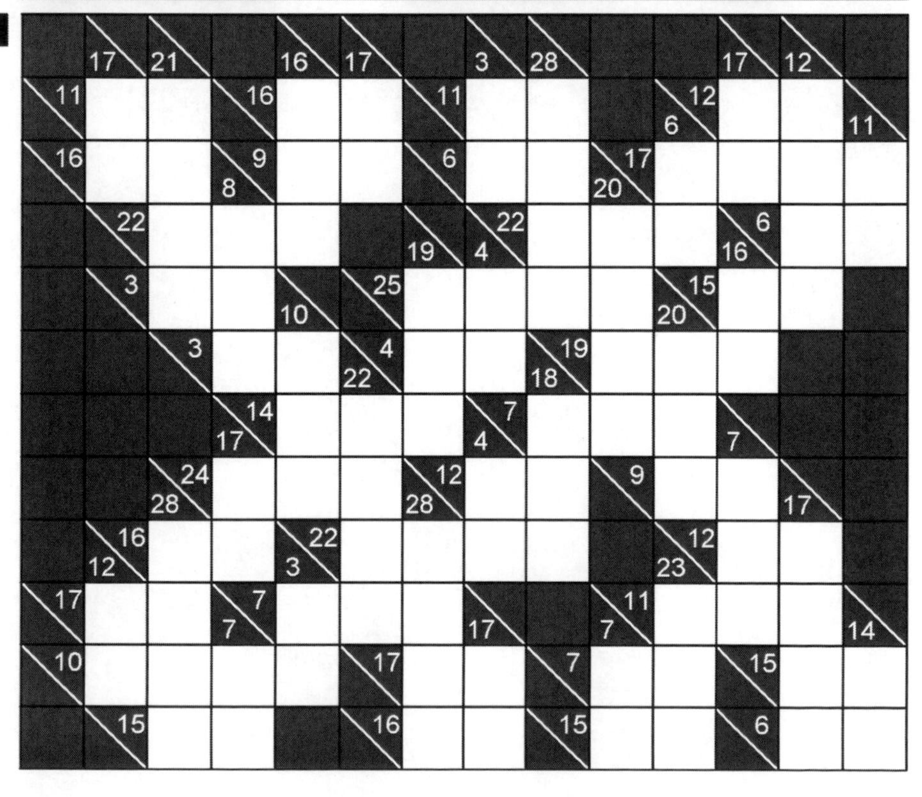

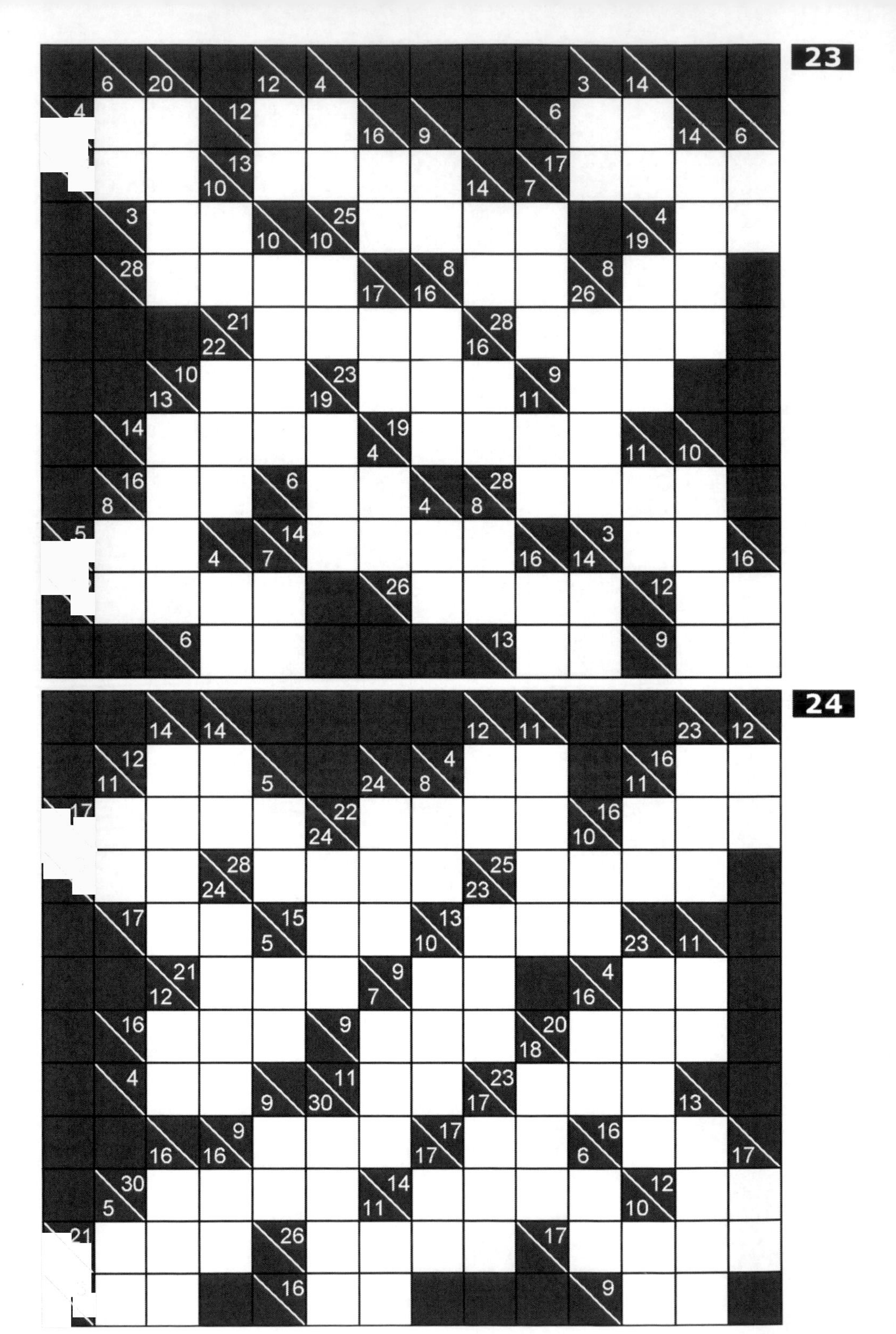
23
24

25

26

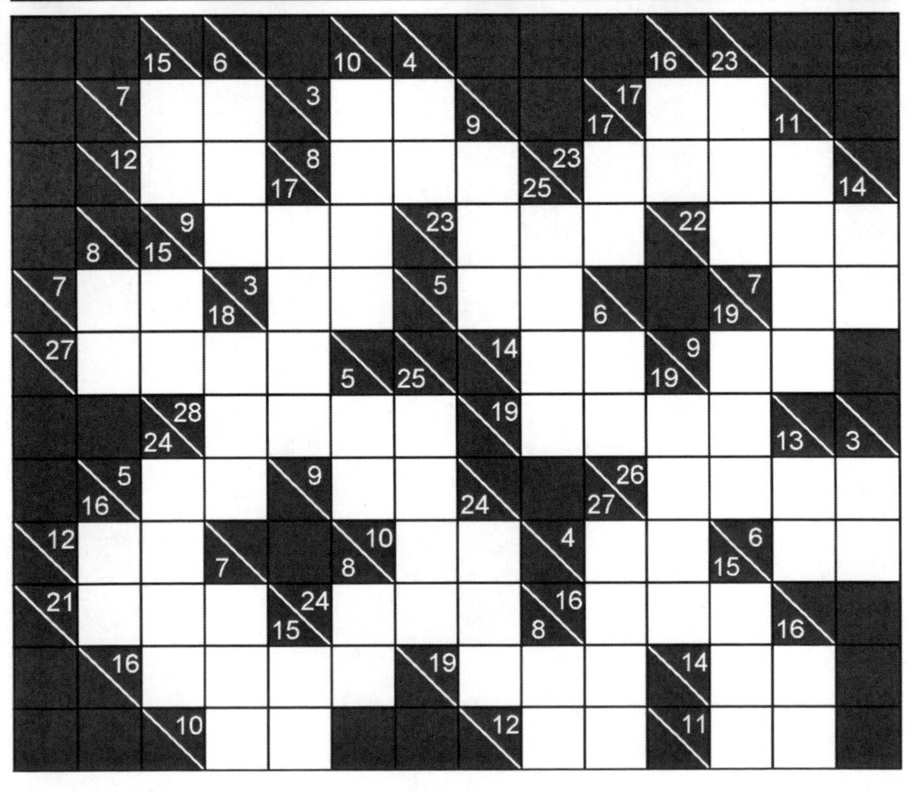

27

28

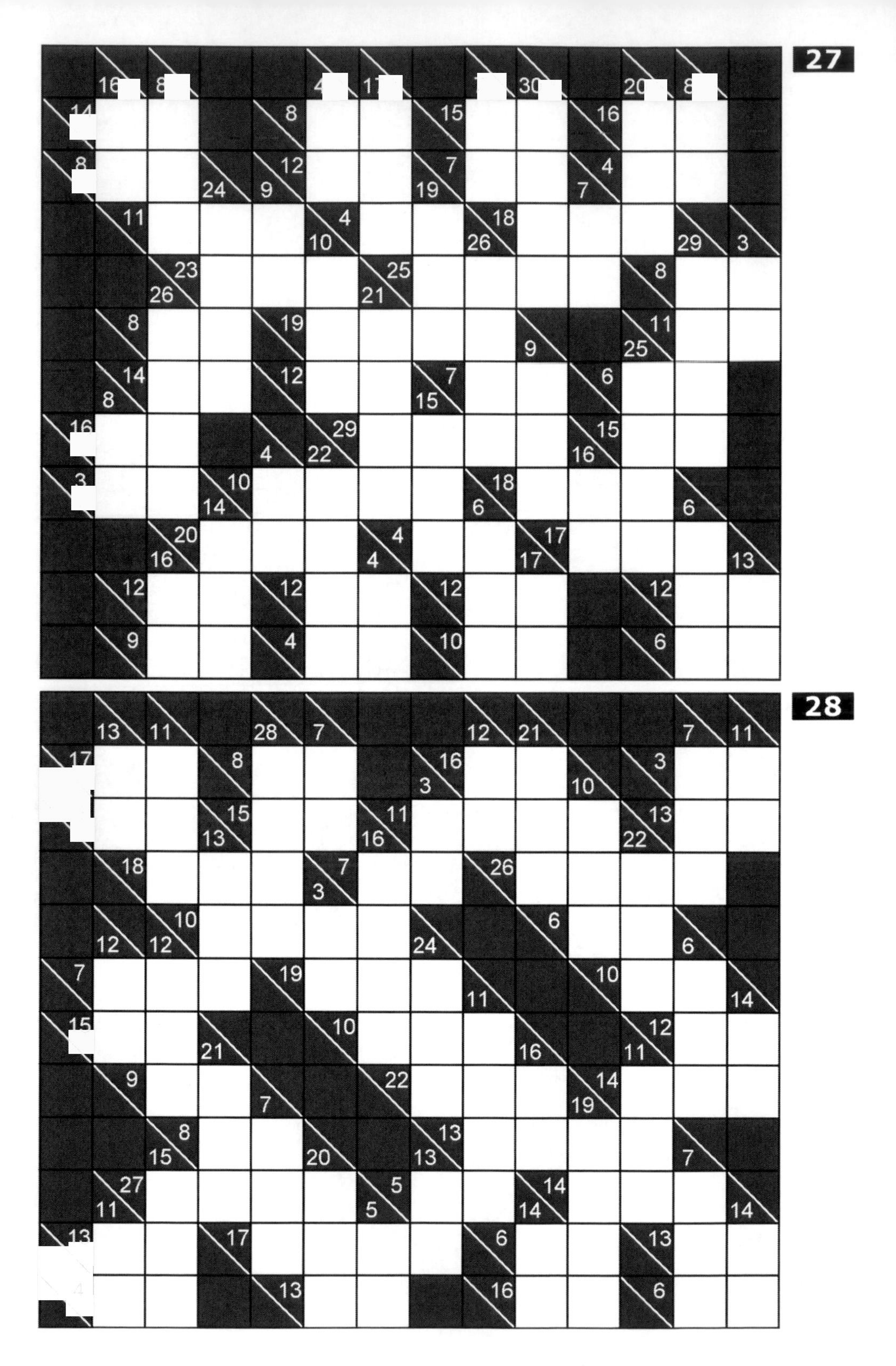

29

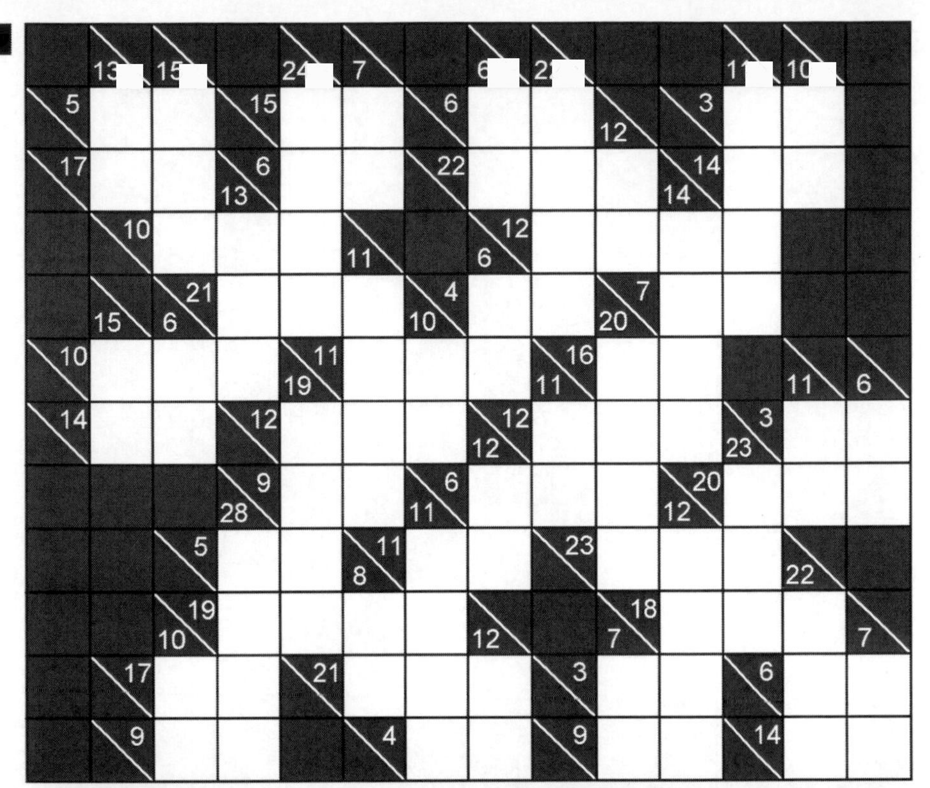

30

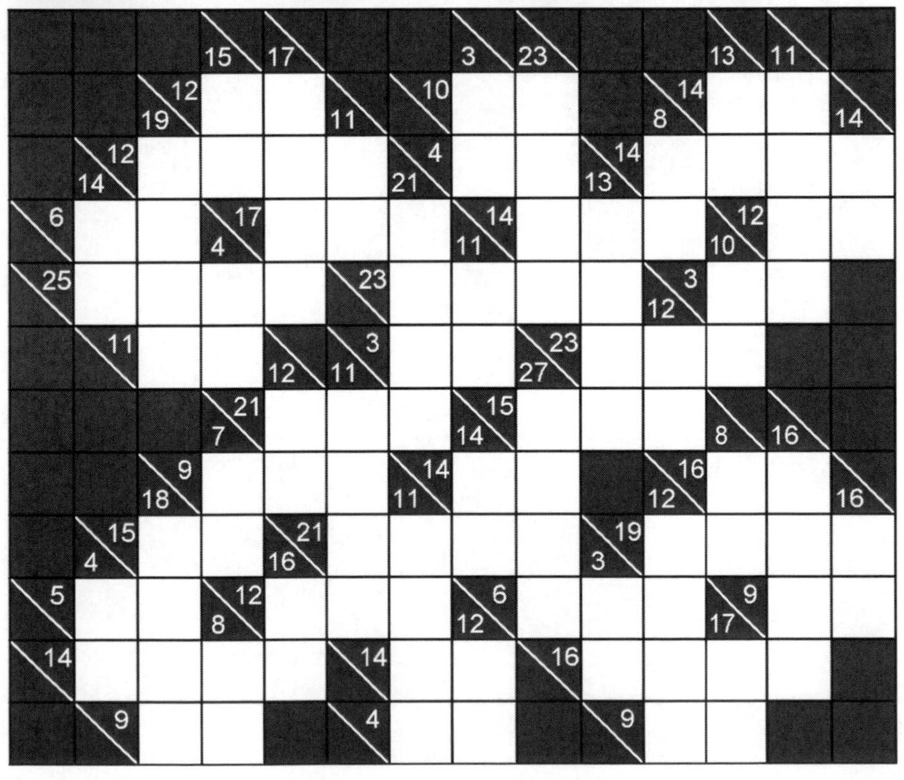

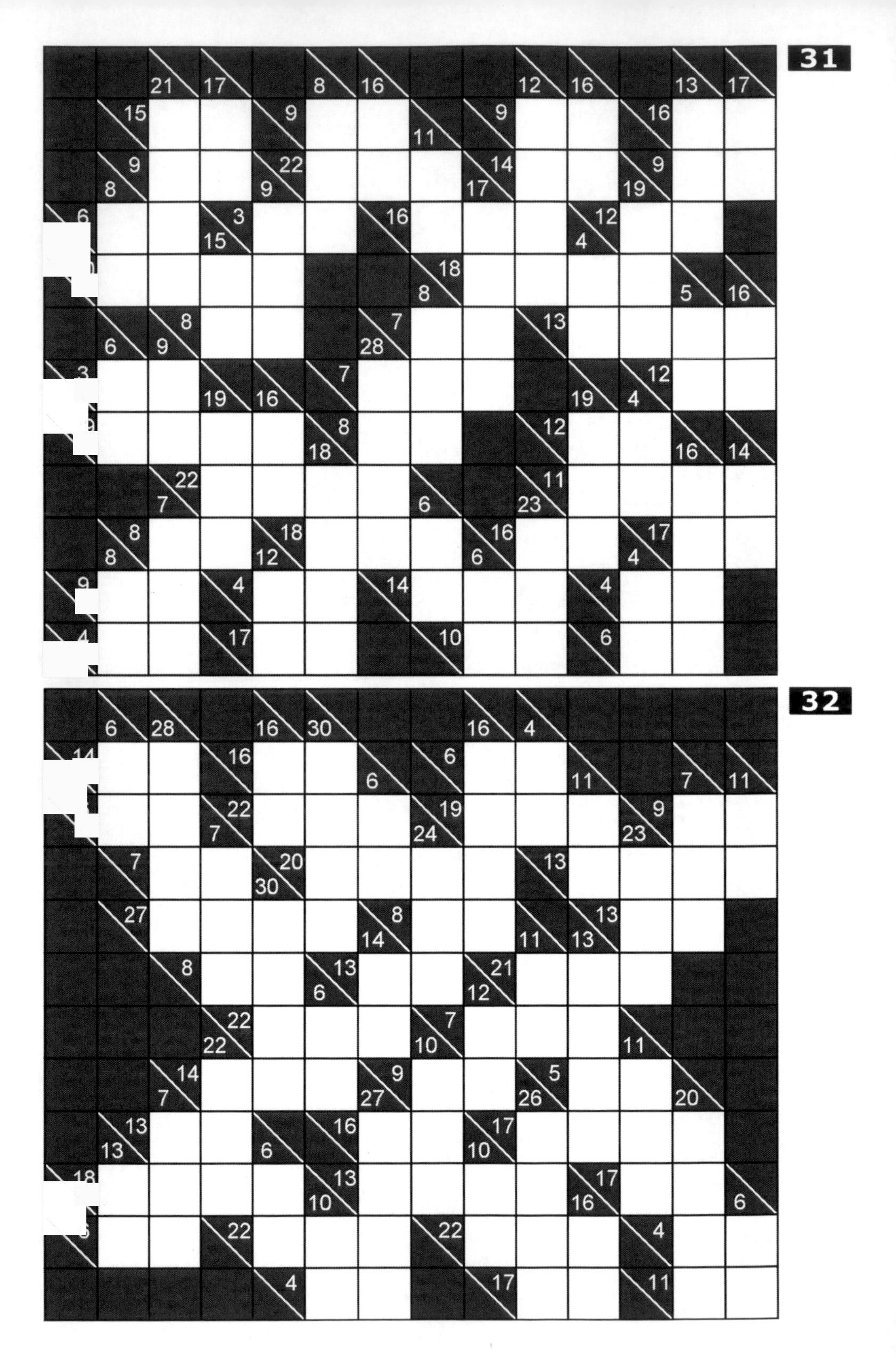
31
32

33

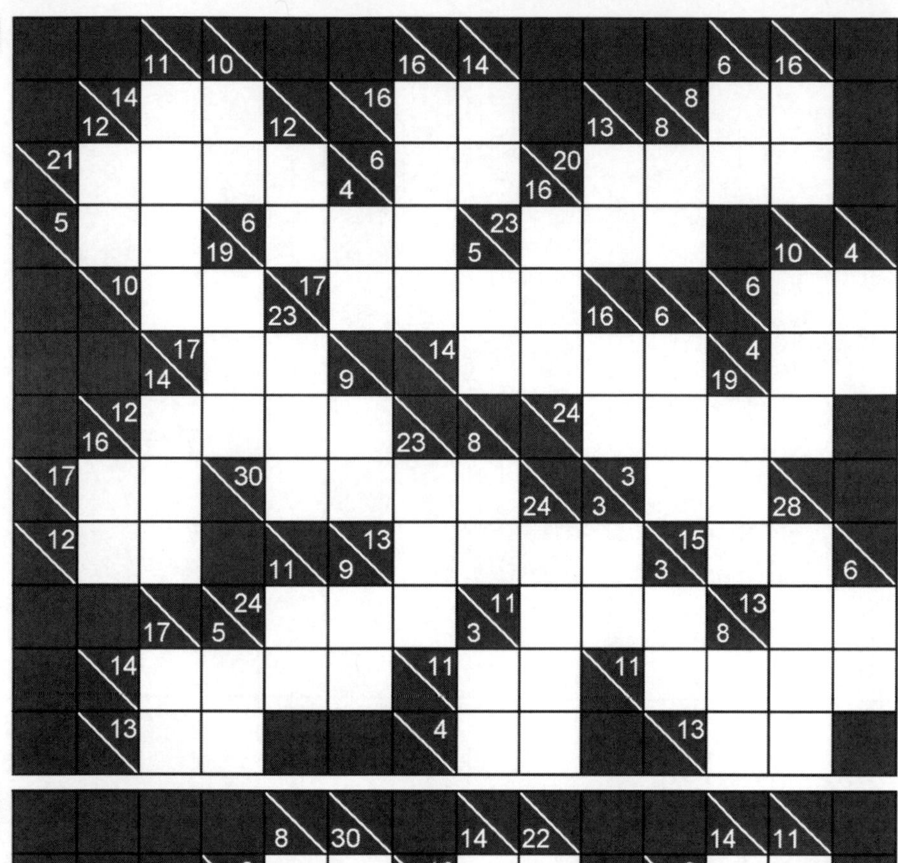

34

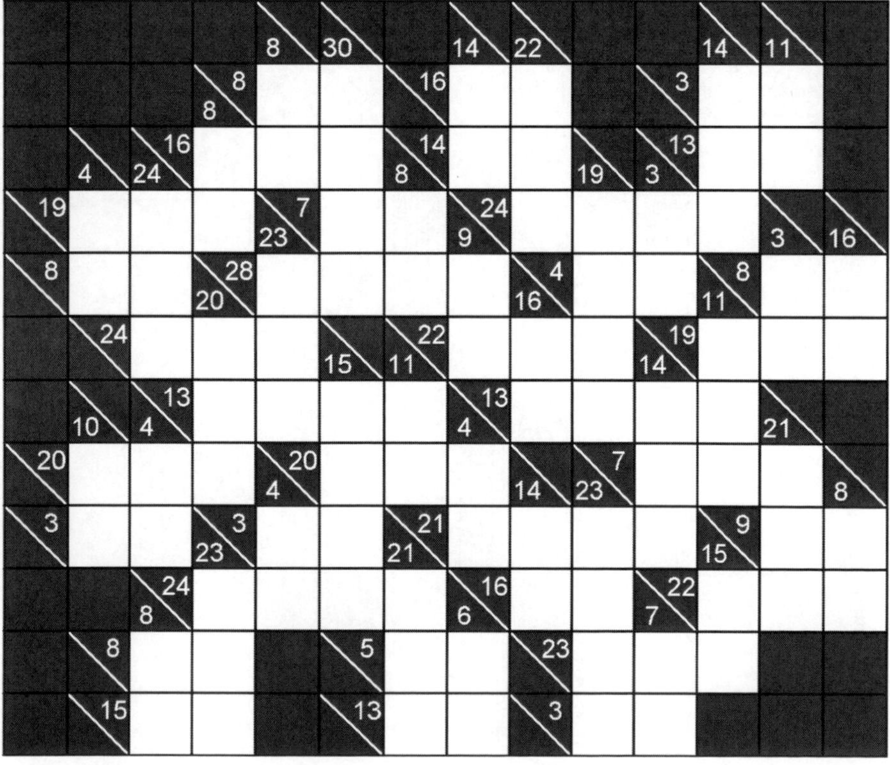

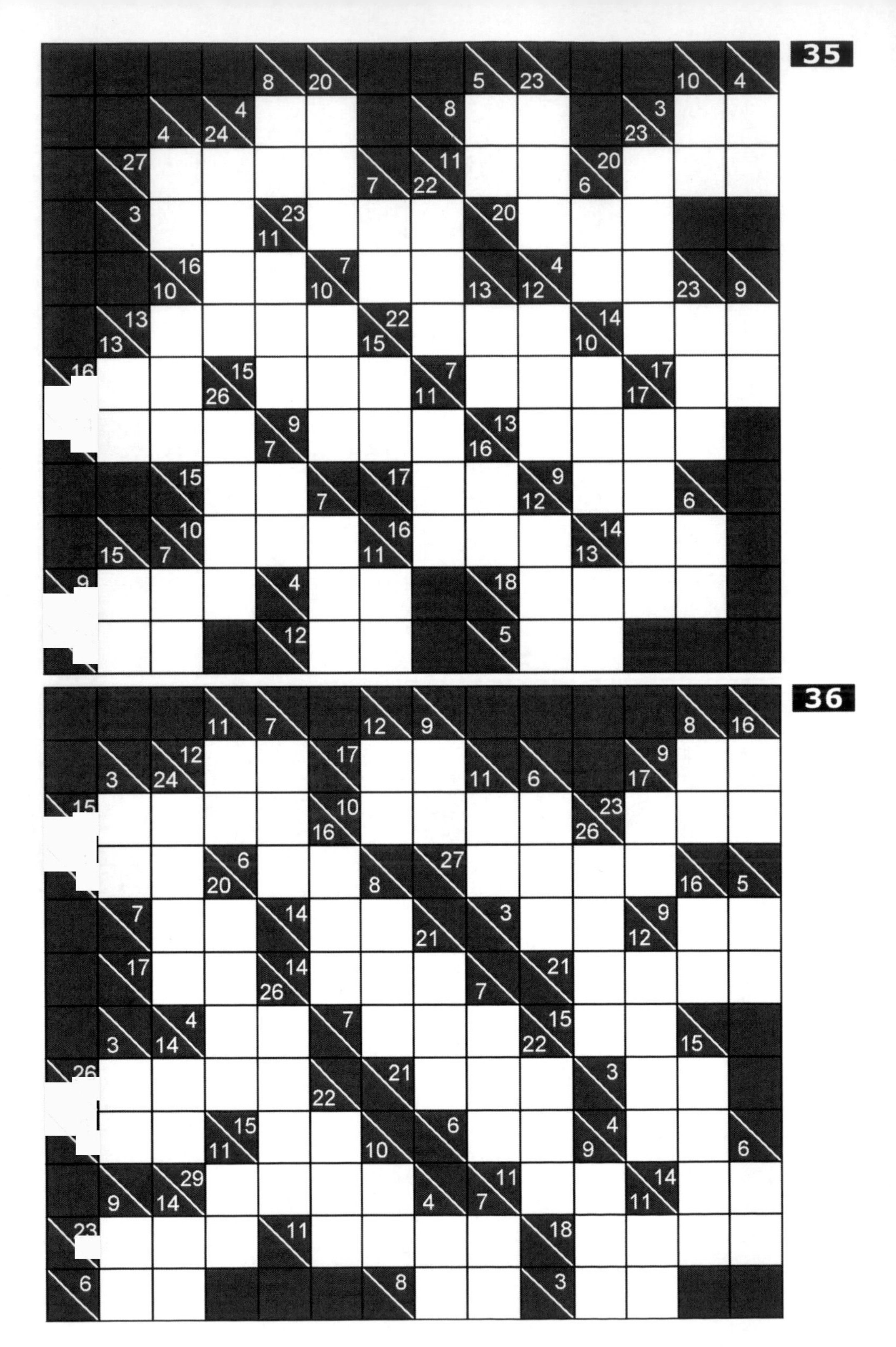
35
36

37

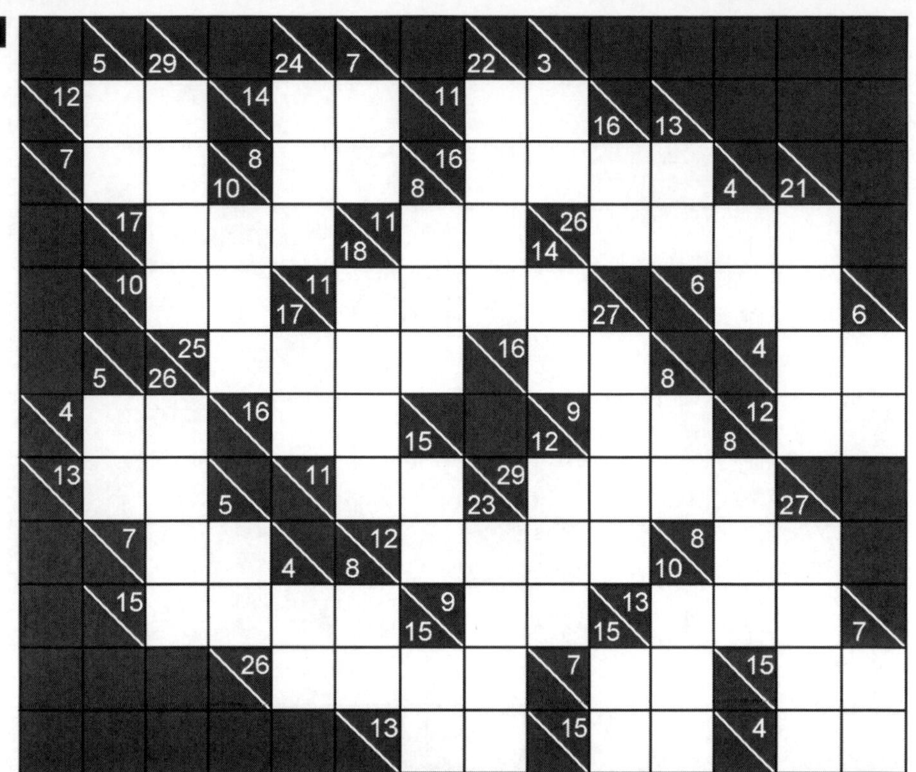

38

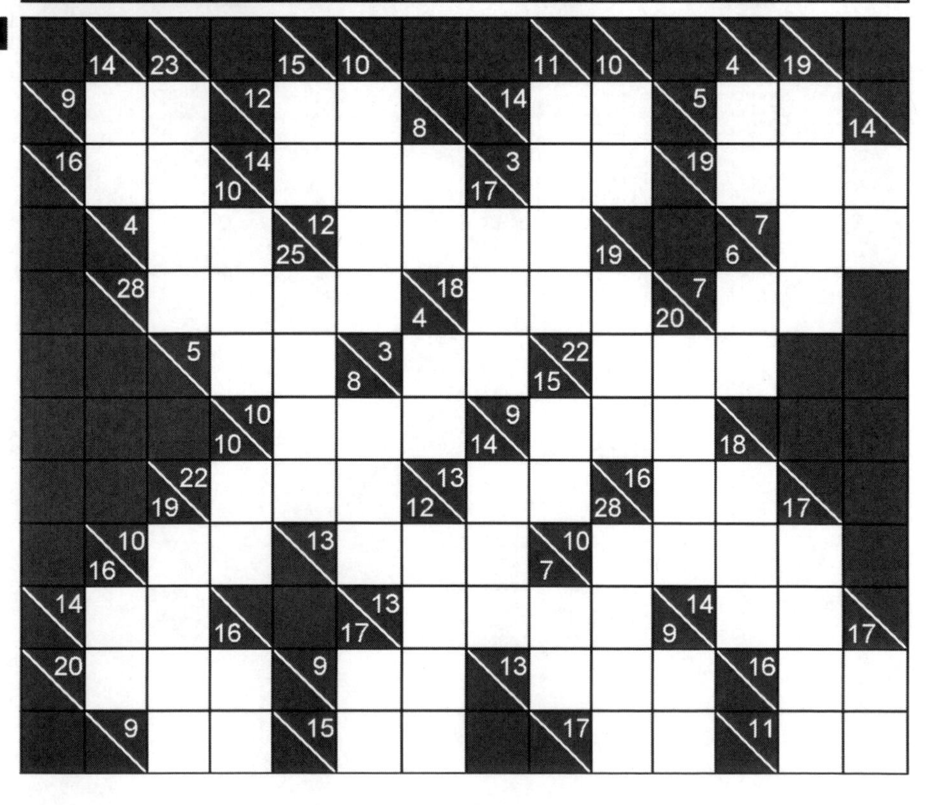

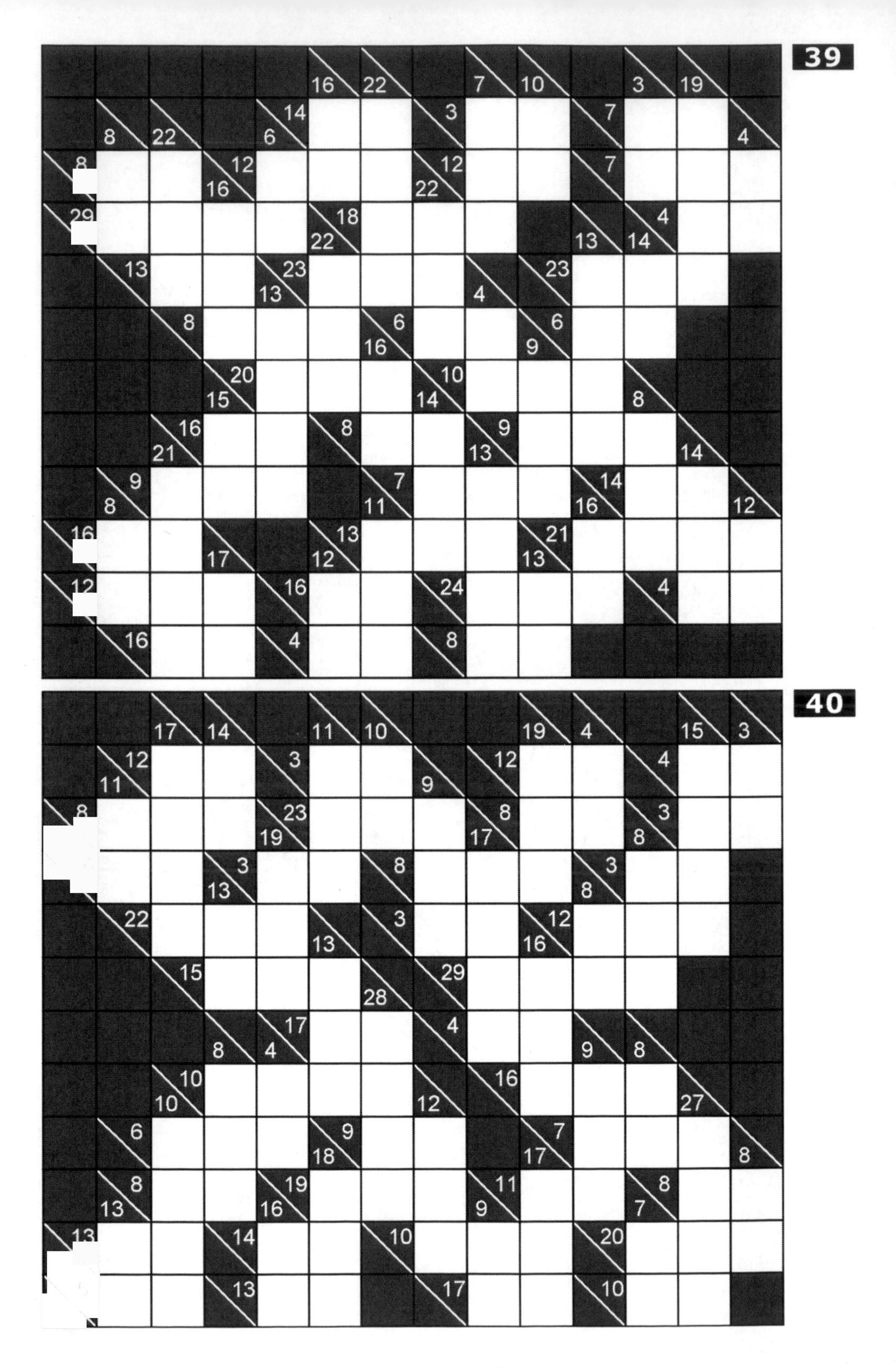
39
40

41

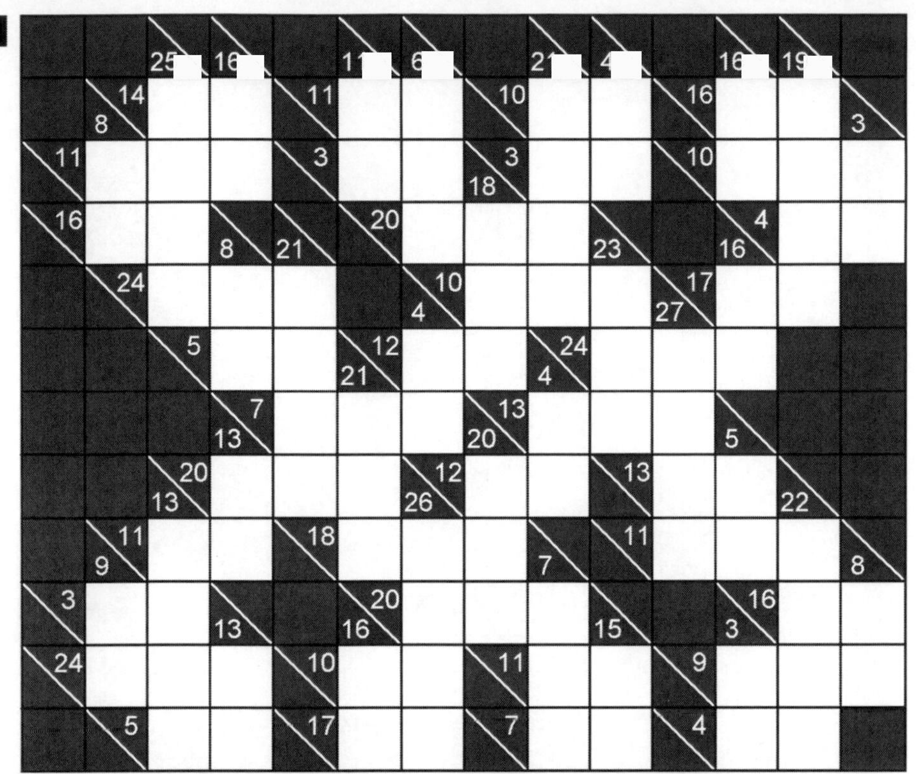

42

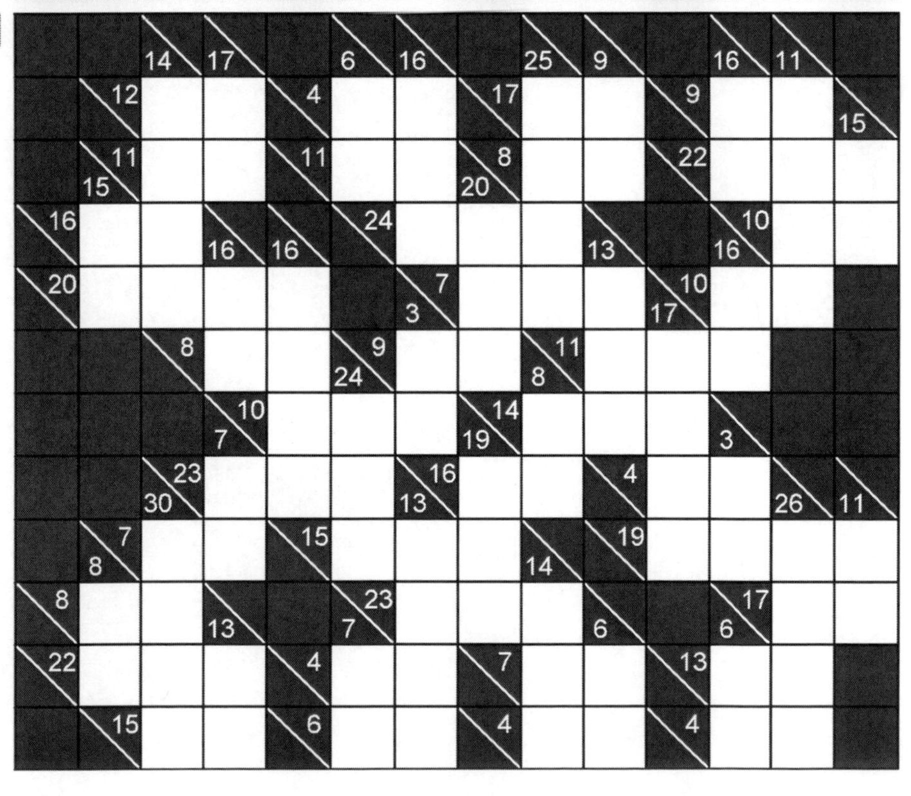

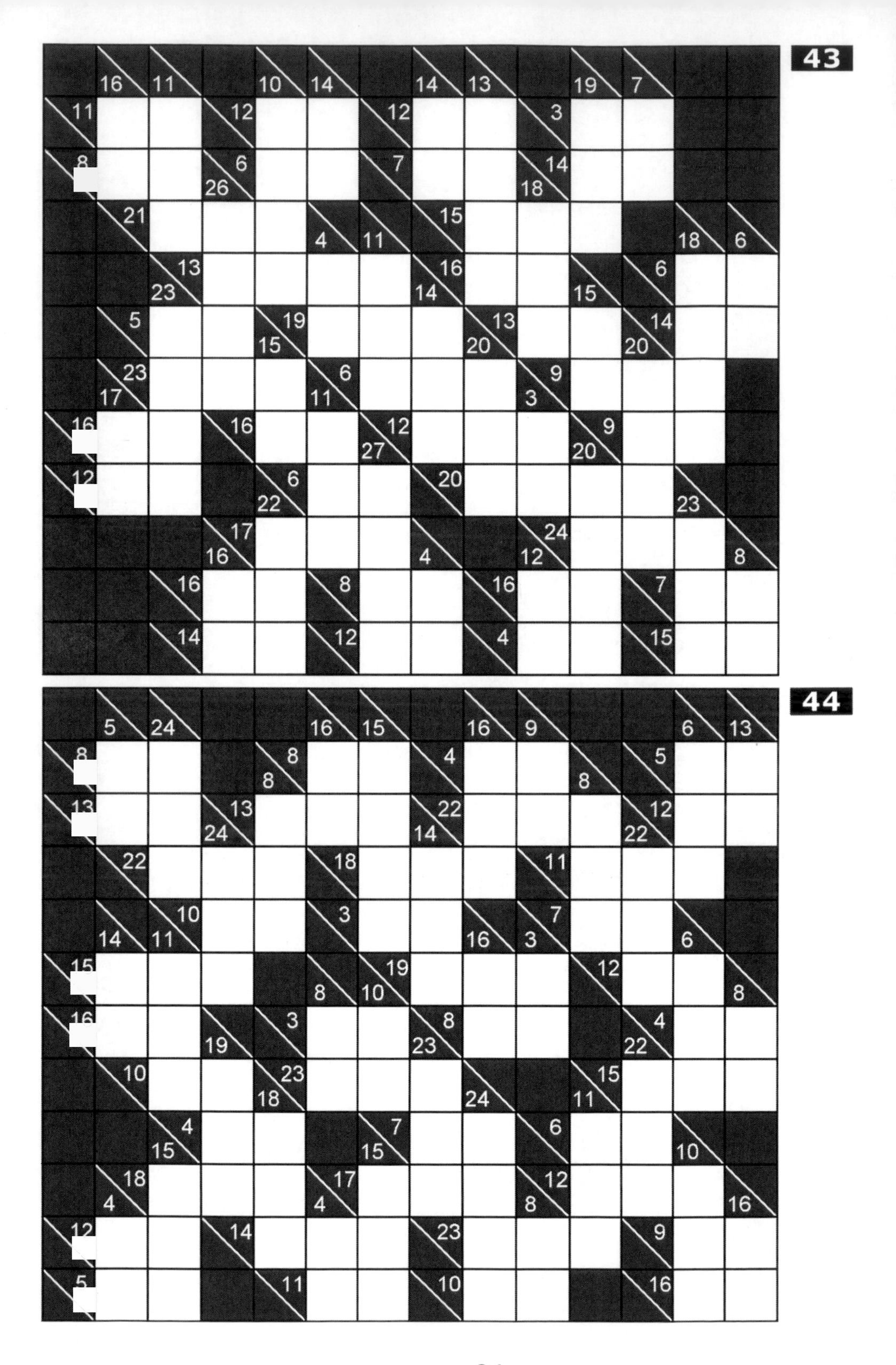

45

46

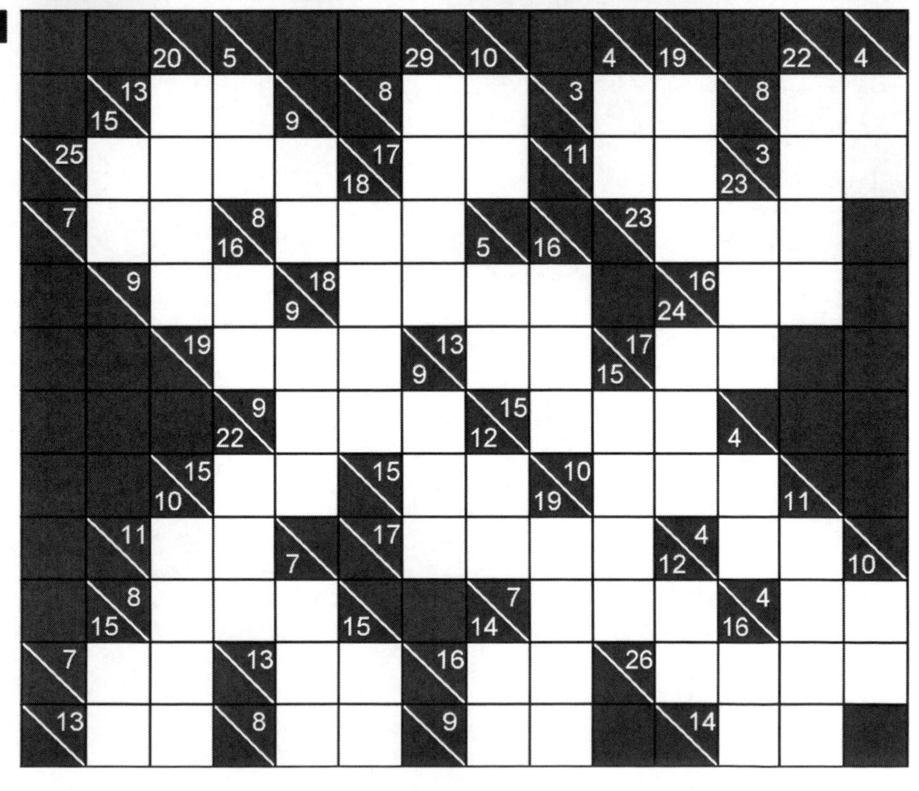

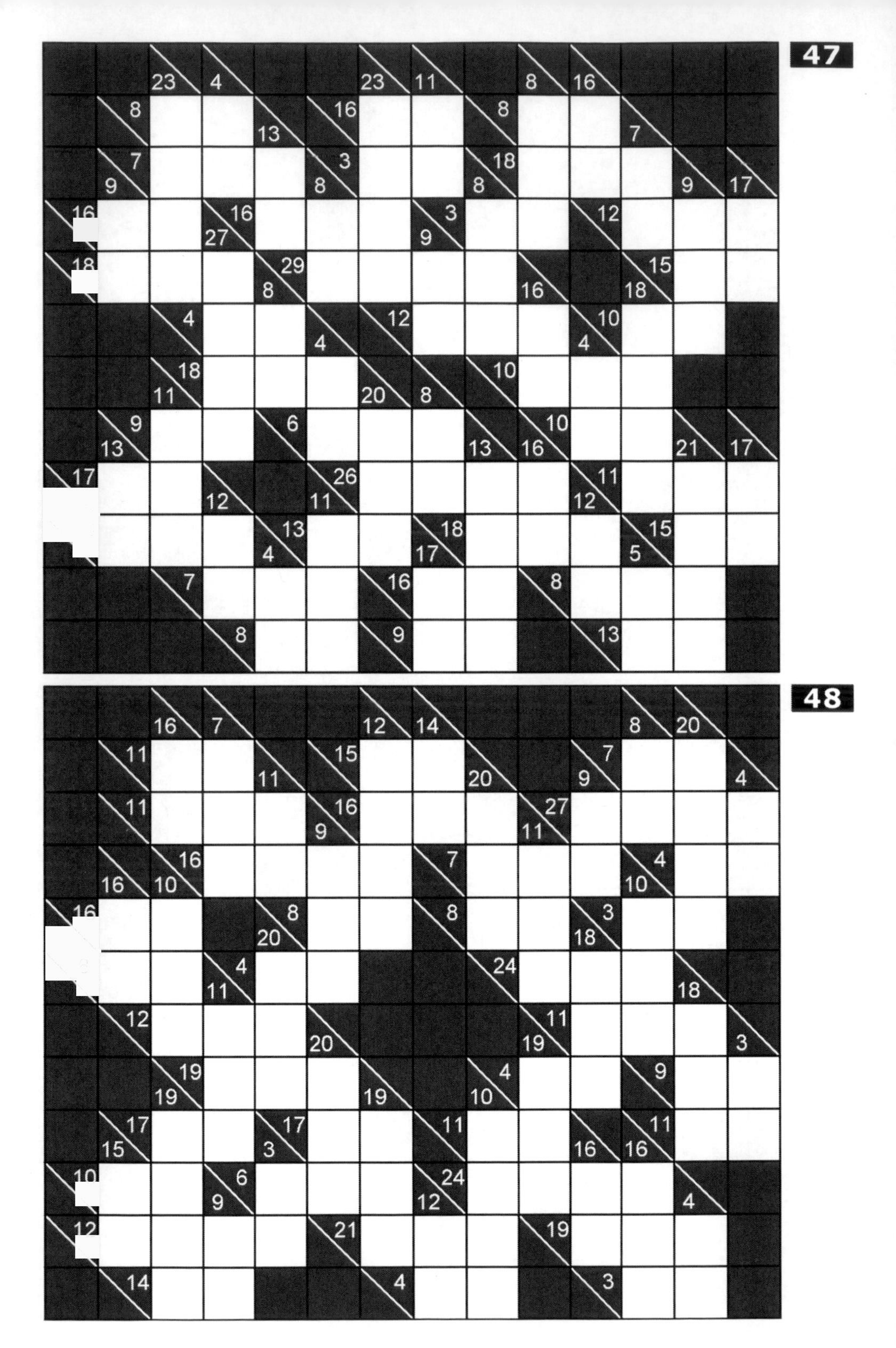
47
48

49

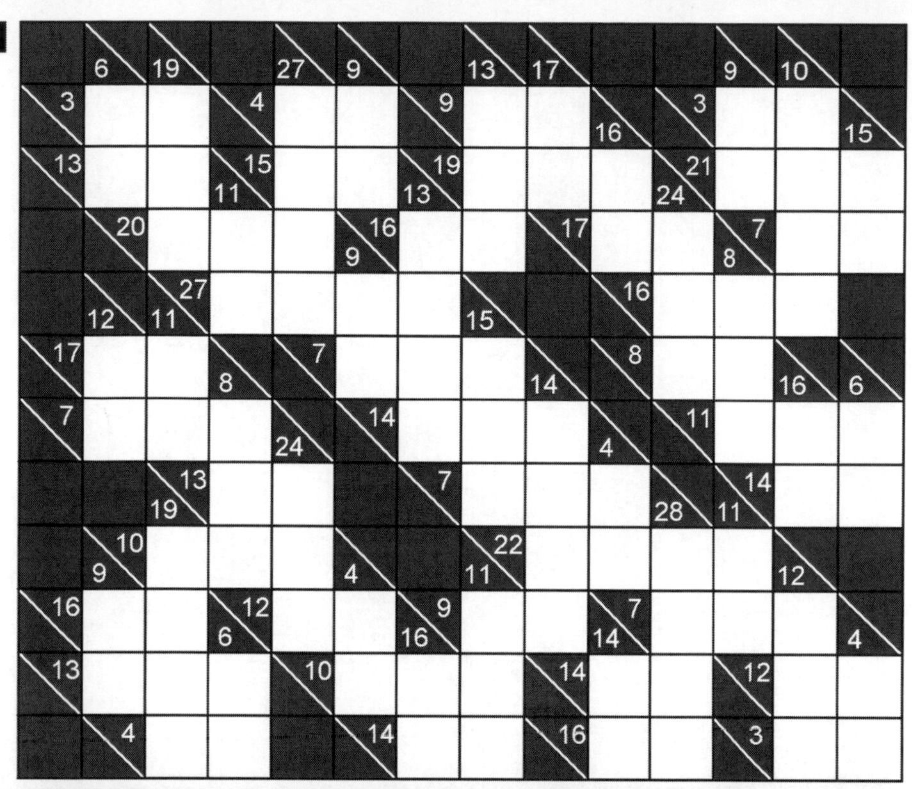

50

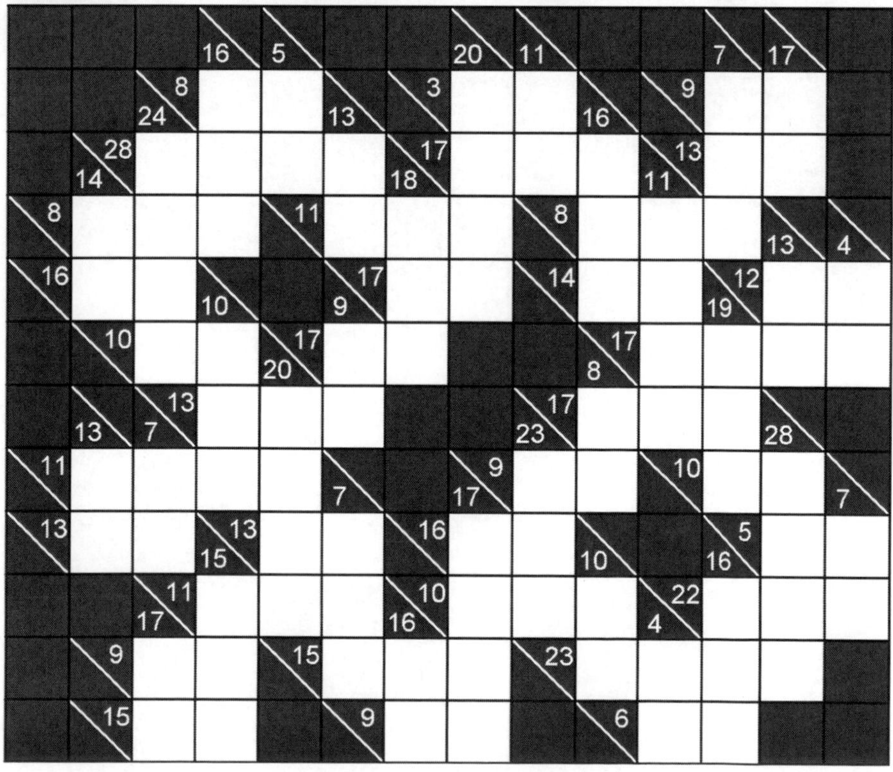

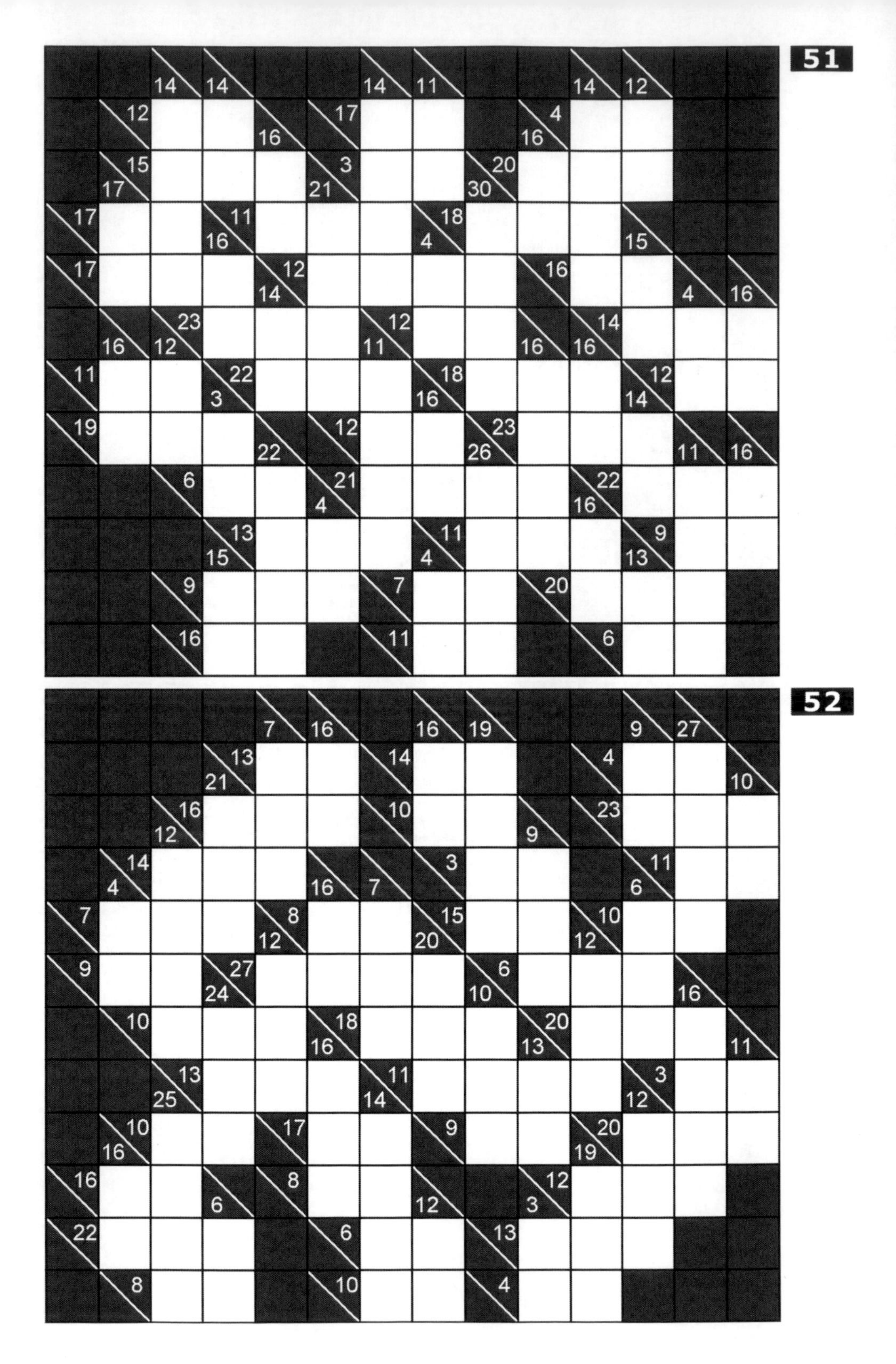
51
52

53

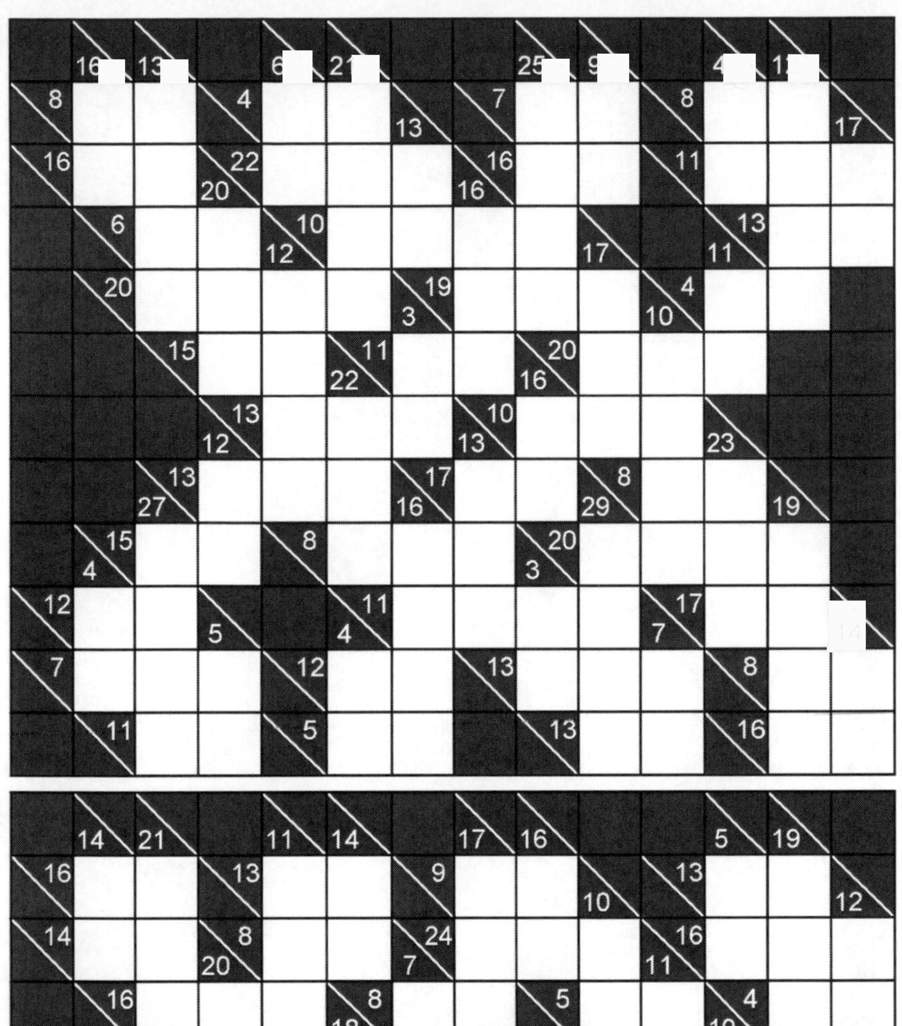

54

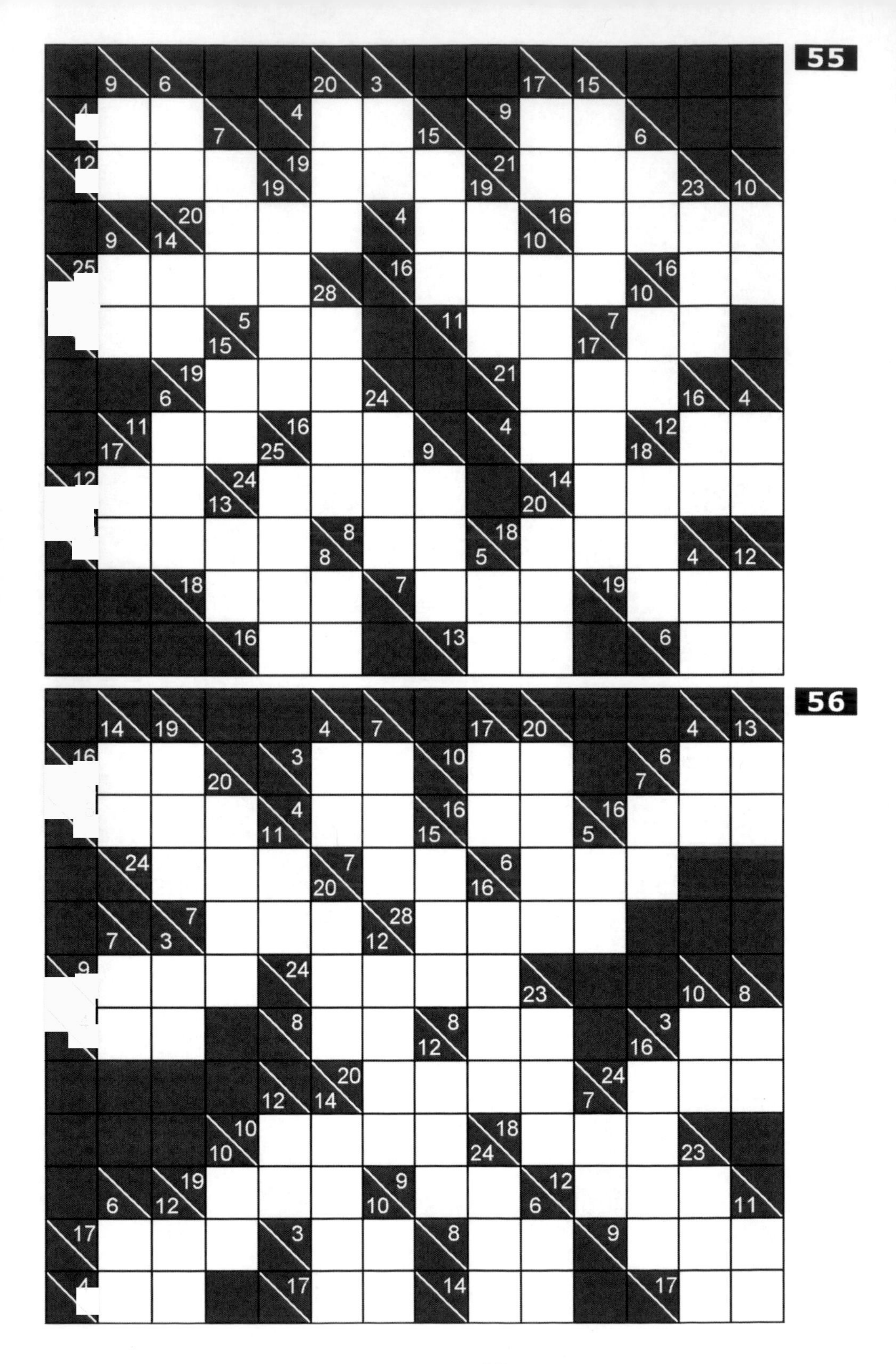

57

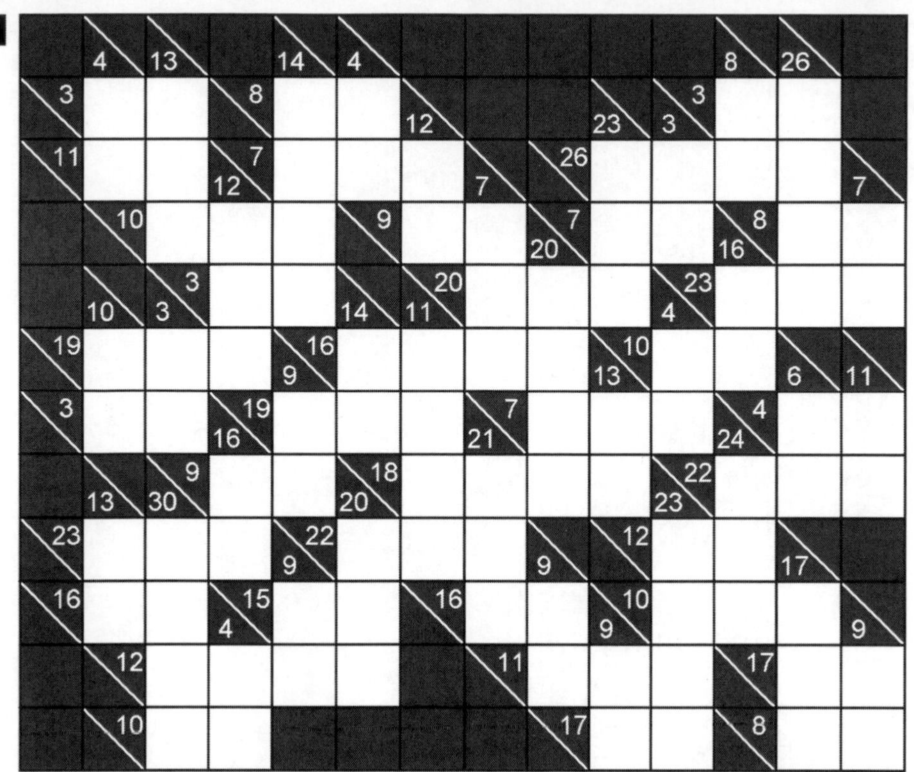

58

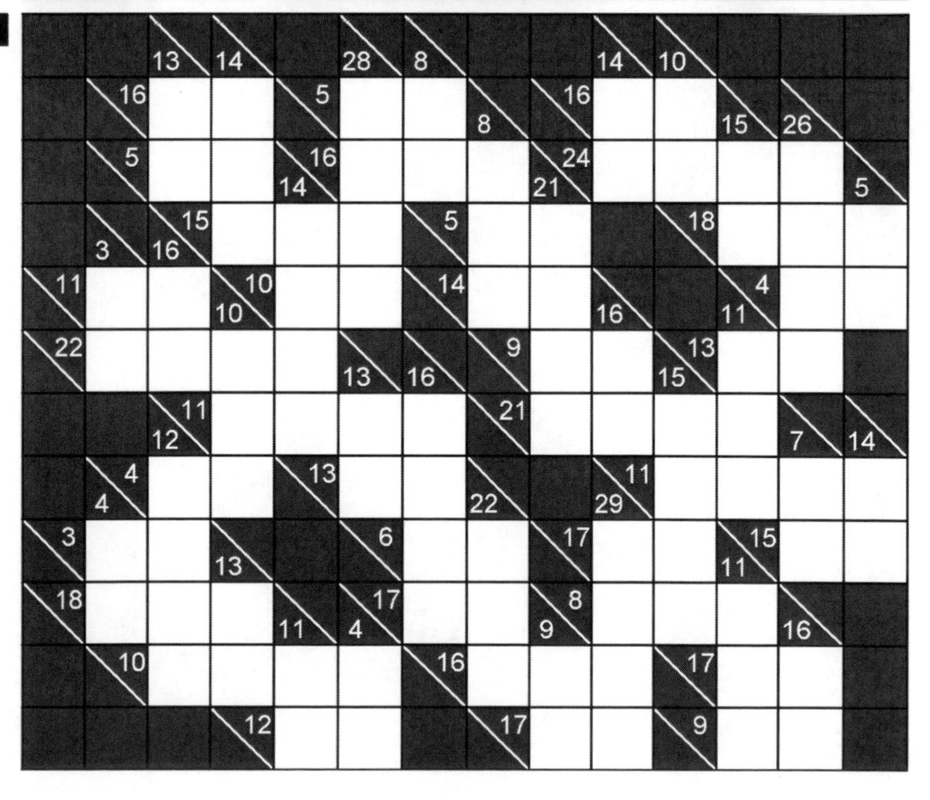

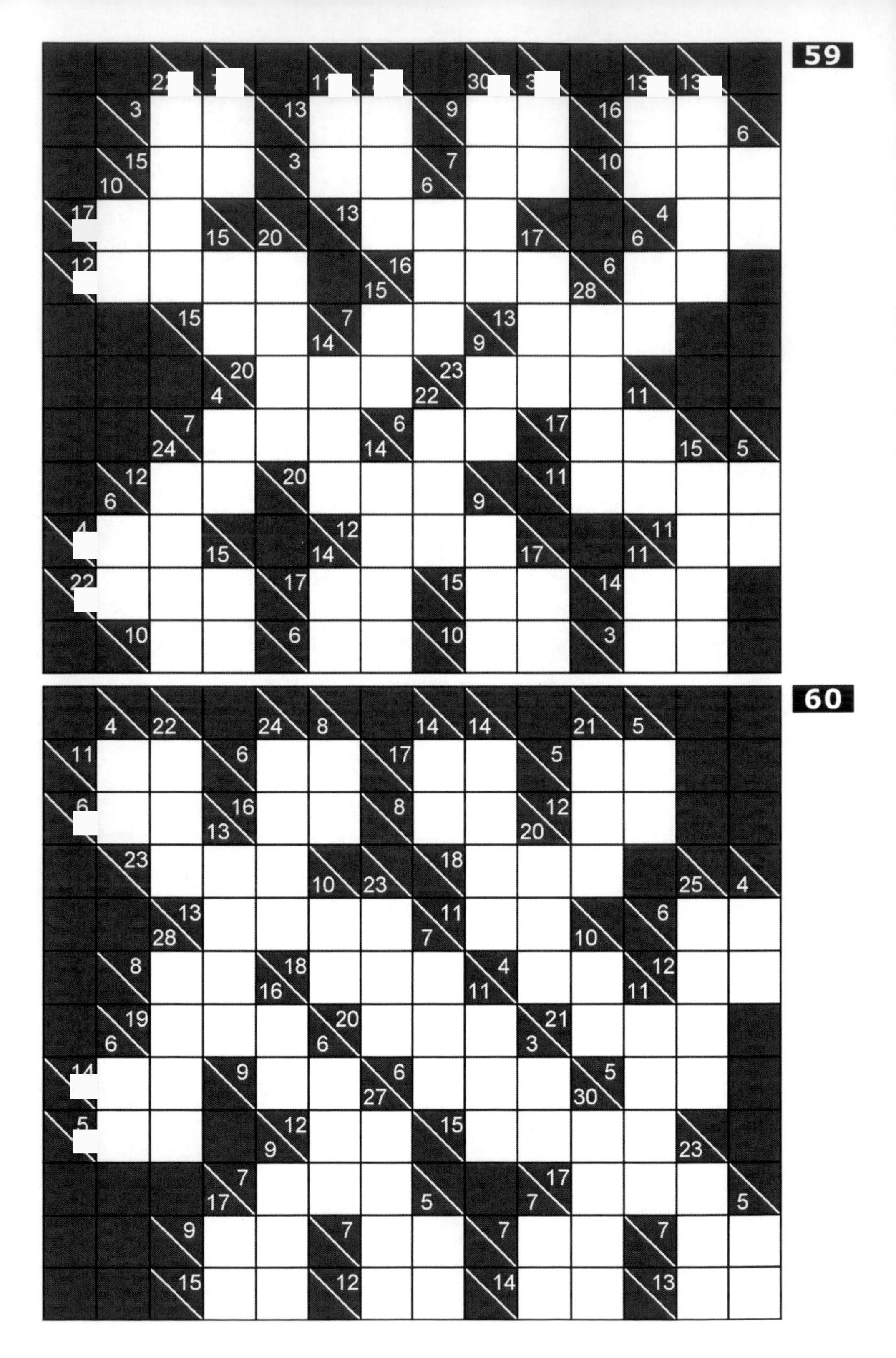

61

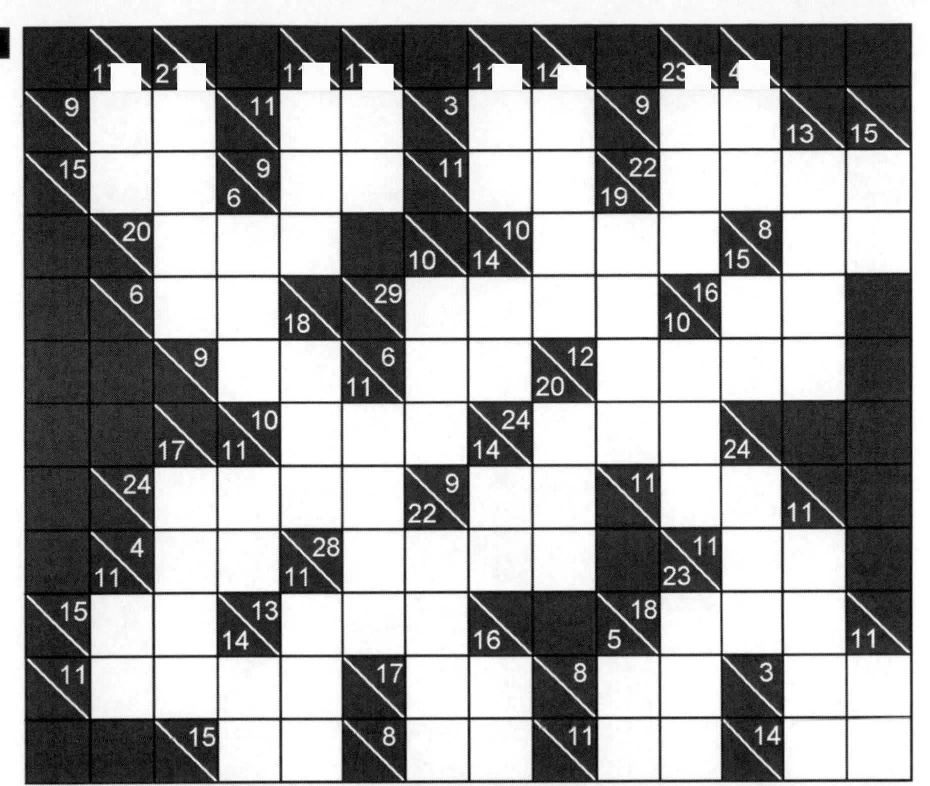

62

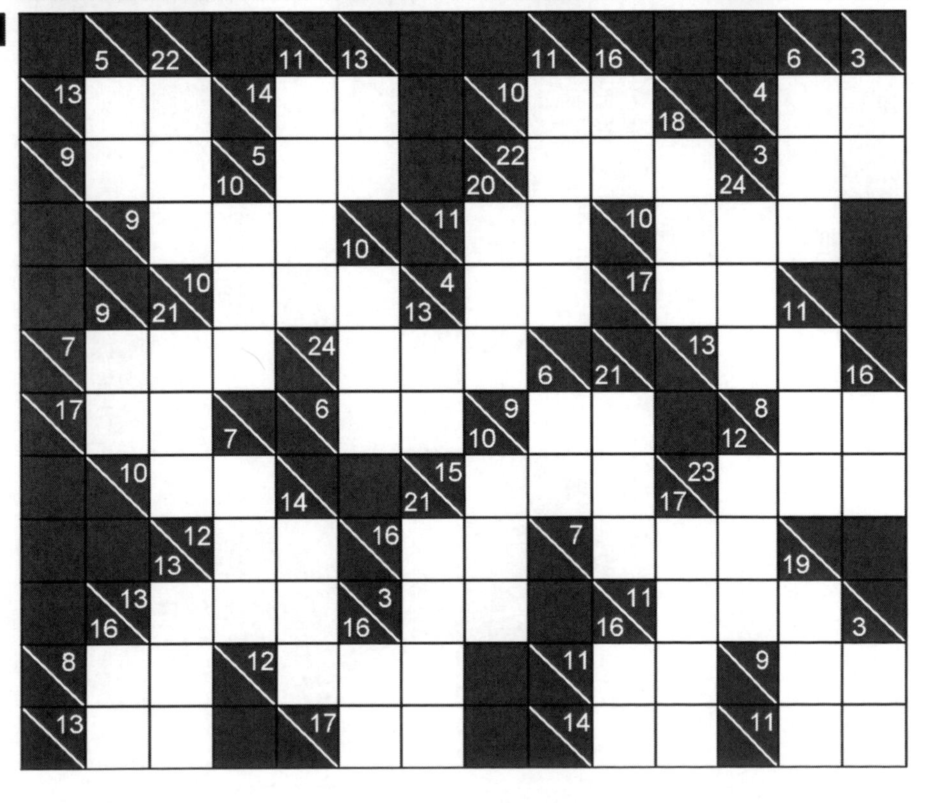

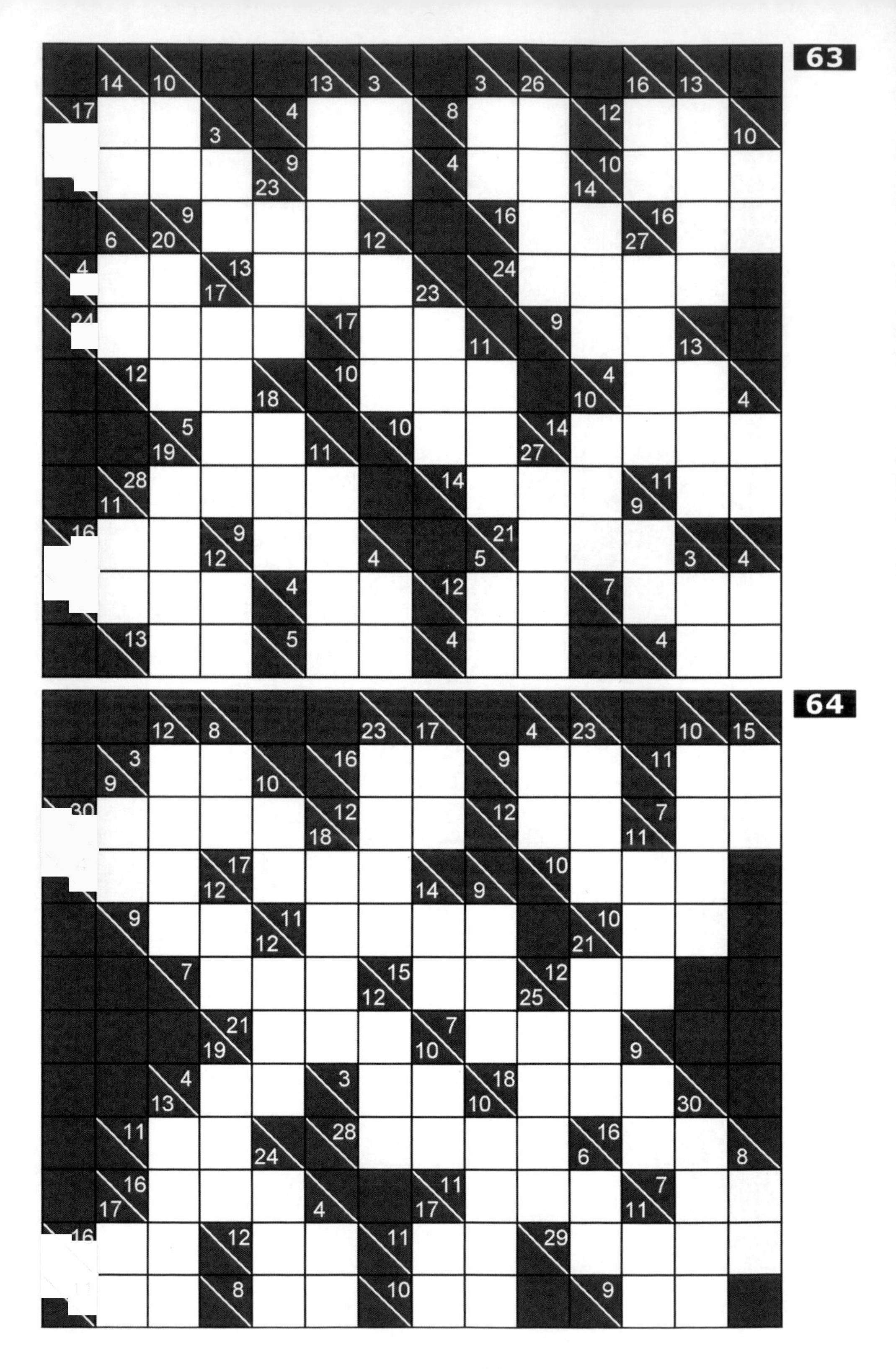
63
64

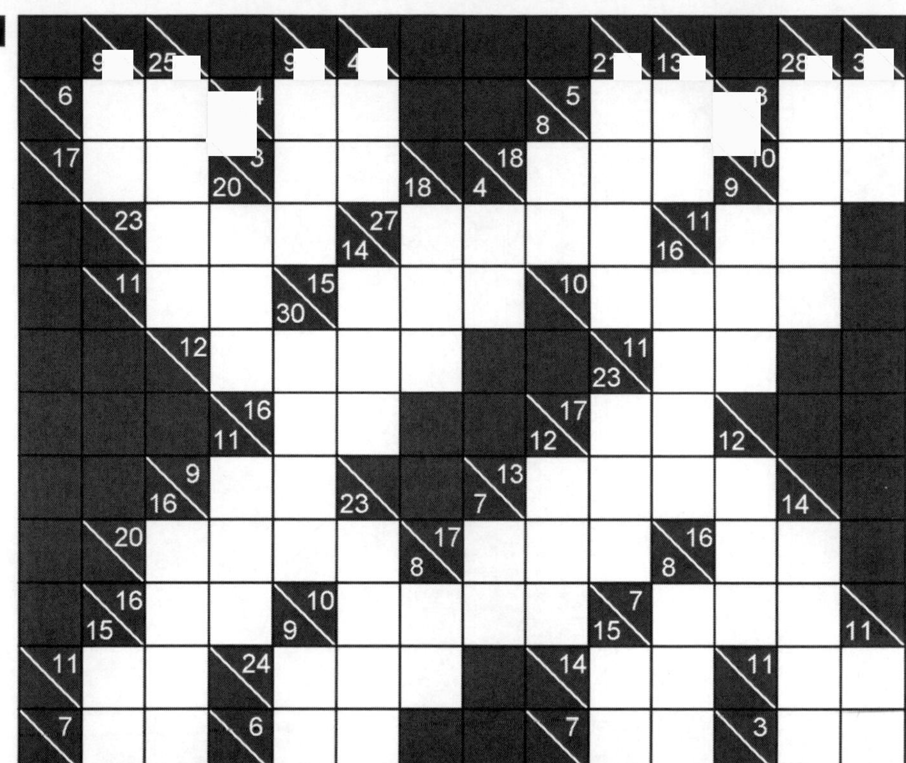

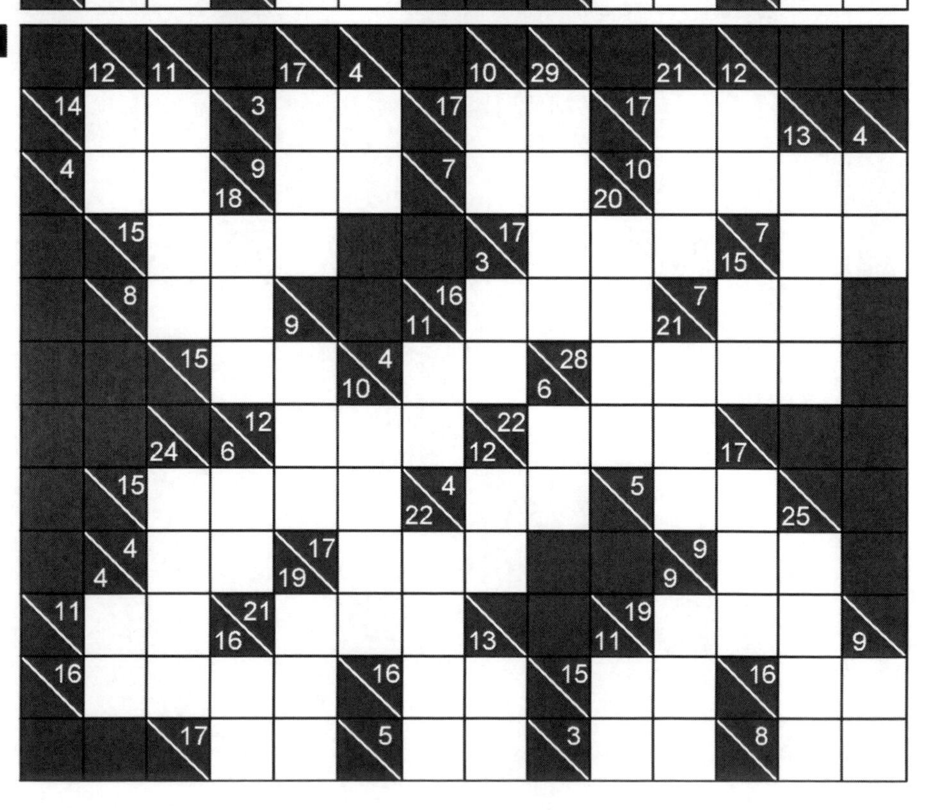

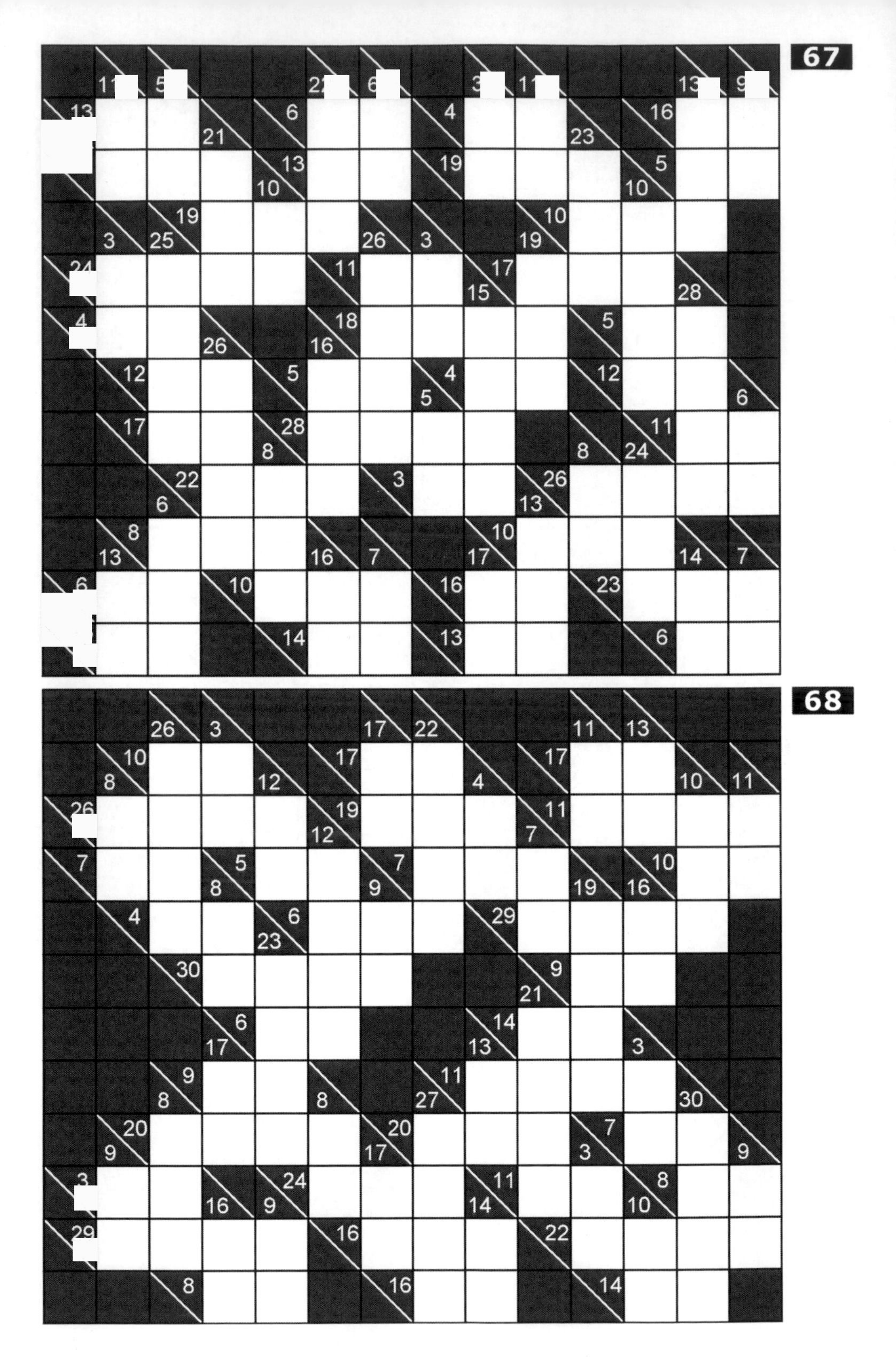

69

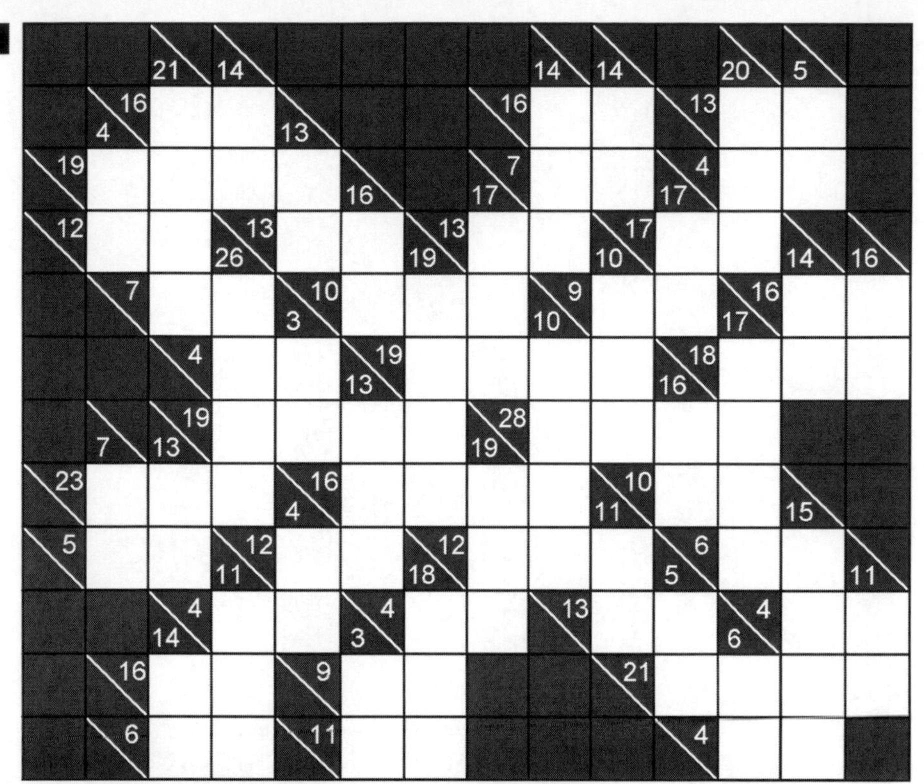

70

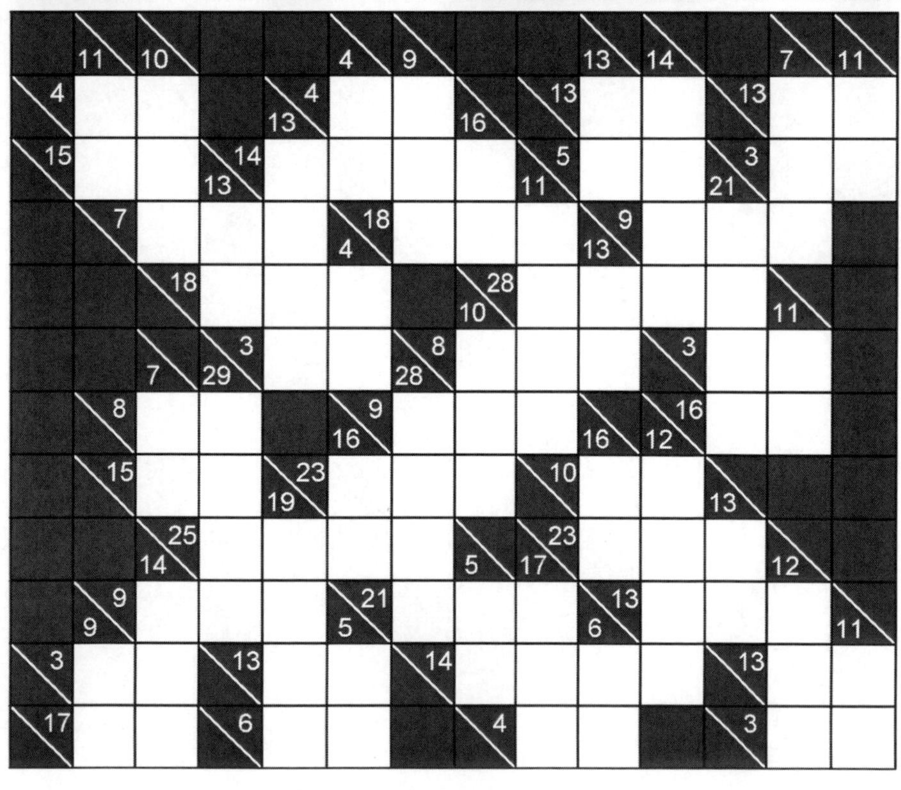

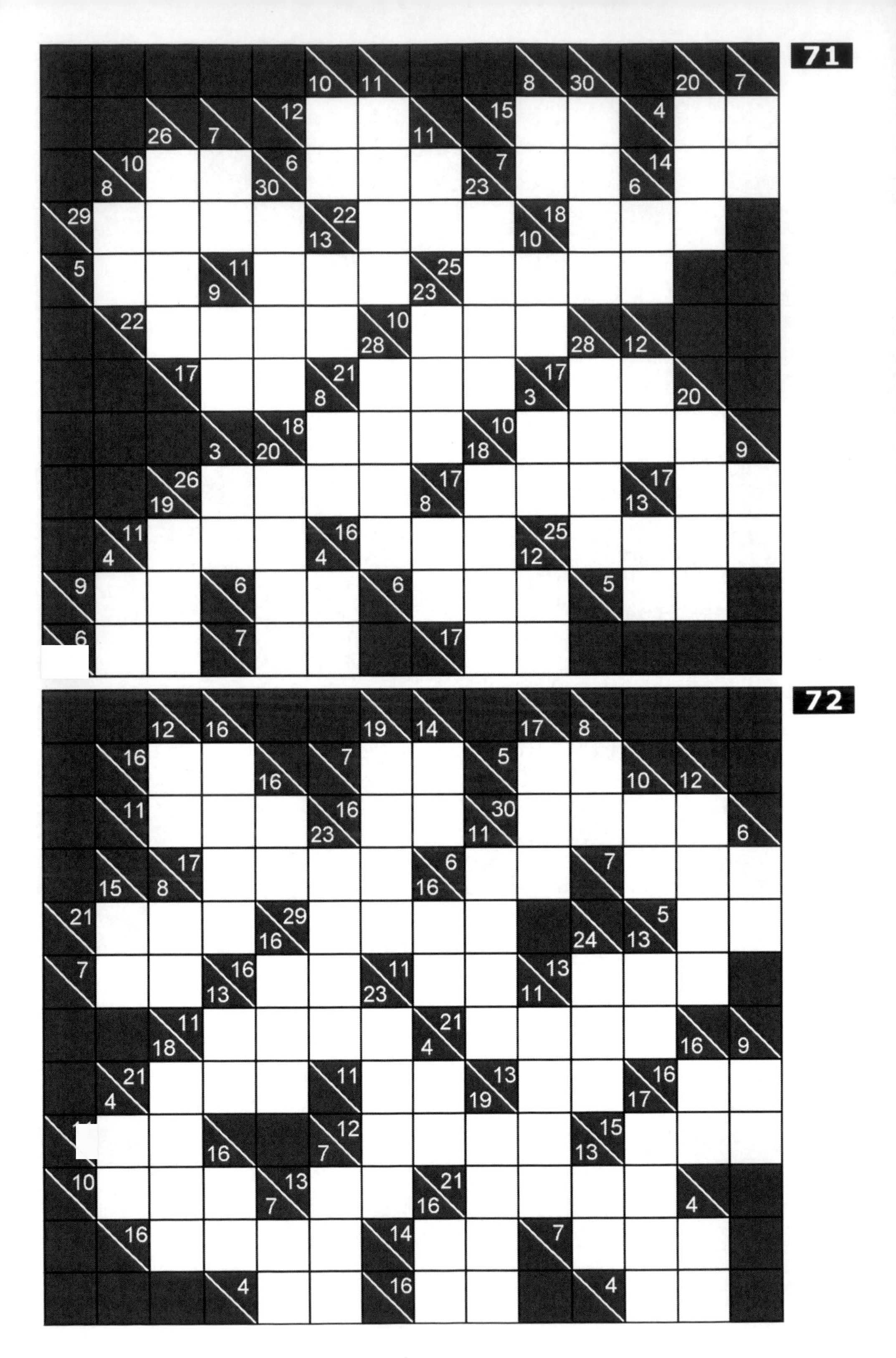
71
72

73

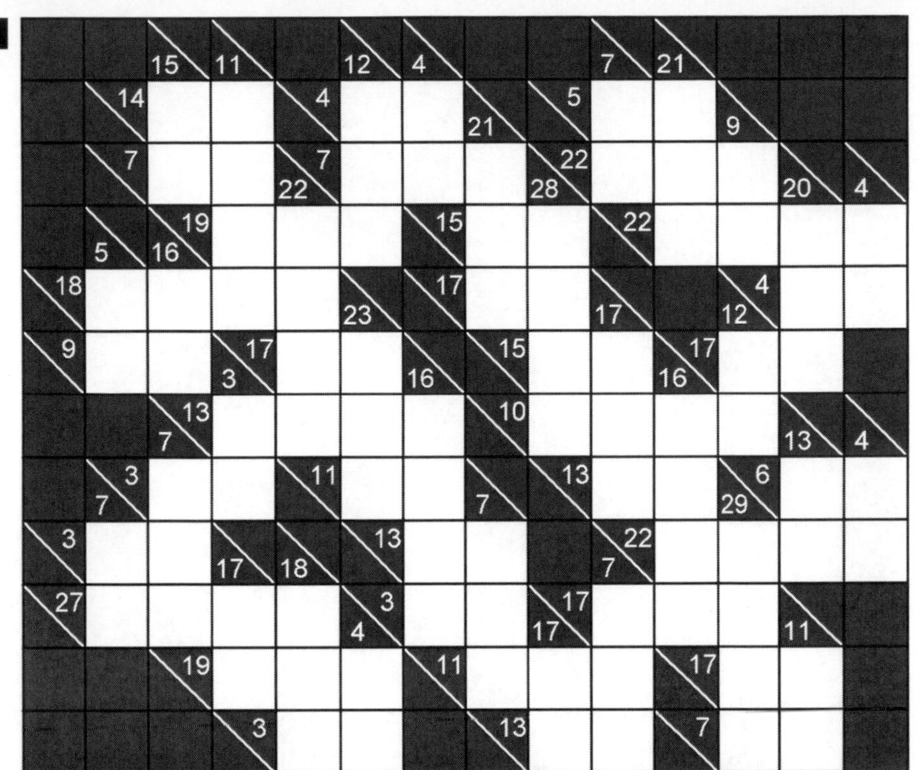

74

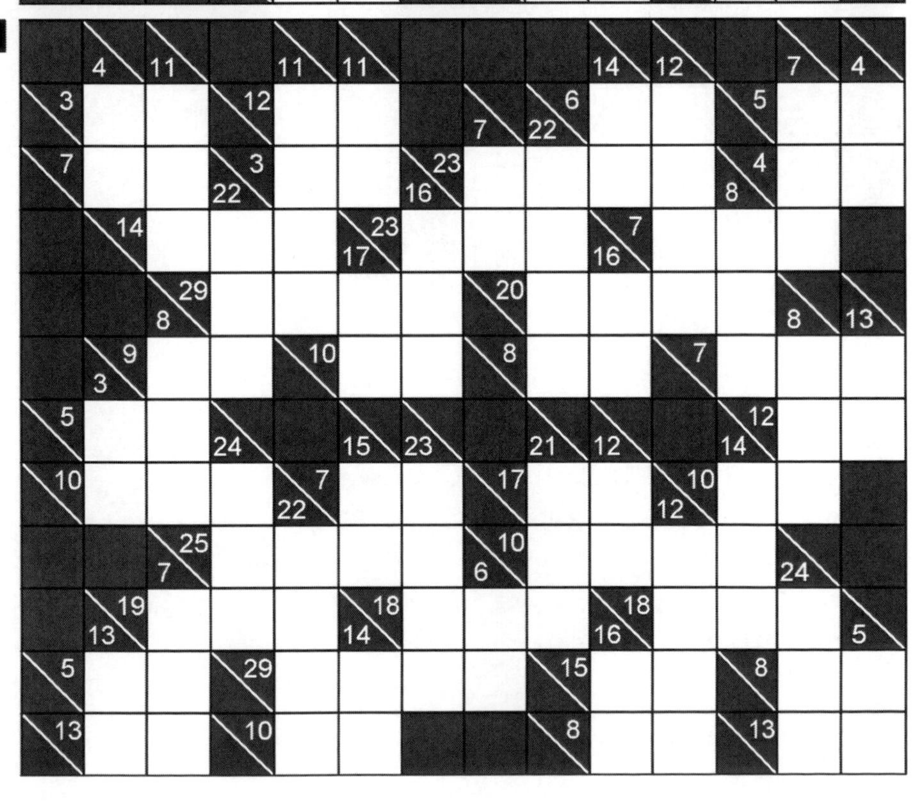

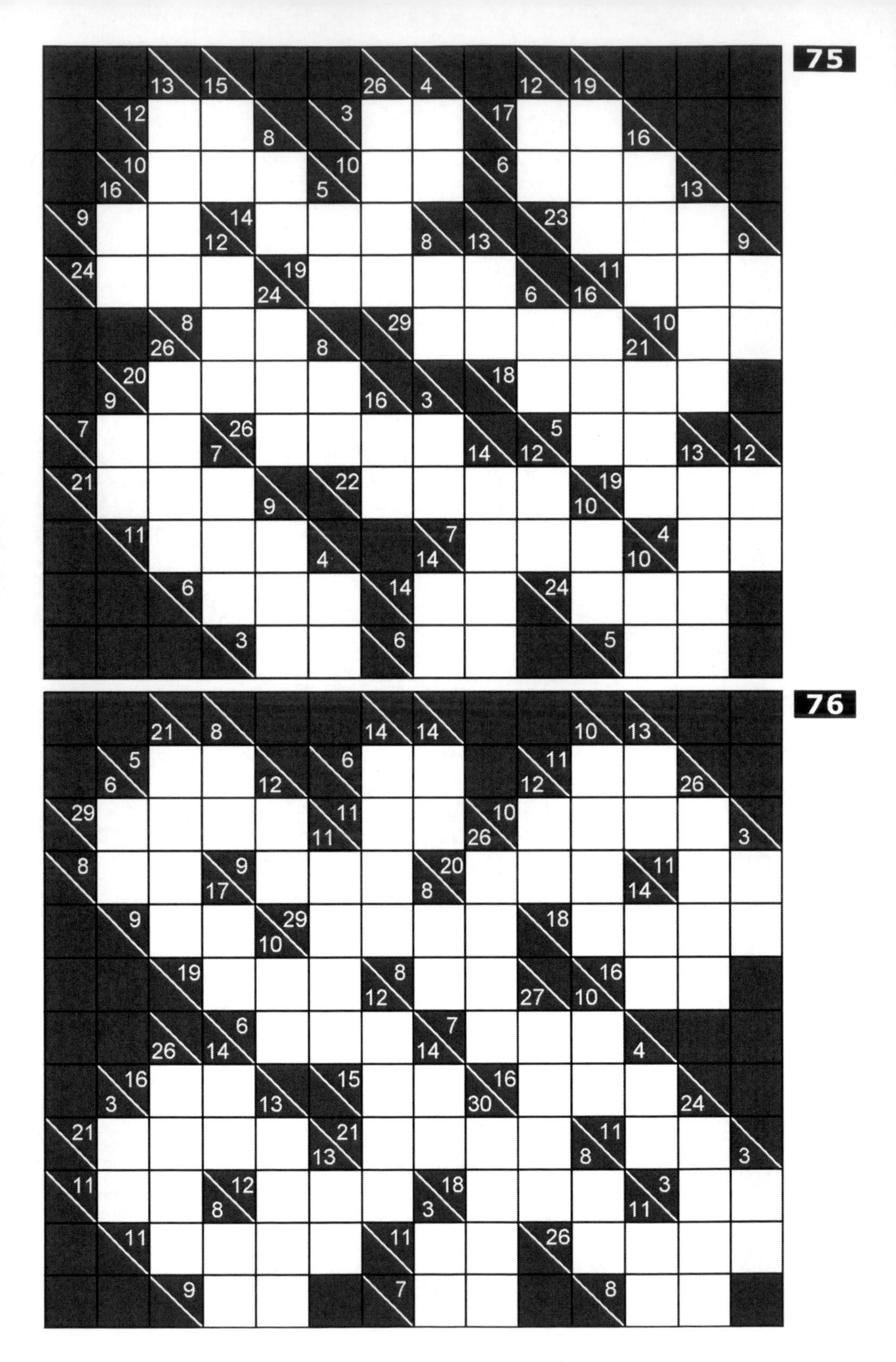
75
76

77

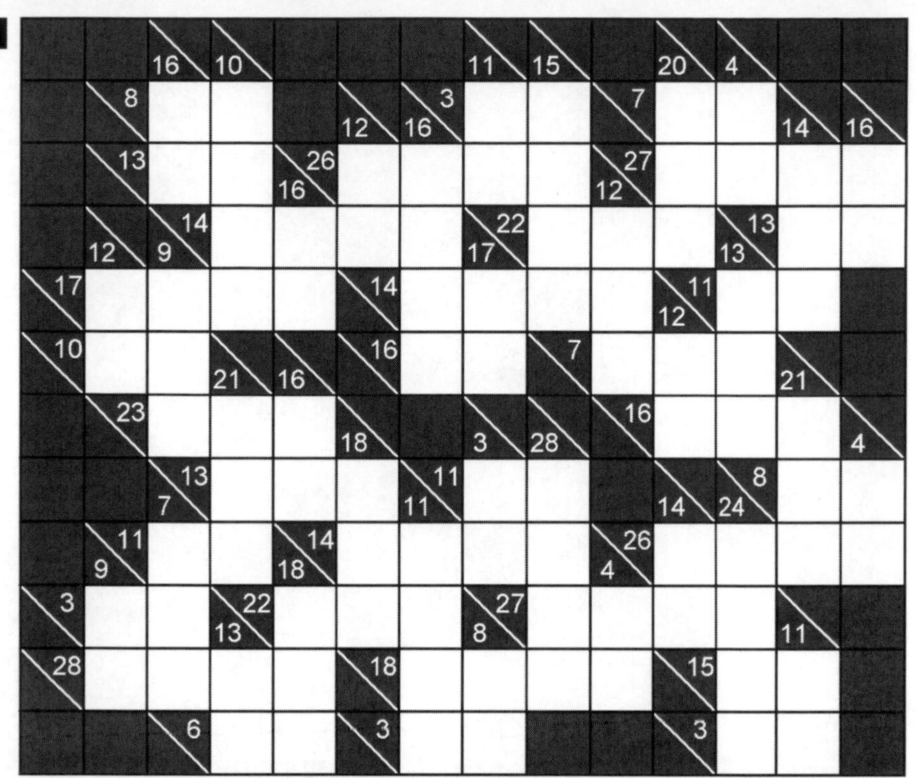

78

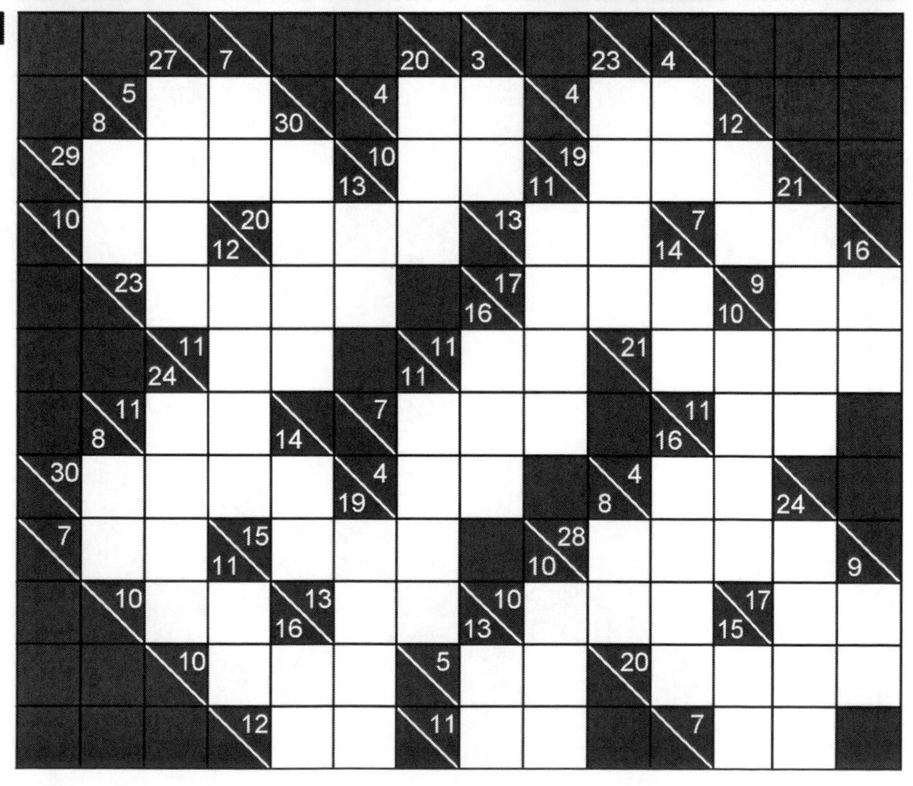

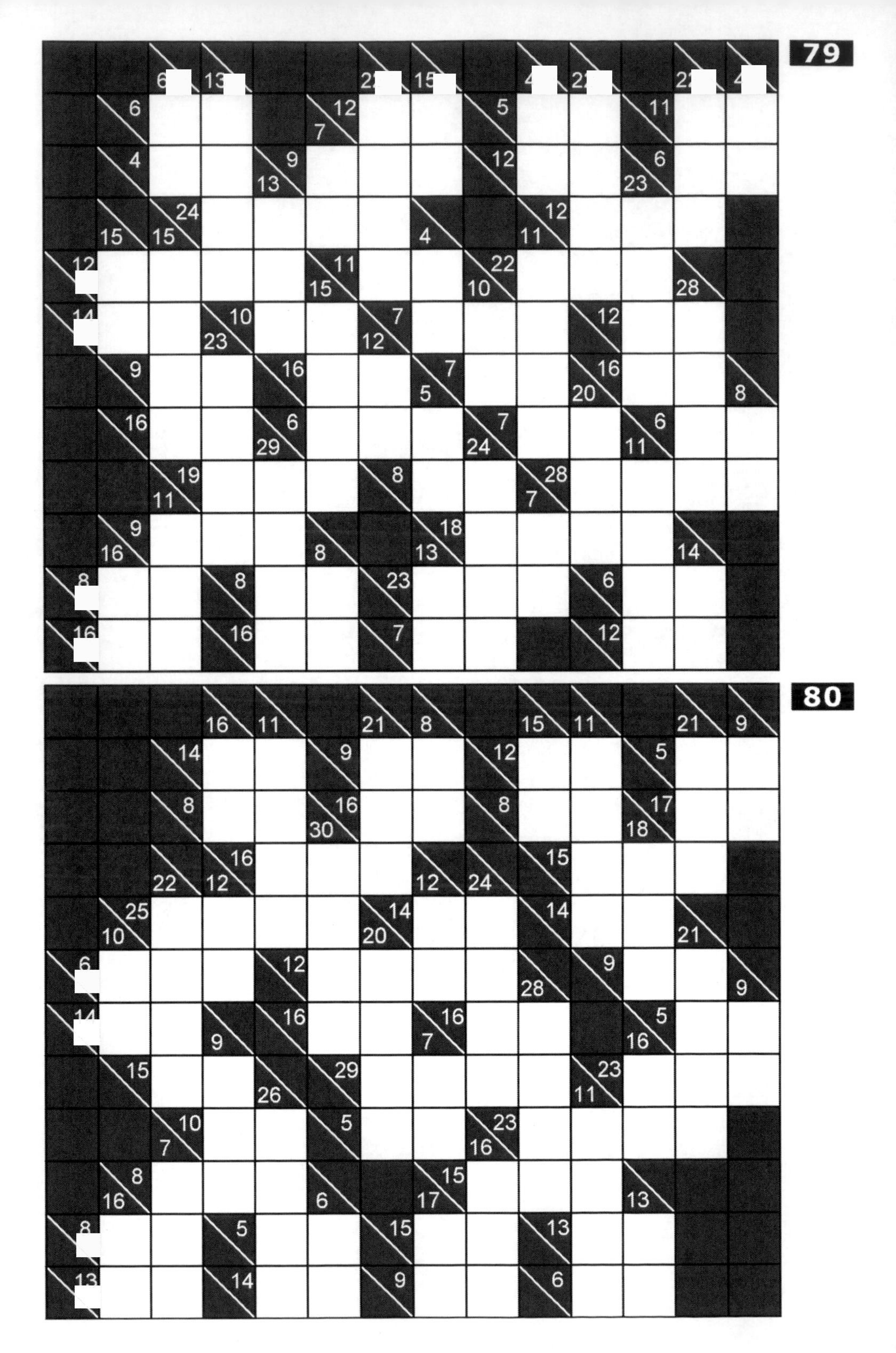
79
80

81

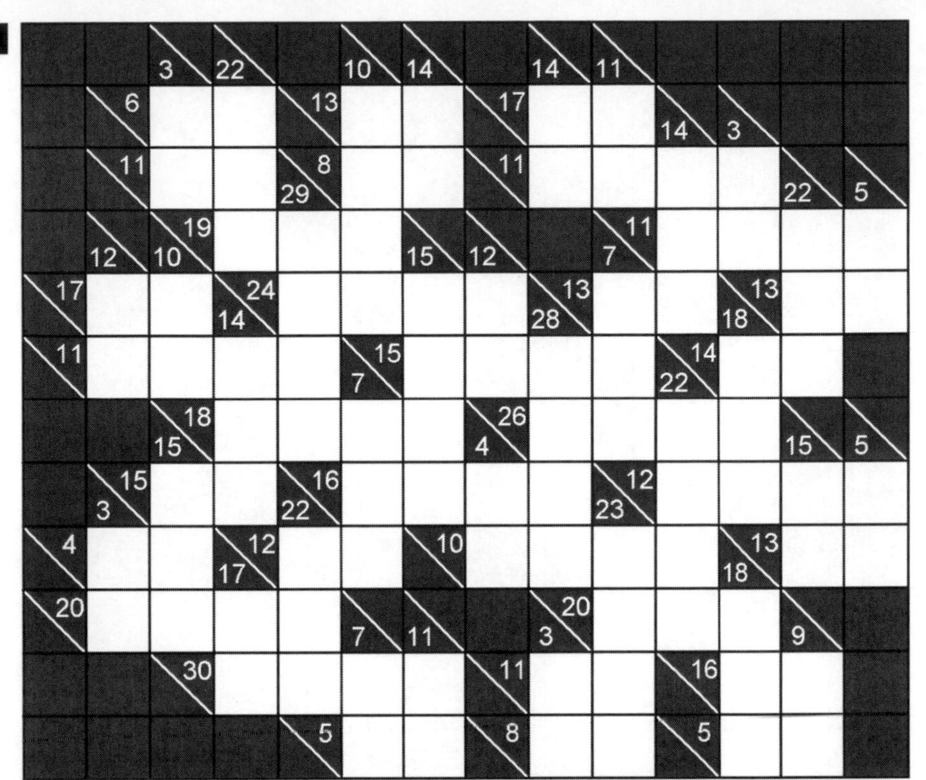

82

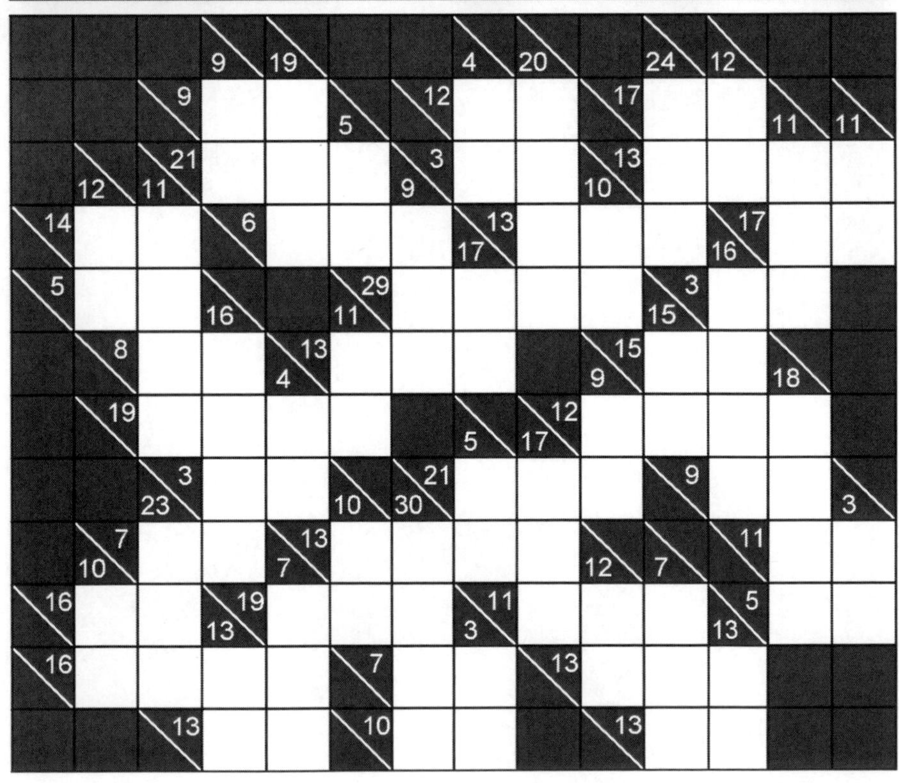

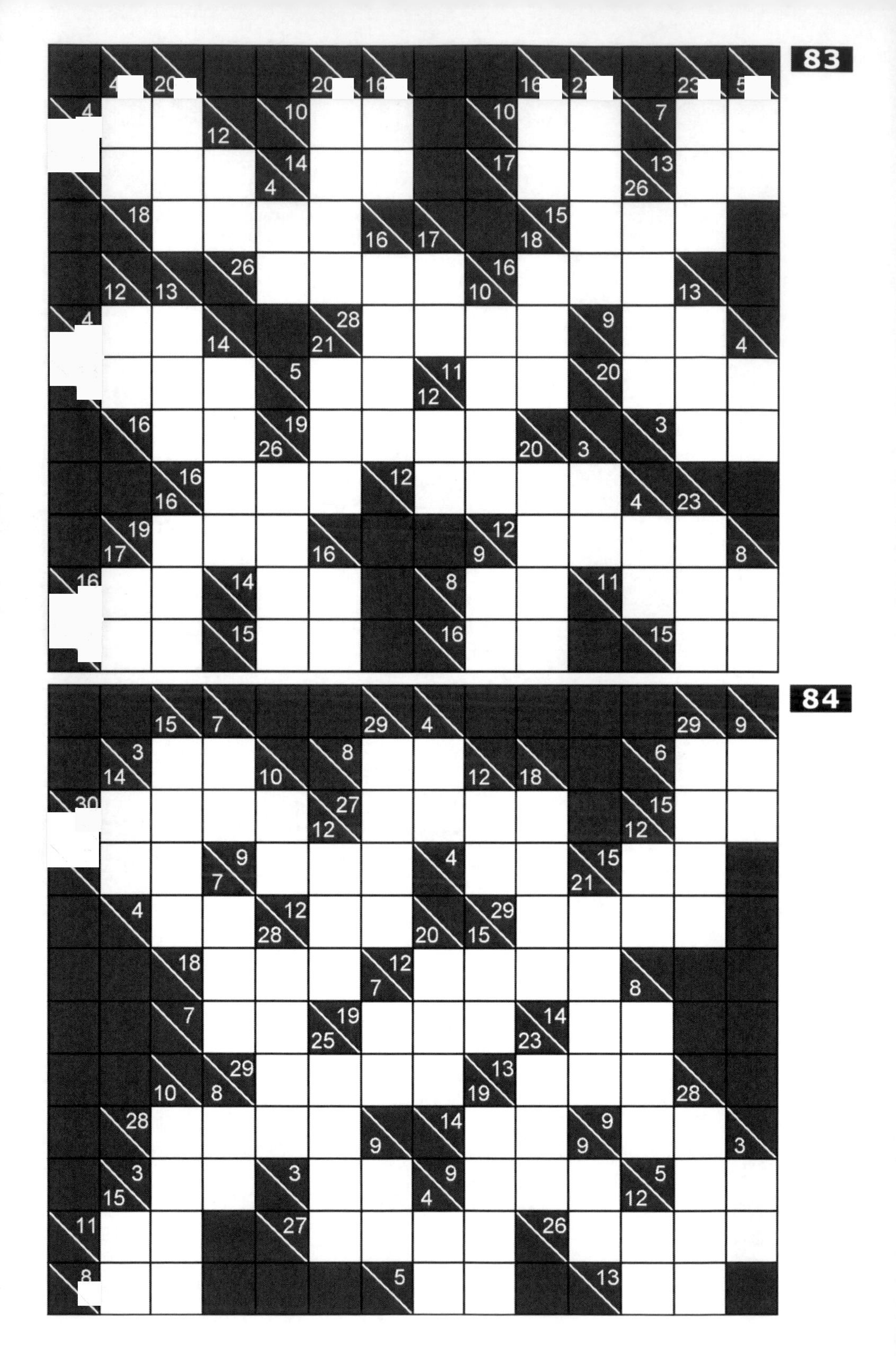
83
84

85

86

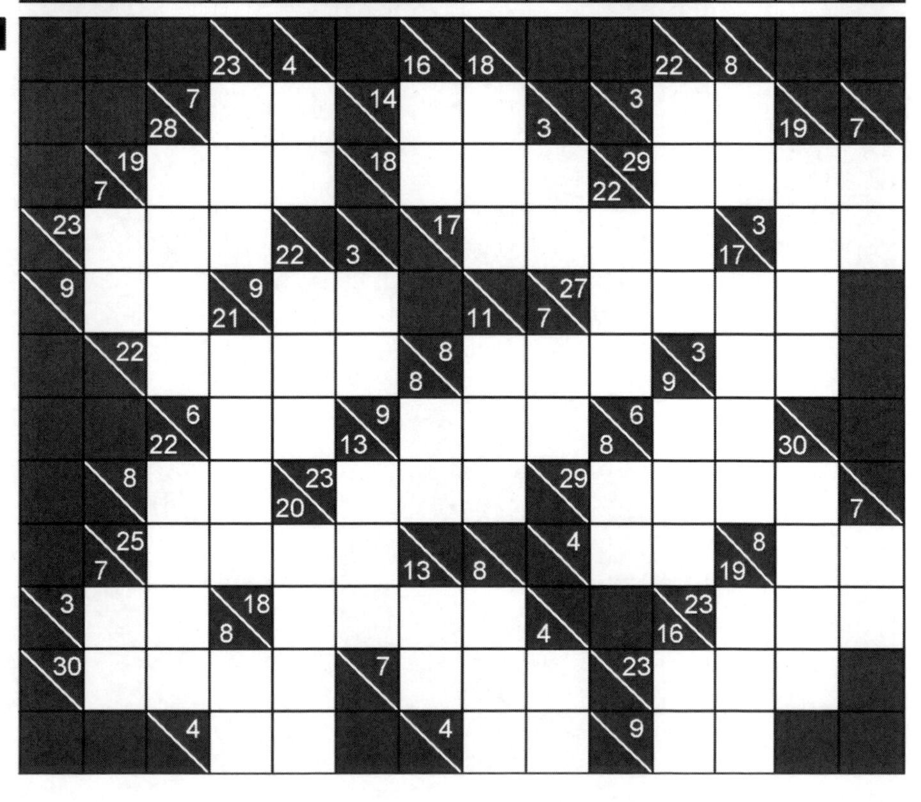

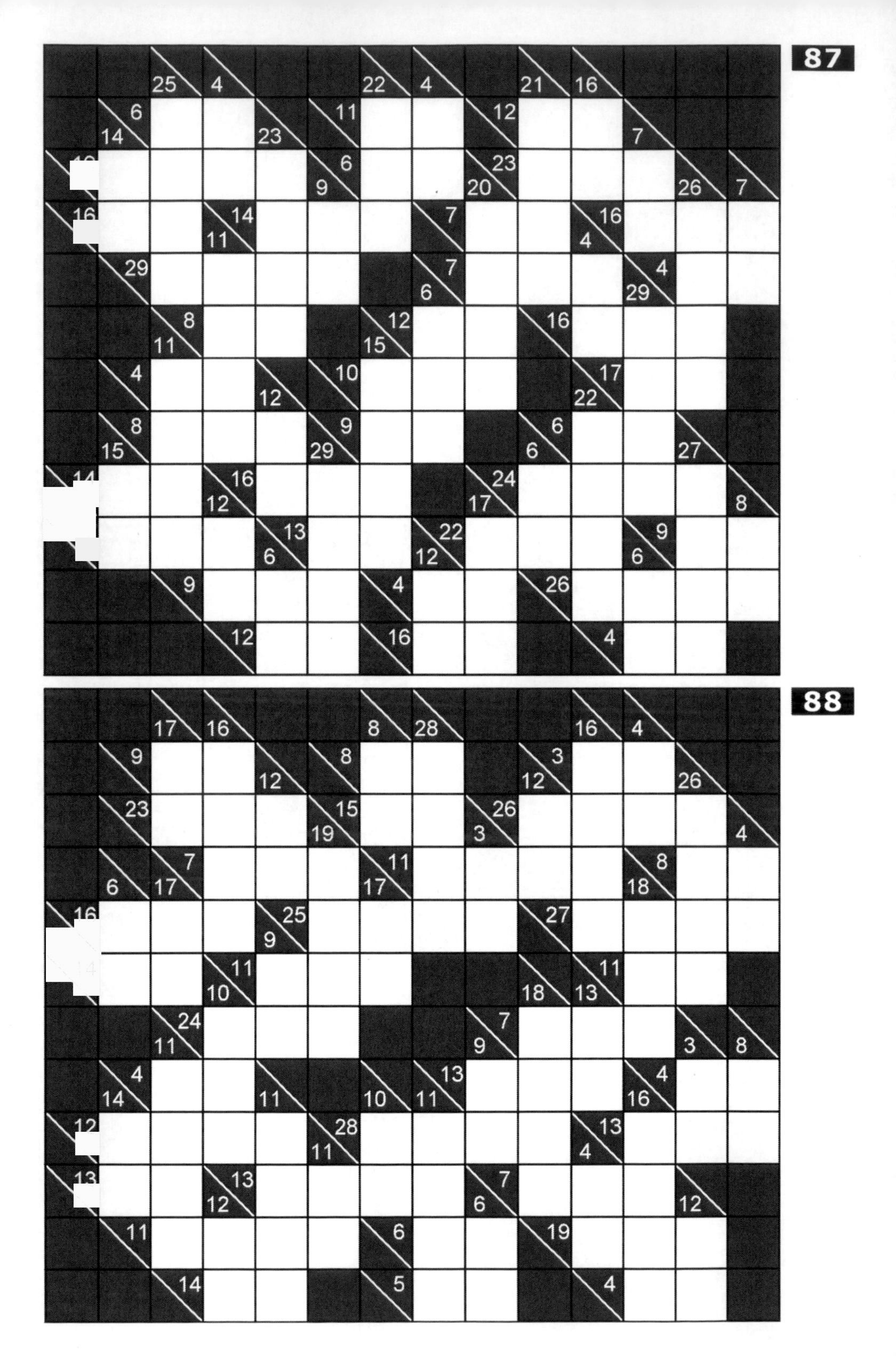
87
88

89

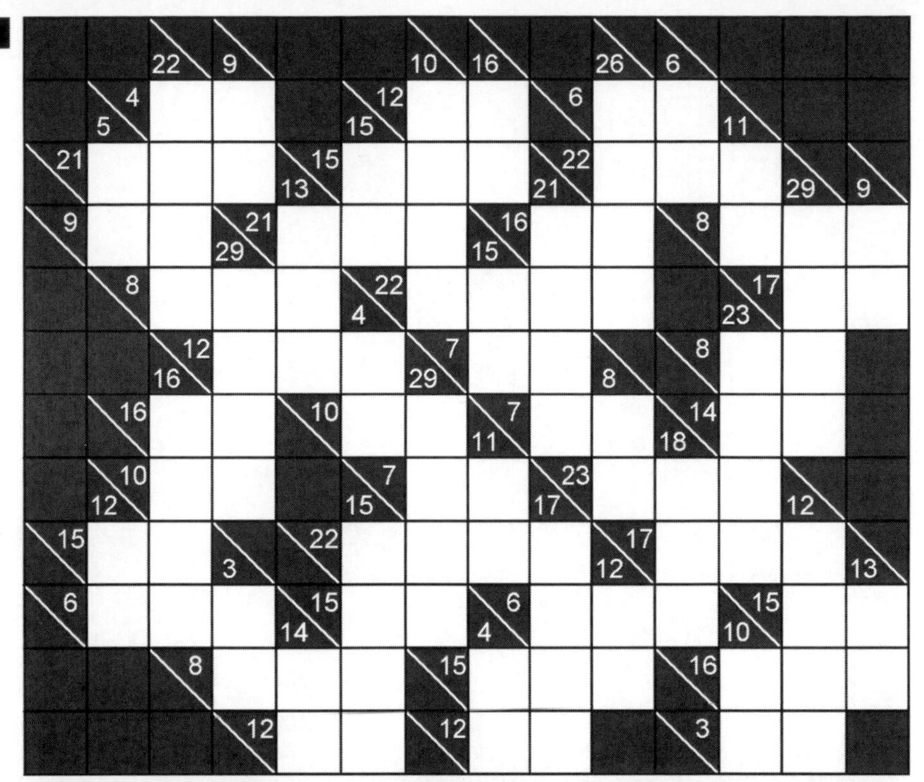

90

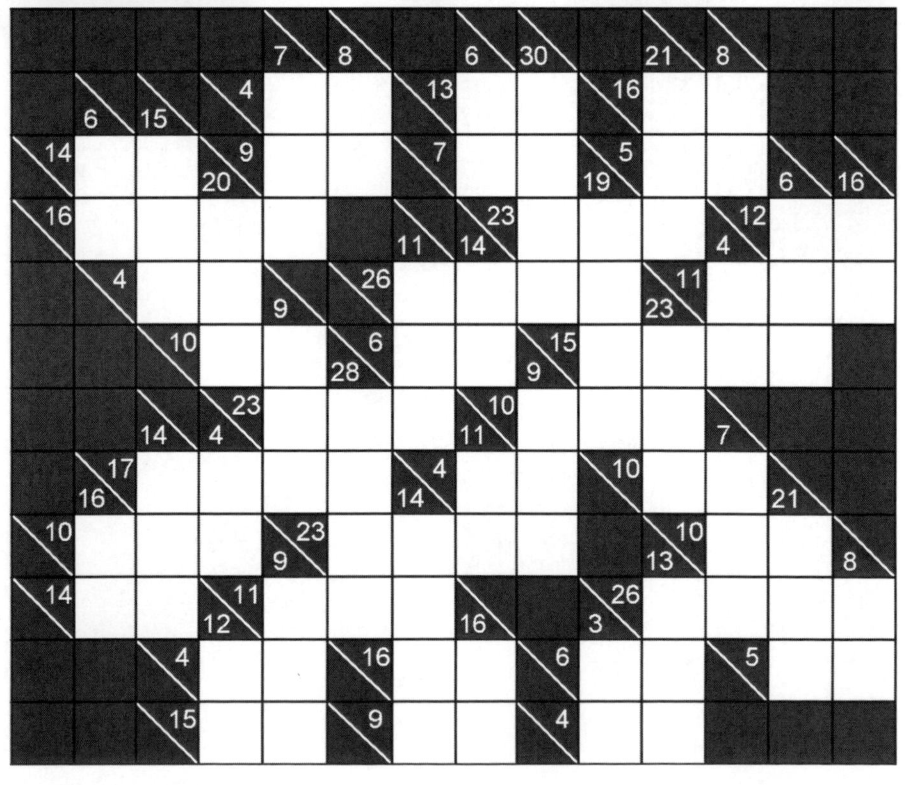

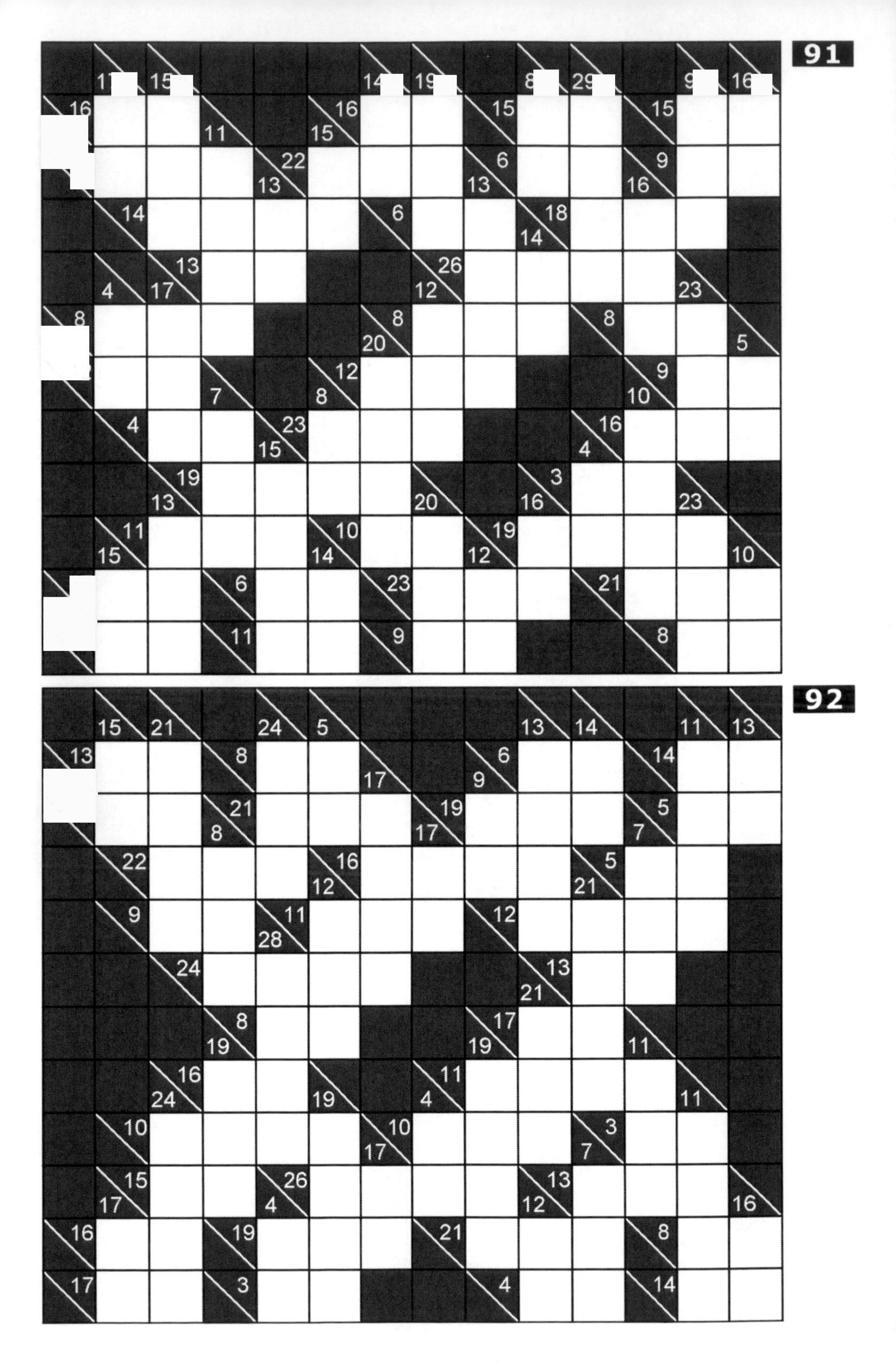

93

94

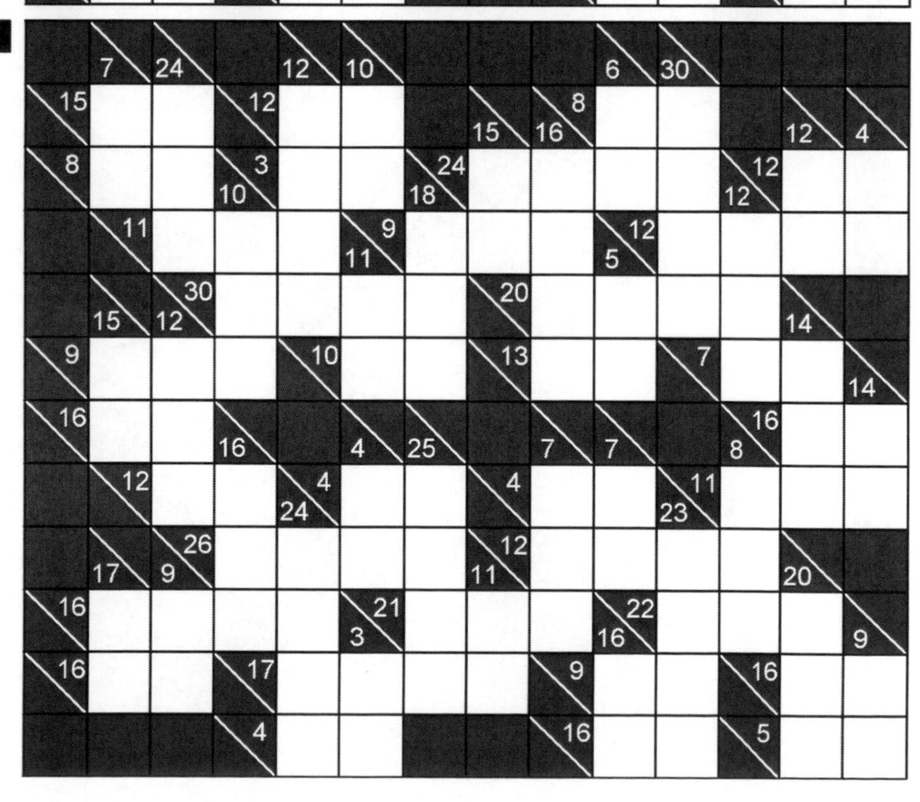

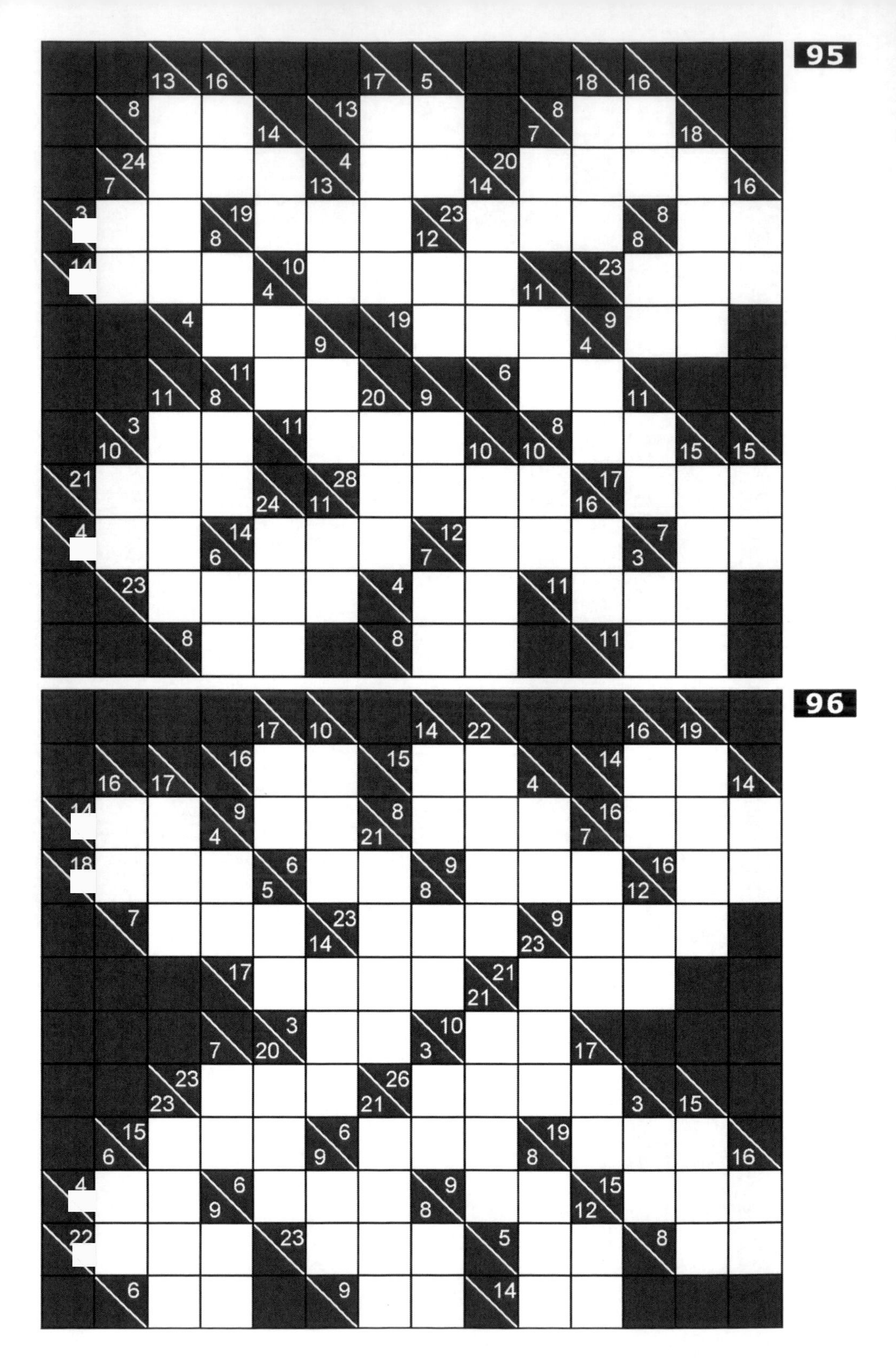
95
96

97

98

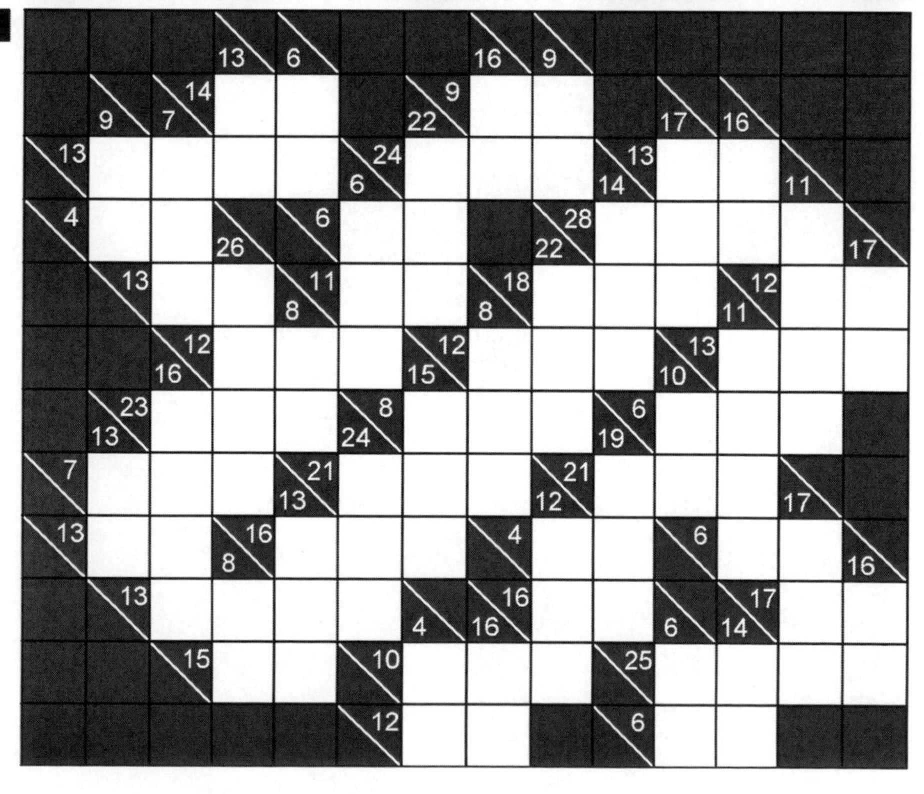

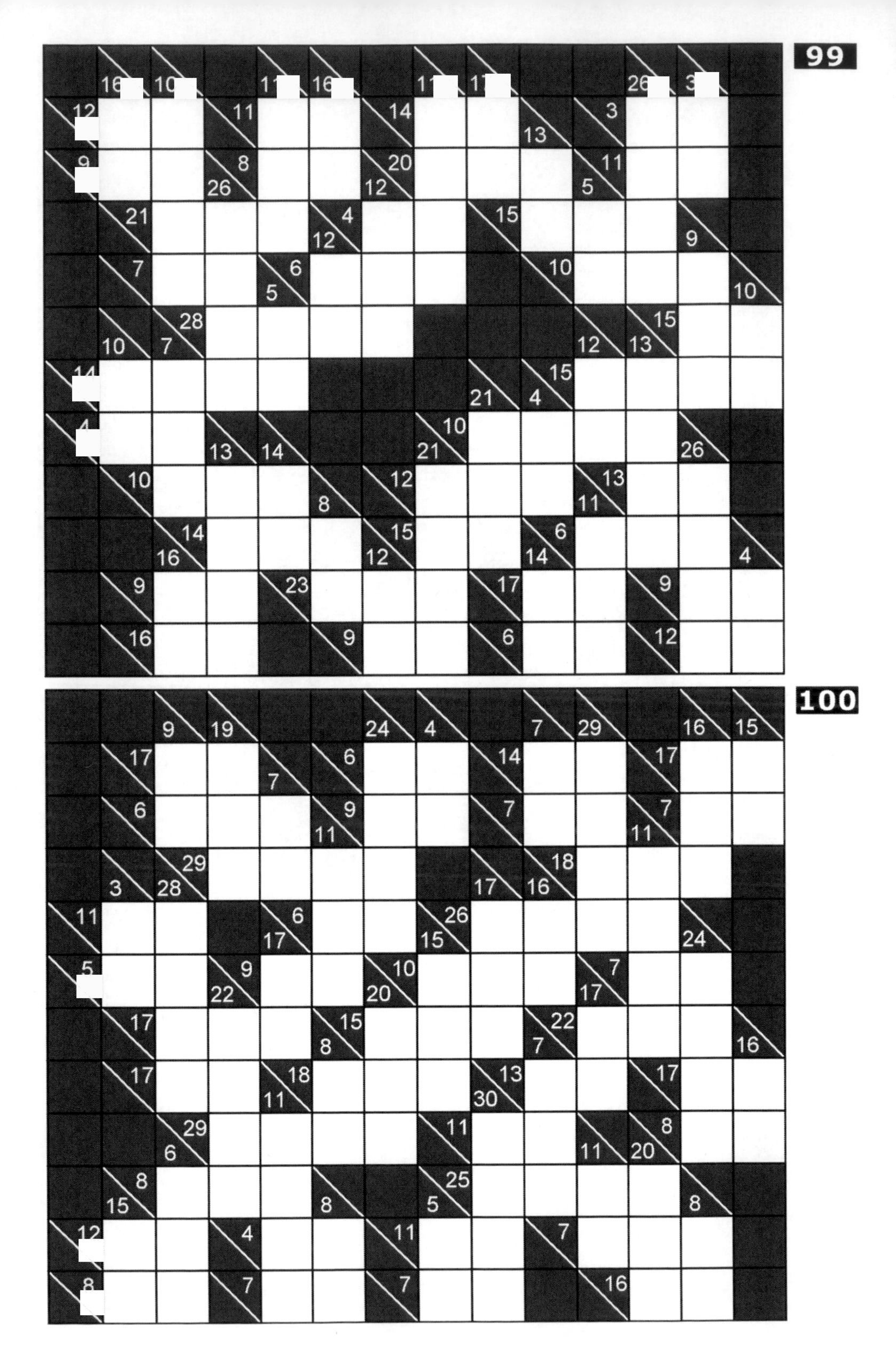

101

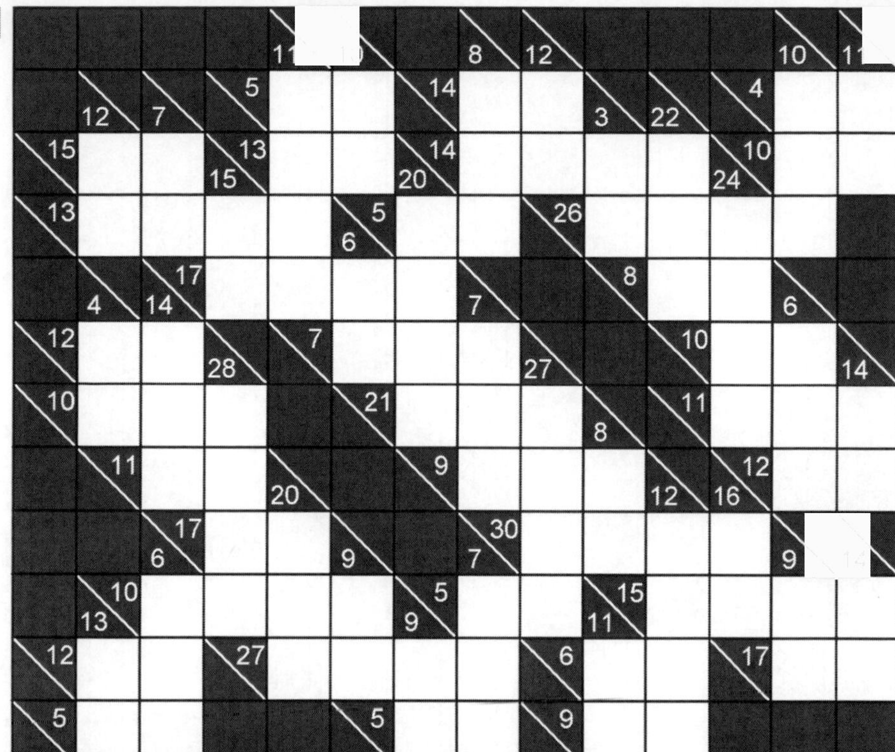

102

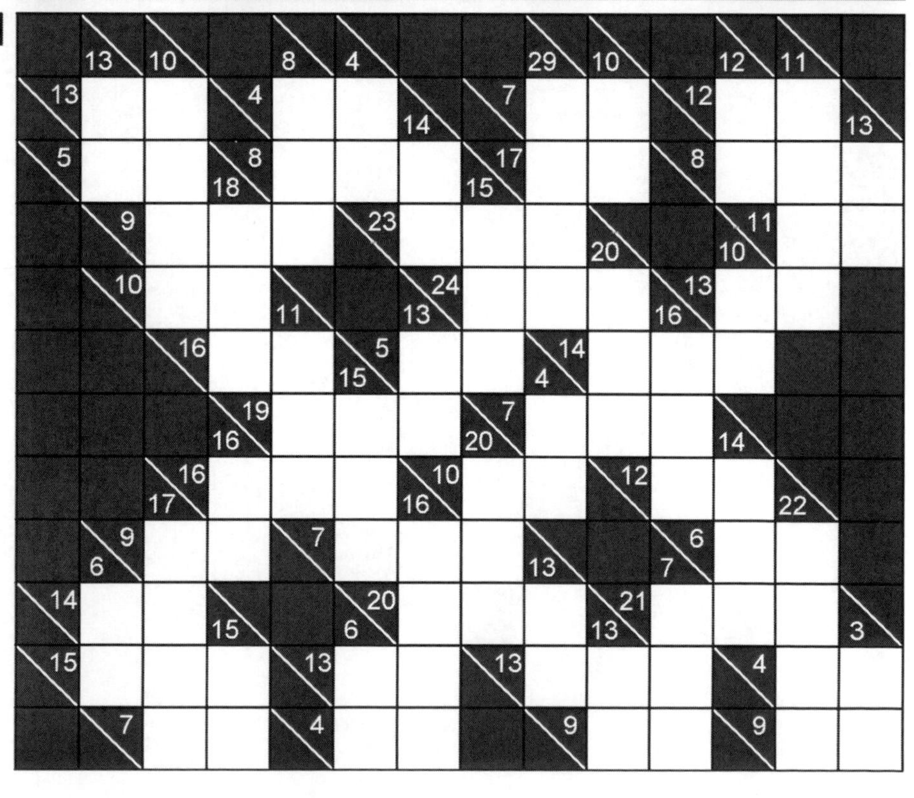

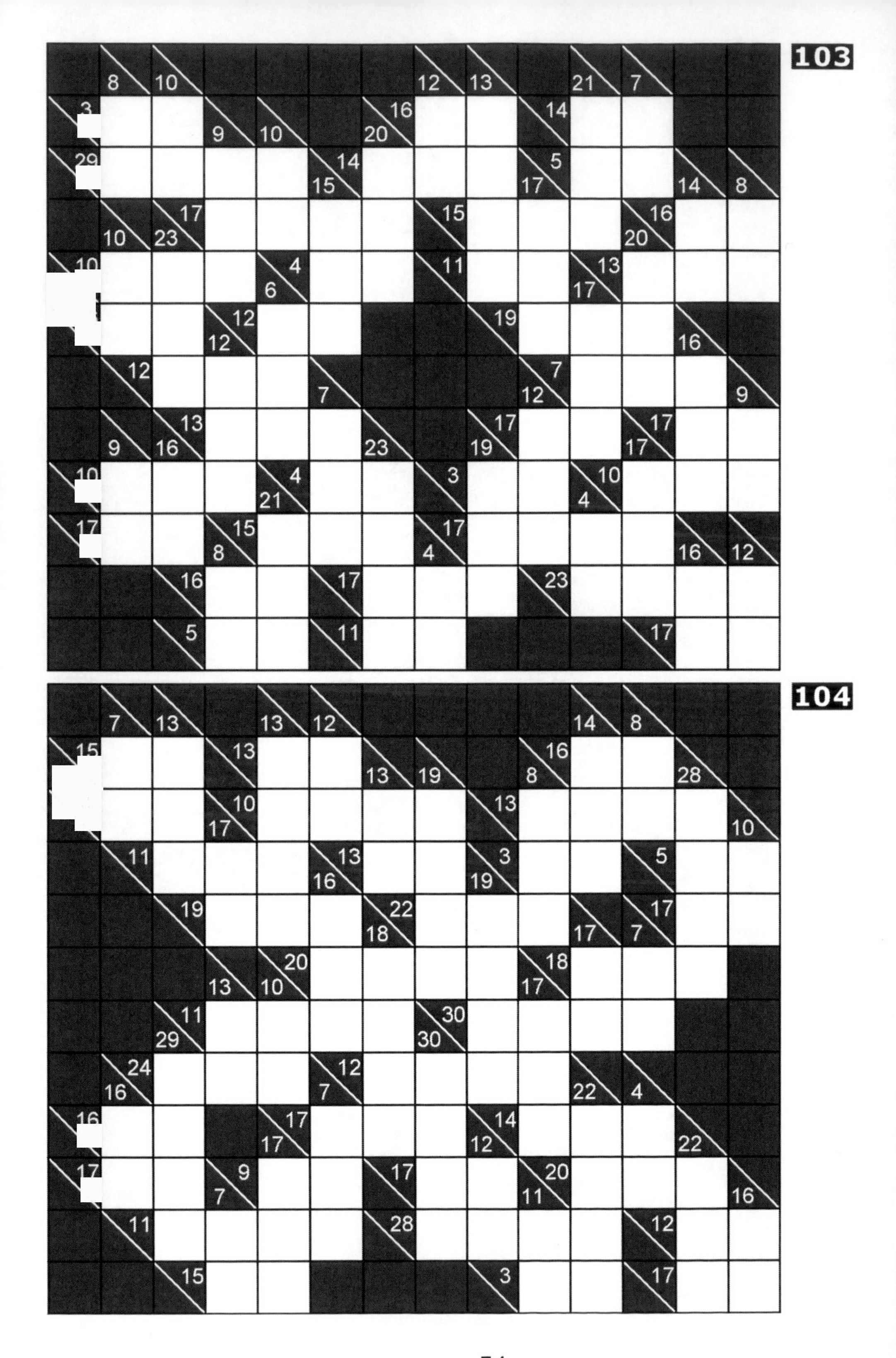

103
104

105

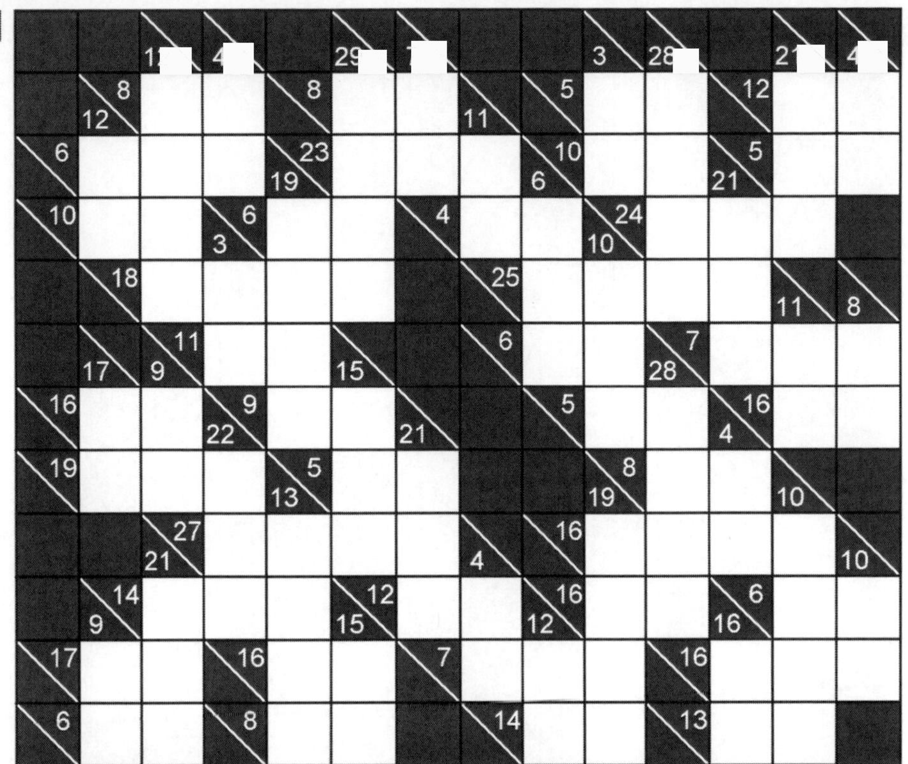

106

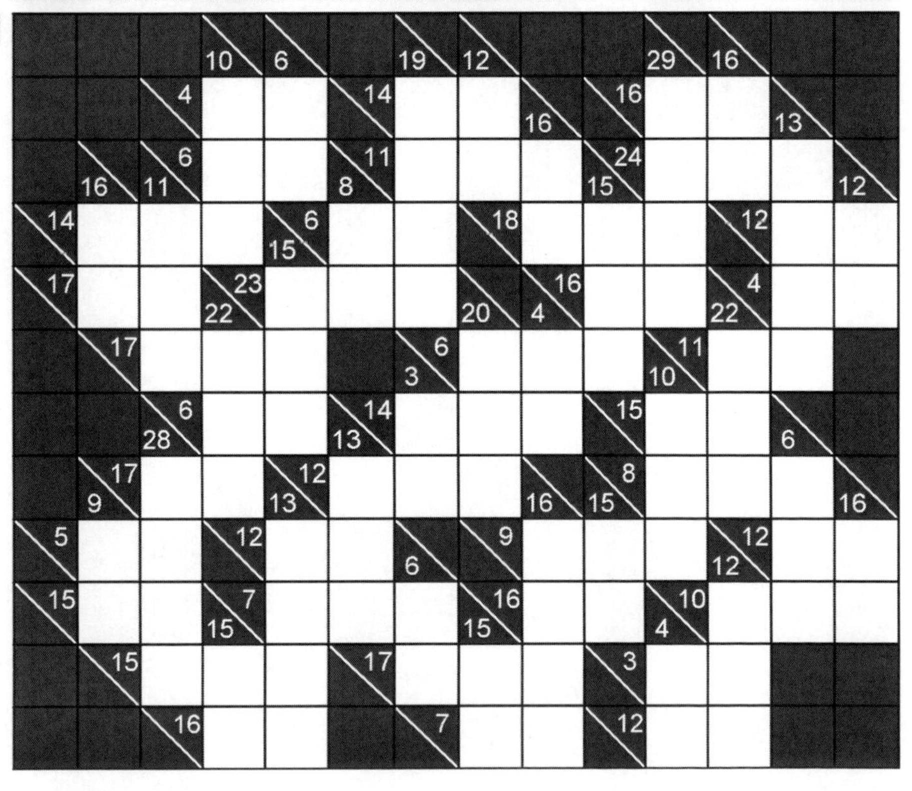

107

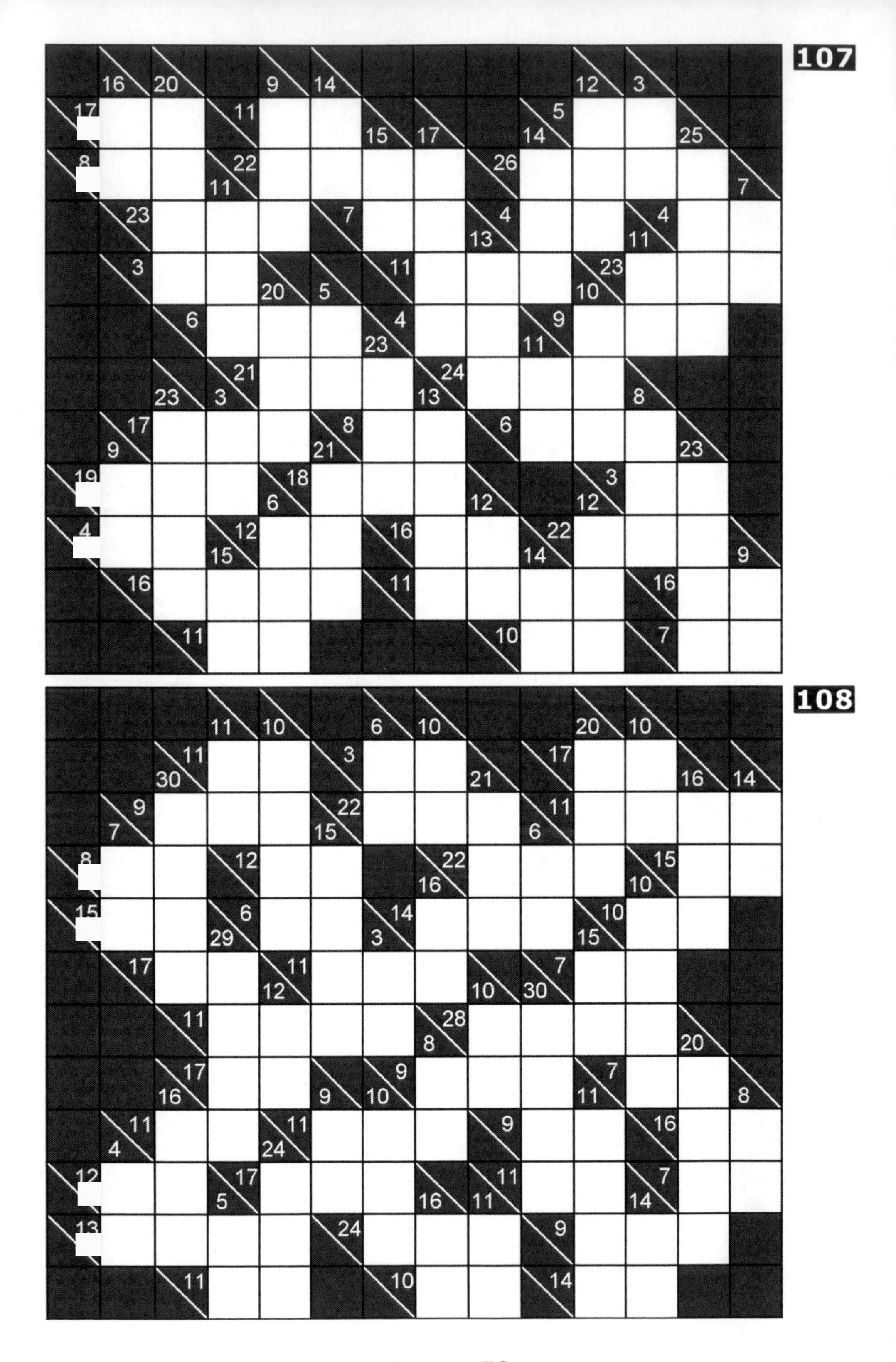

108

109

110

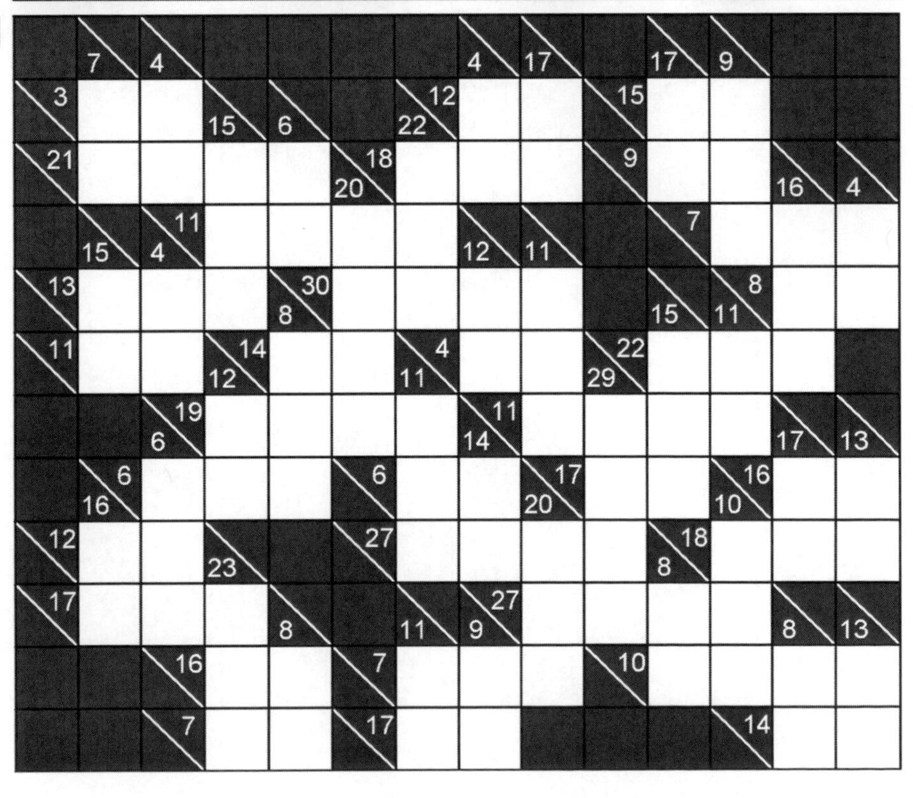

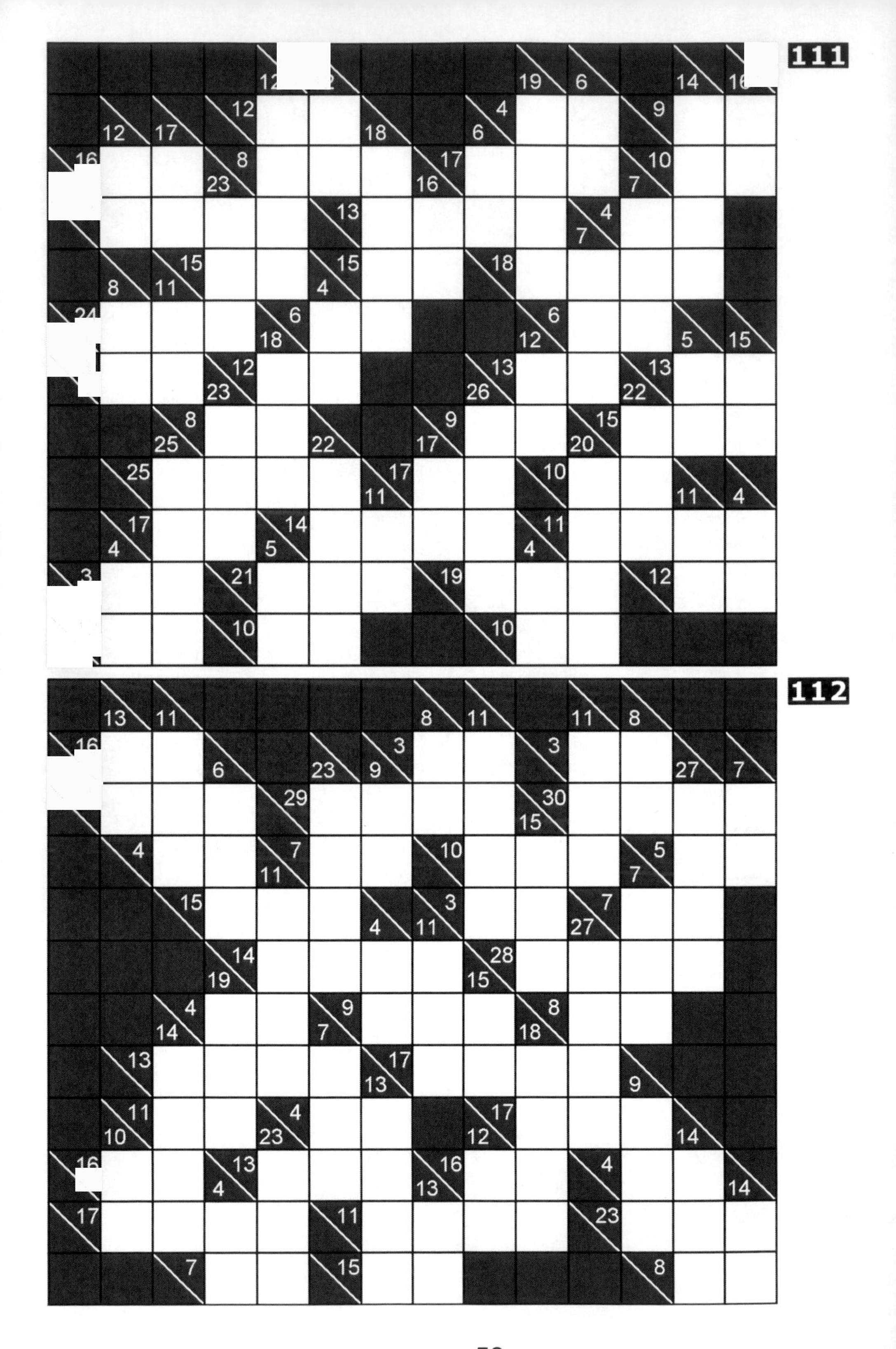
111
112

113

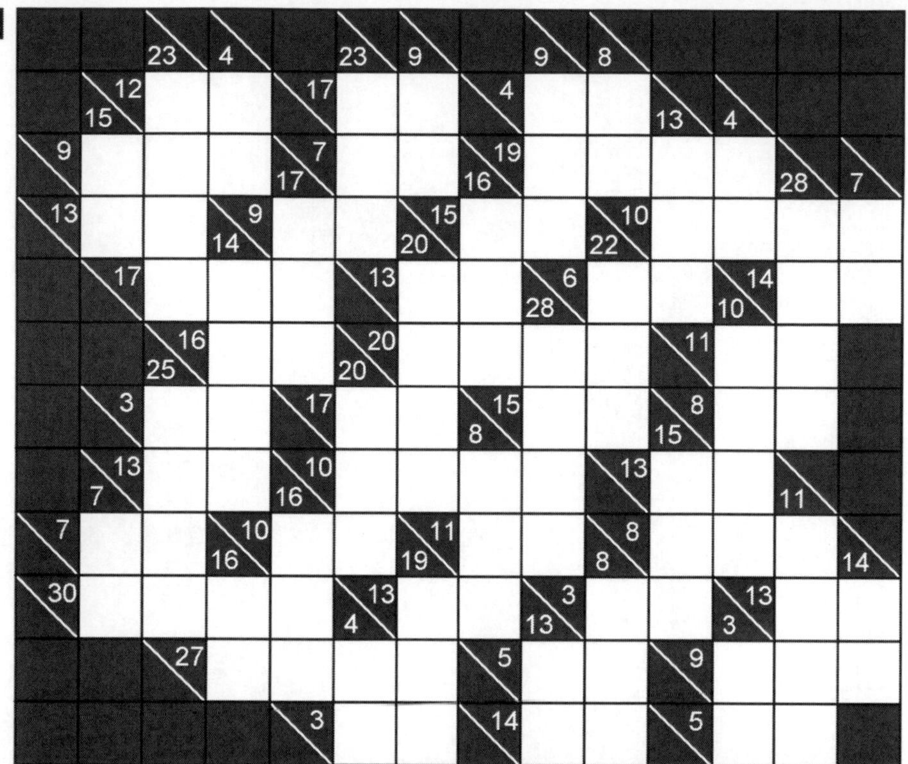

114

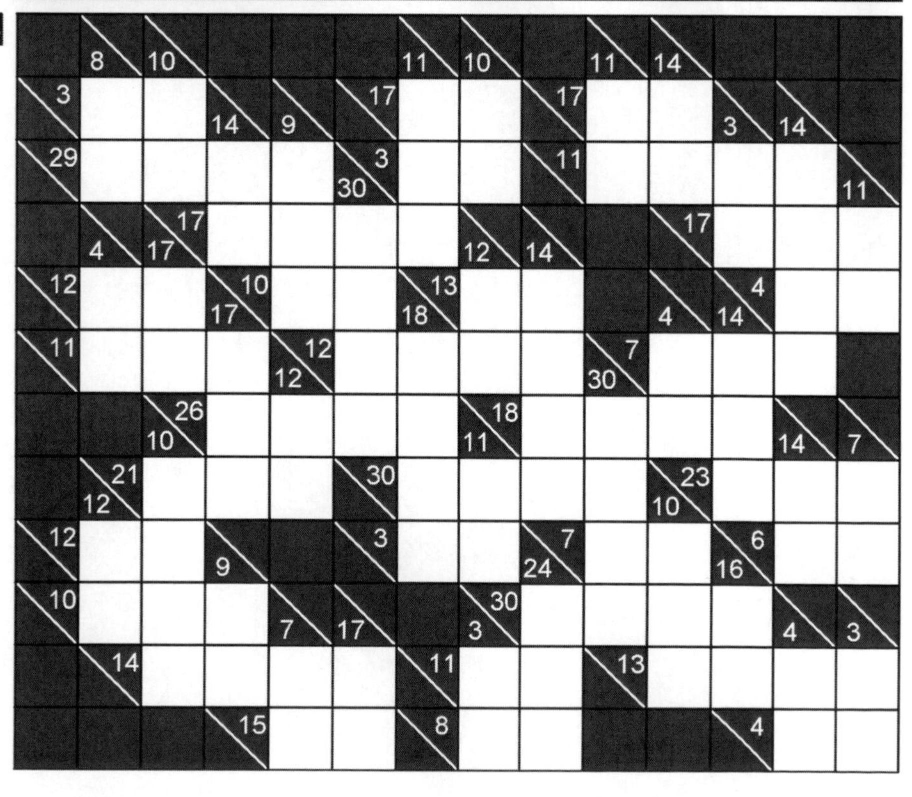

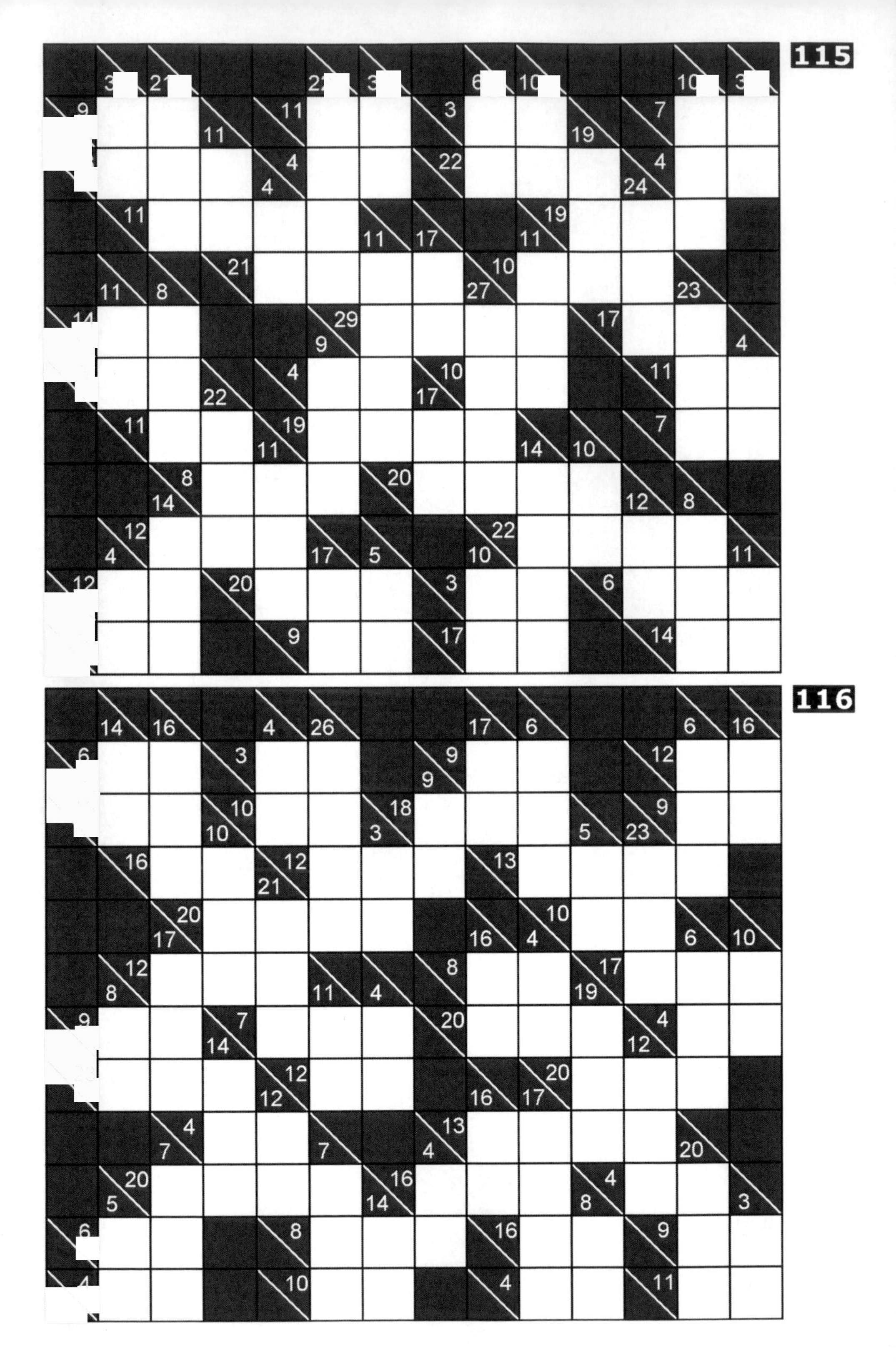
115
116

117

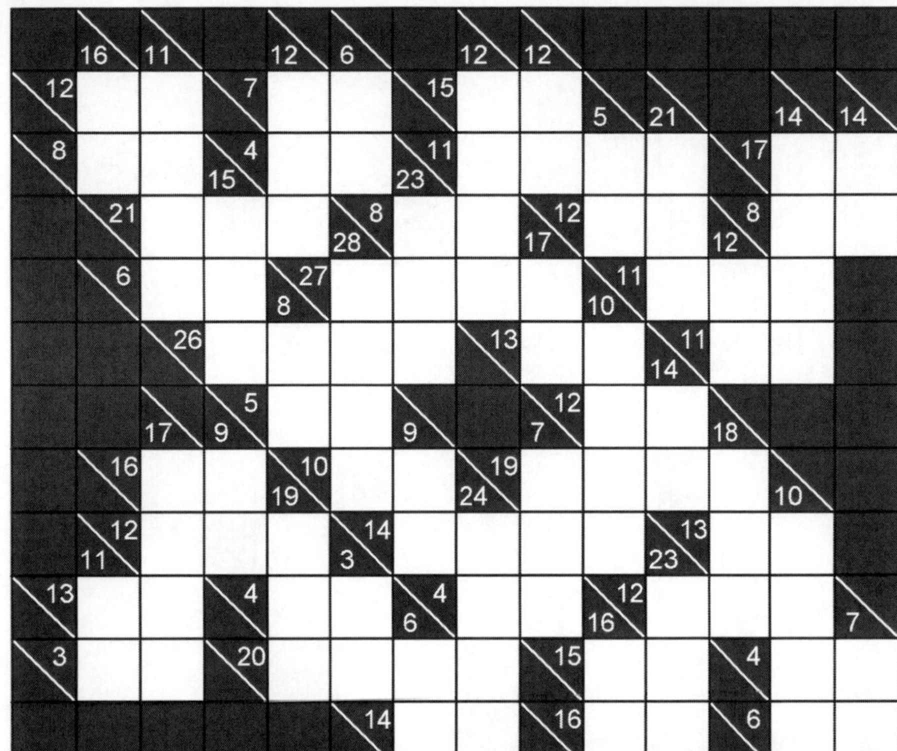

118

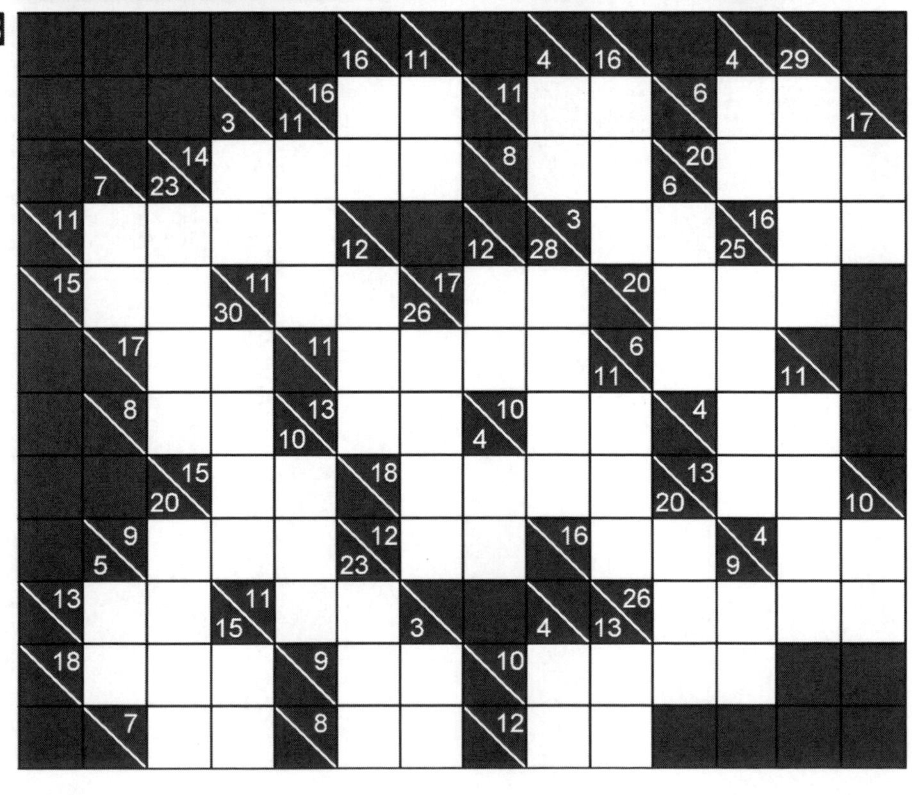

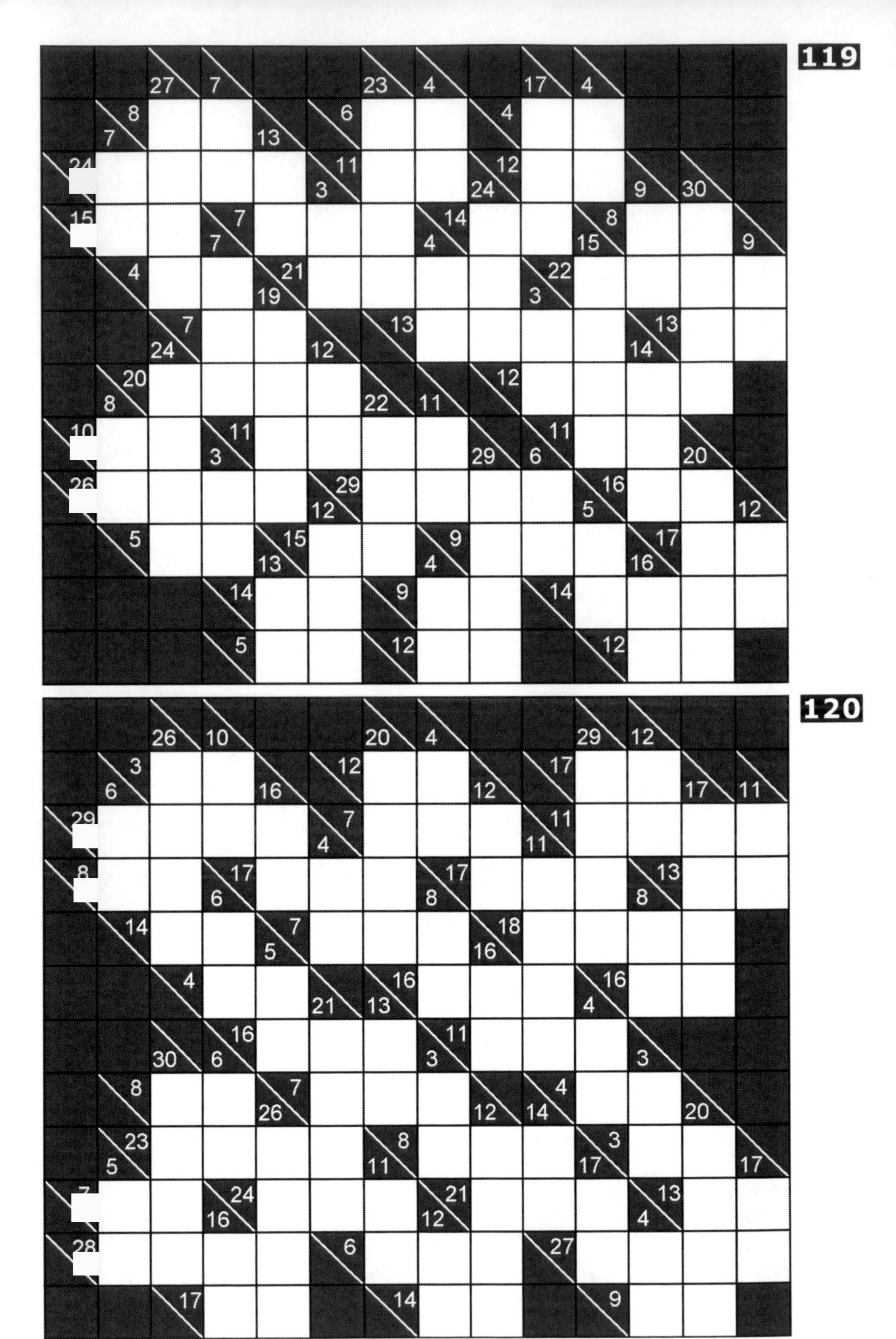

121

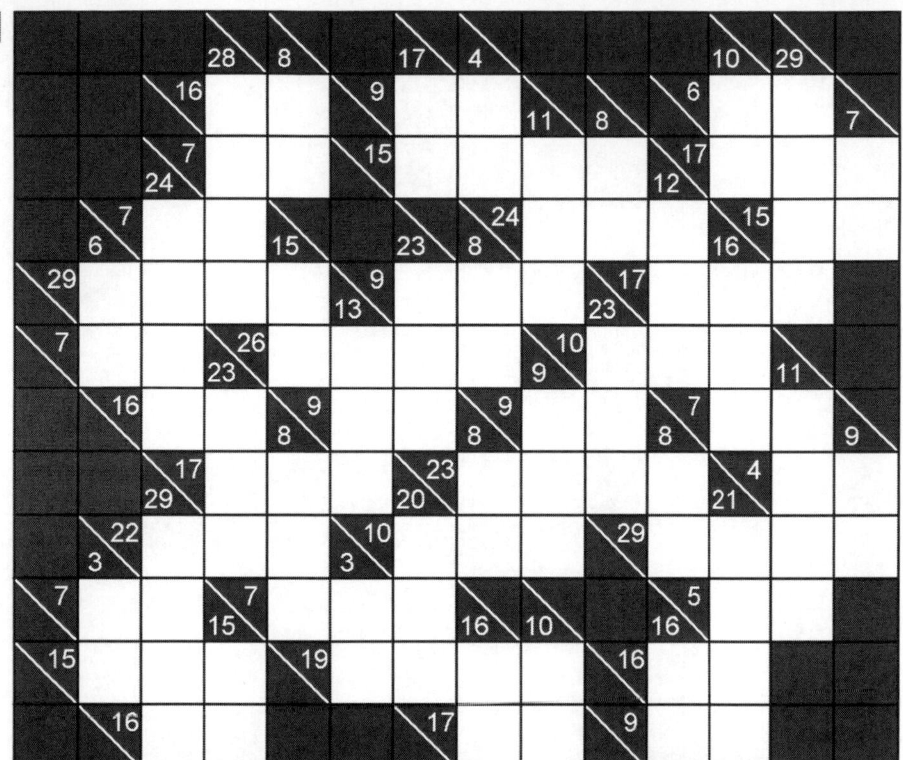

122

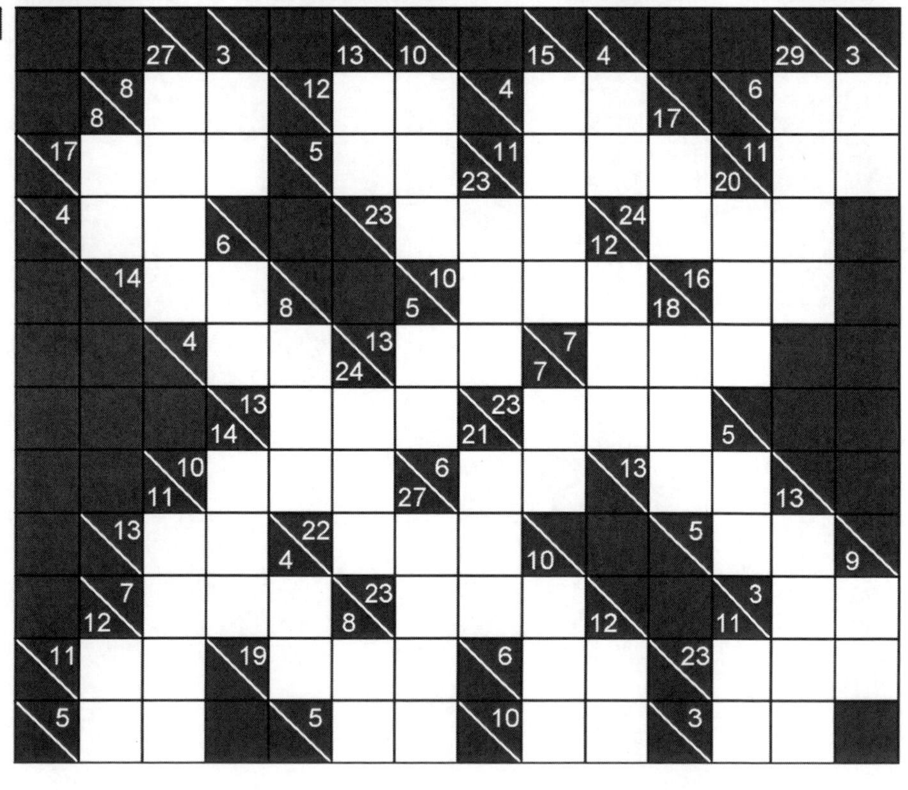

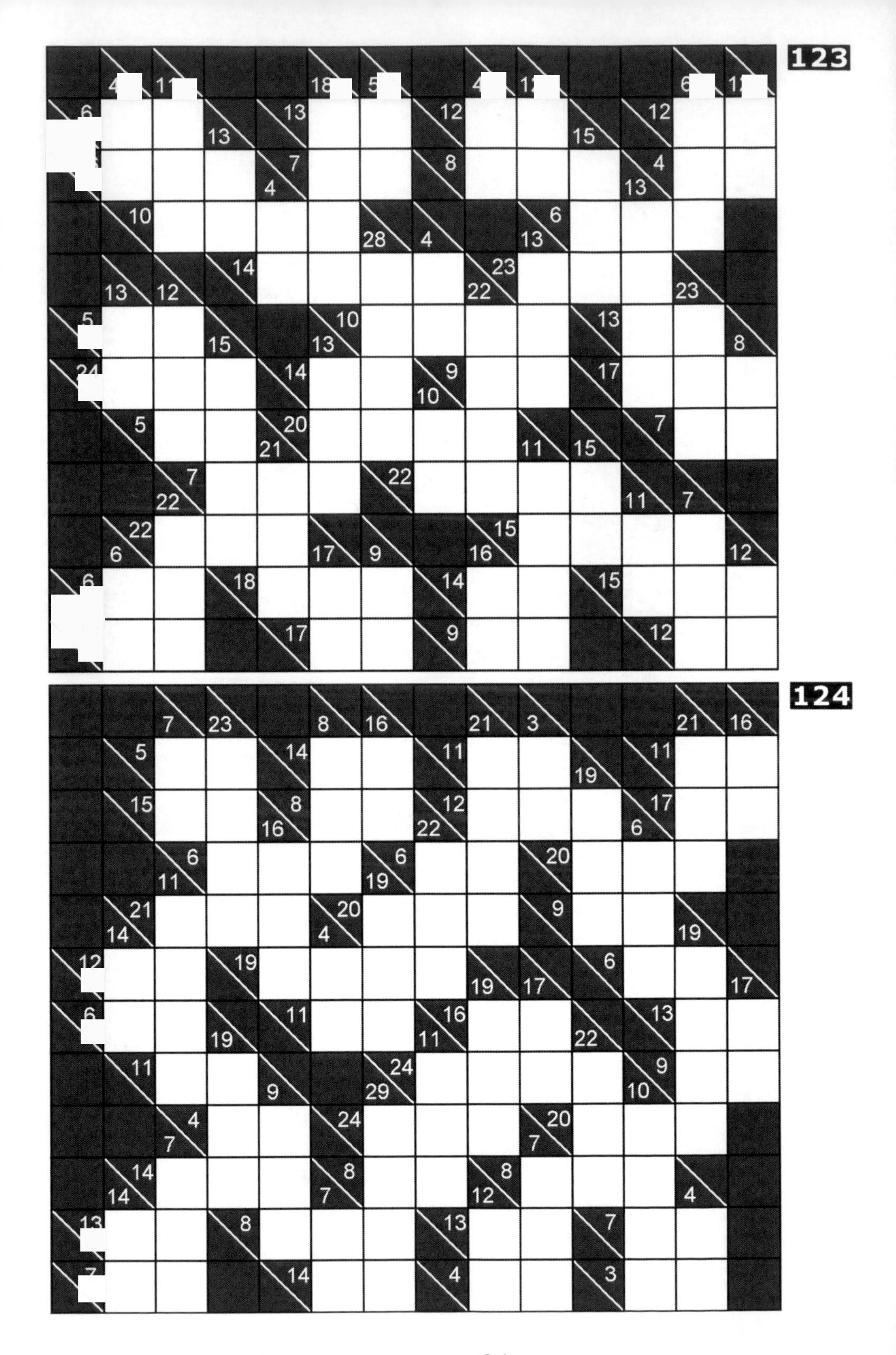

125

126

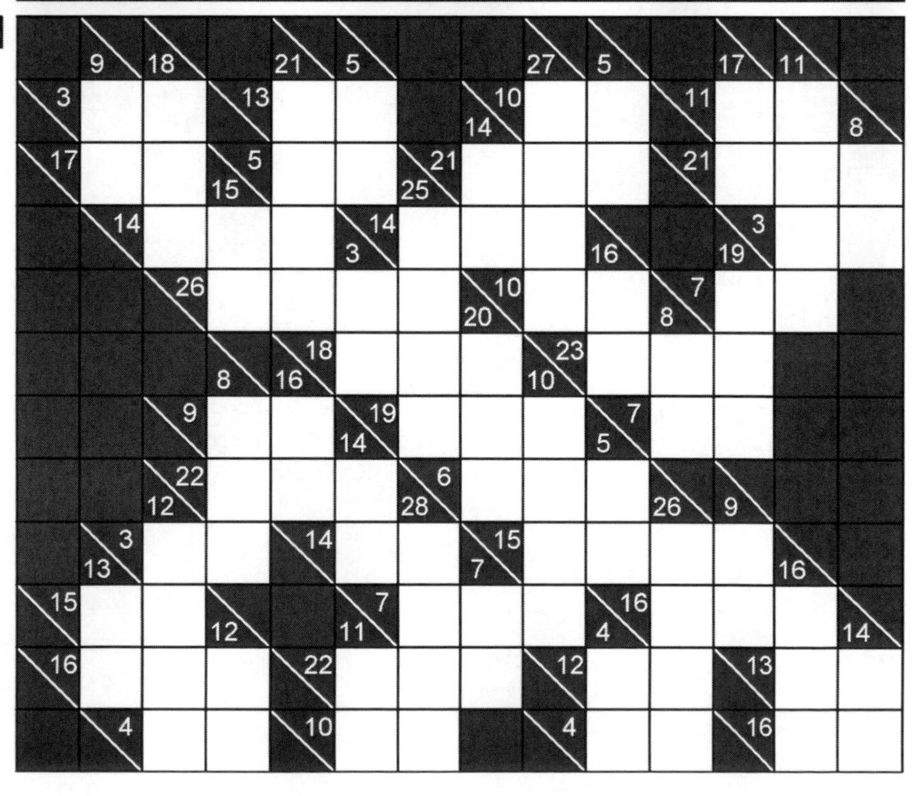

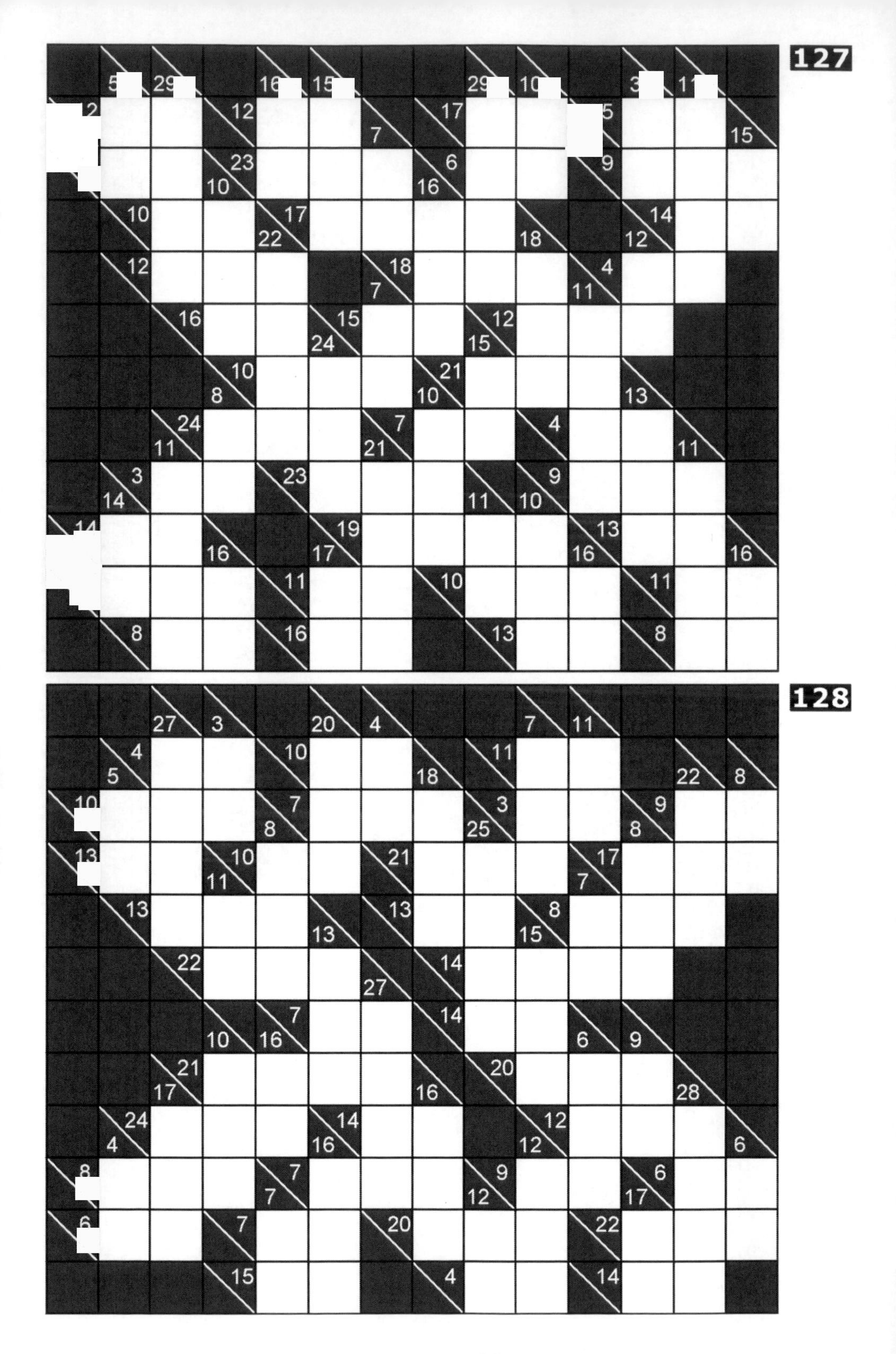

129

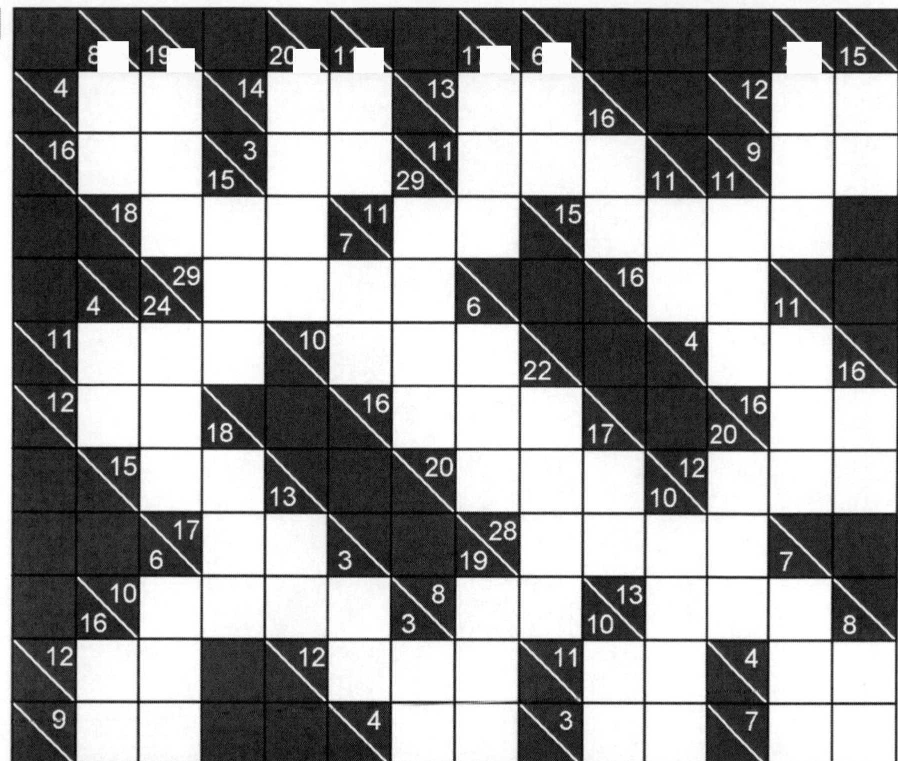

130

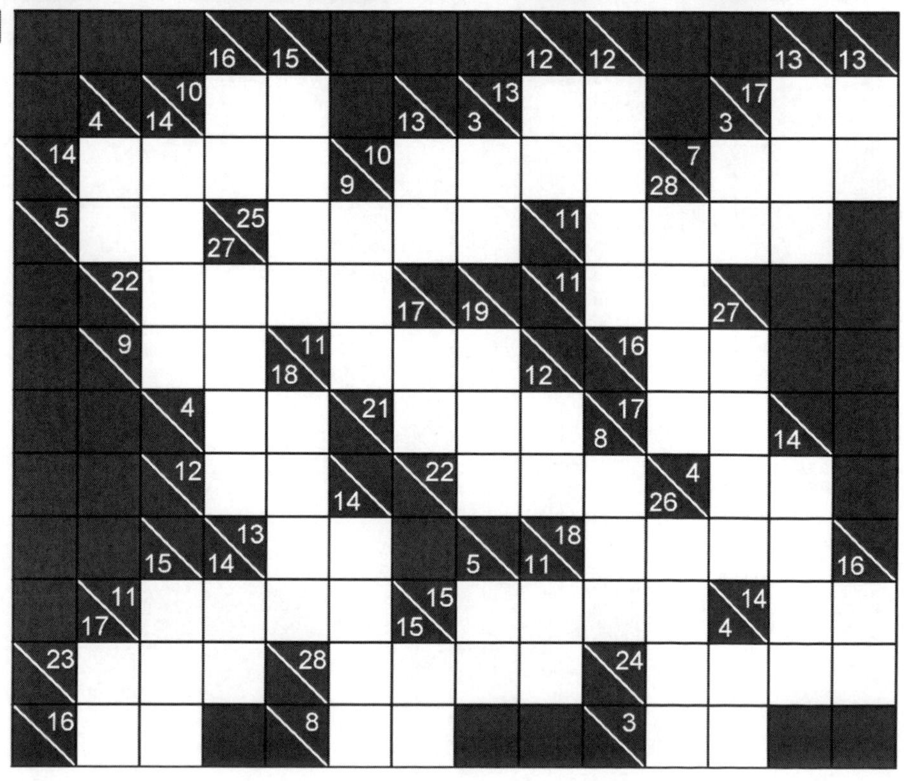

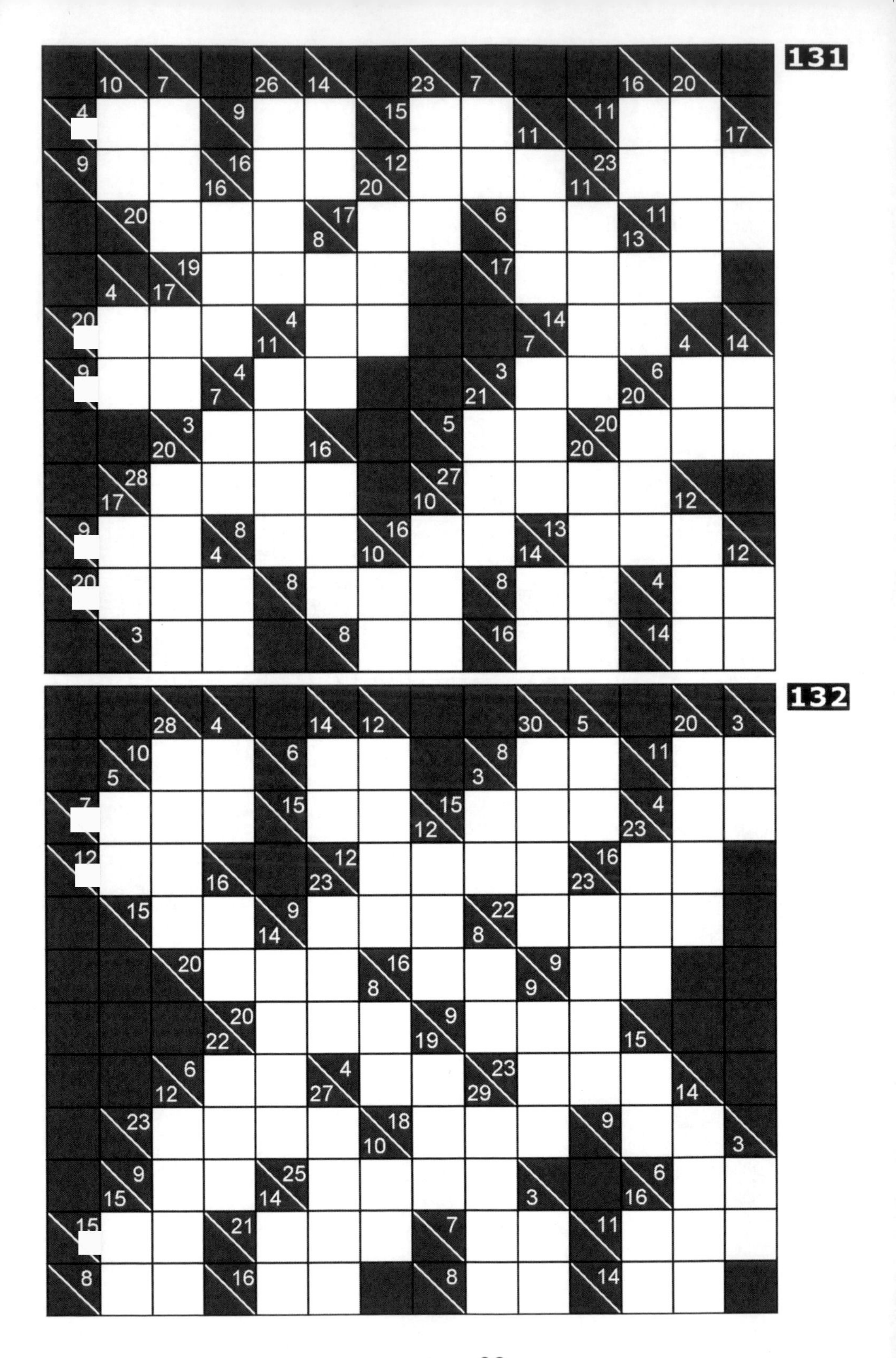
131
132

133

134

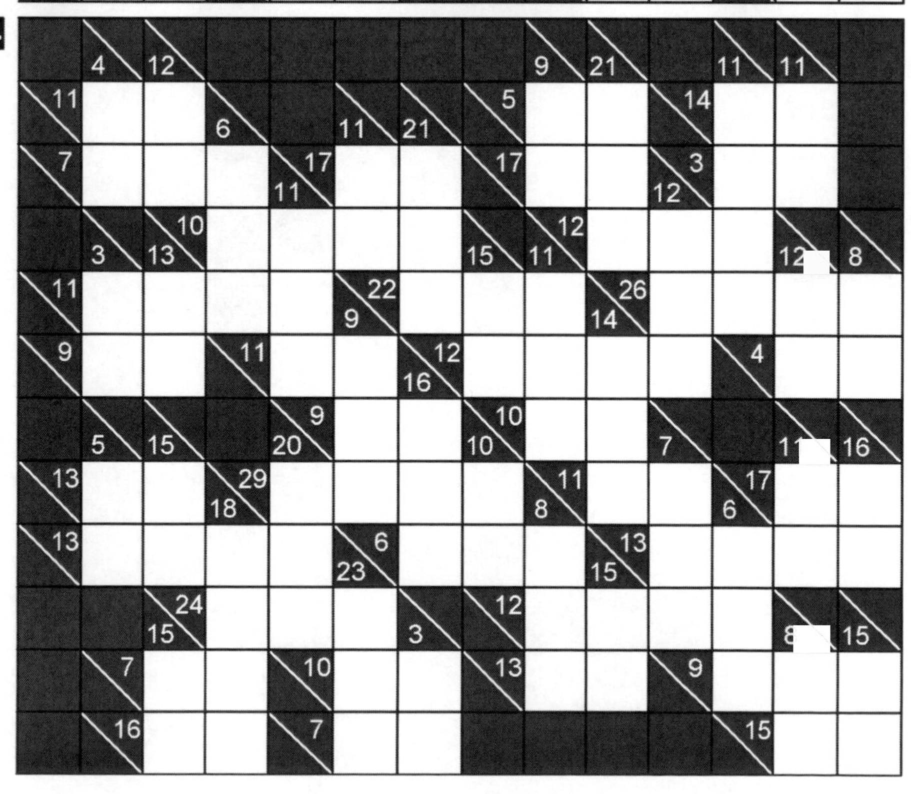

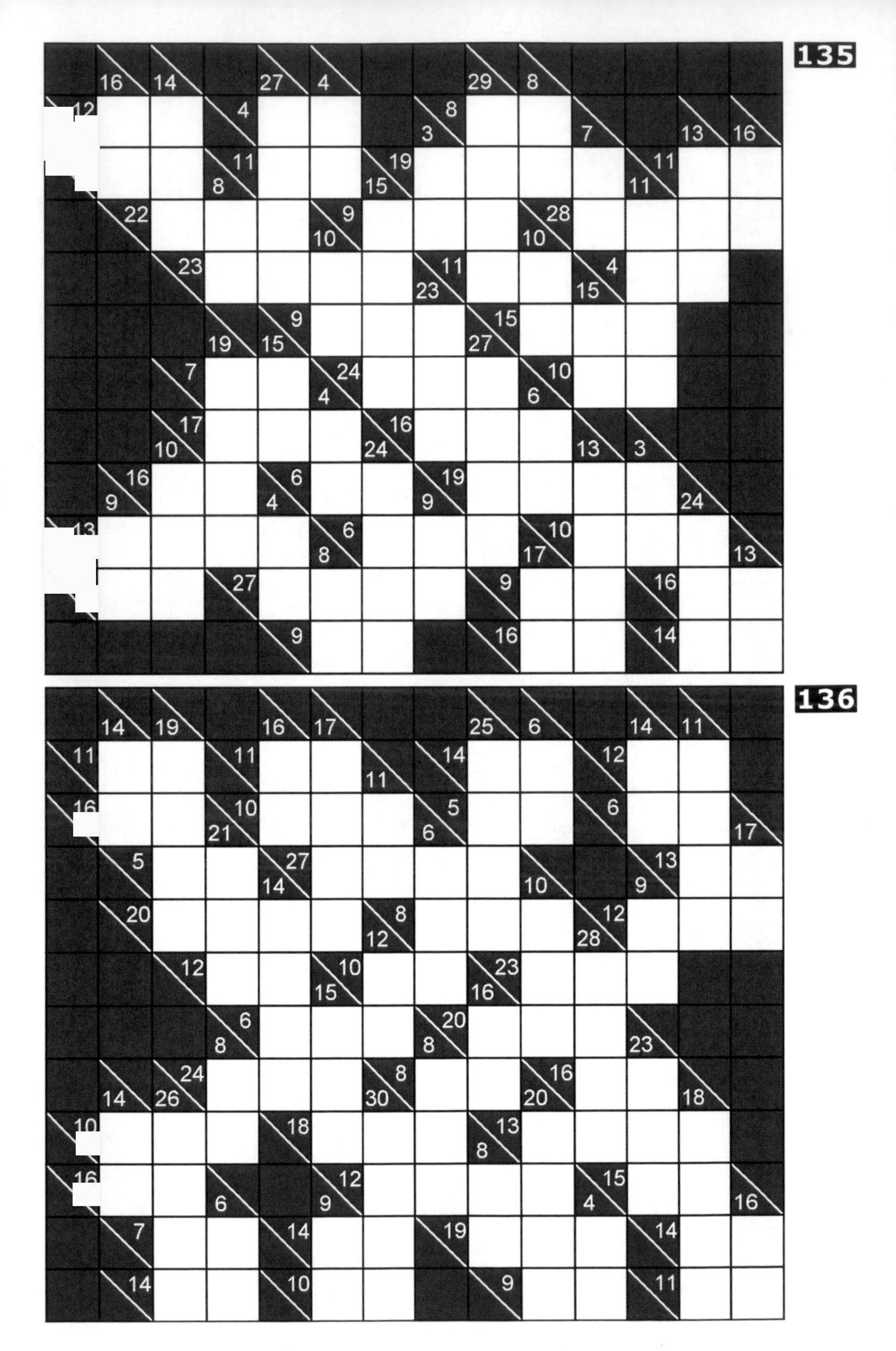
135
136

137

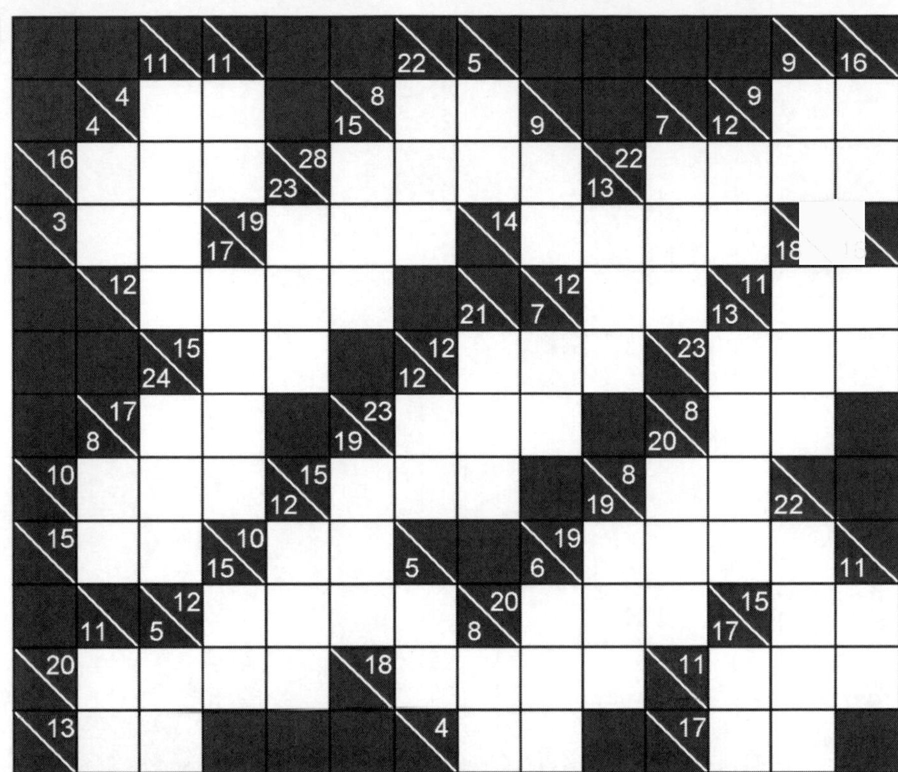

138

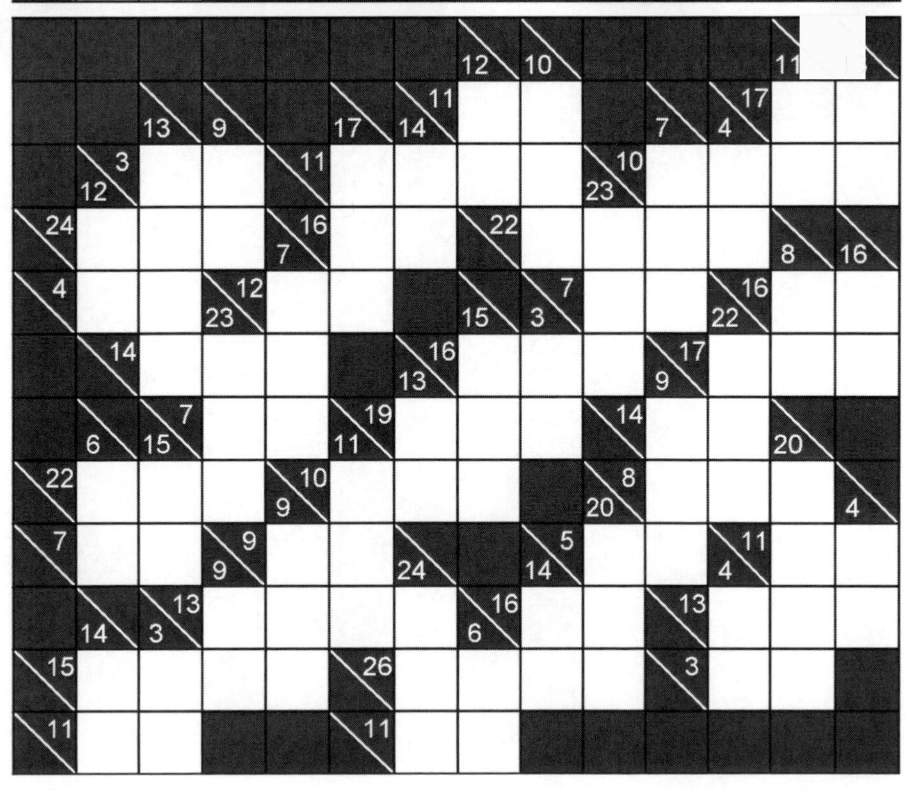

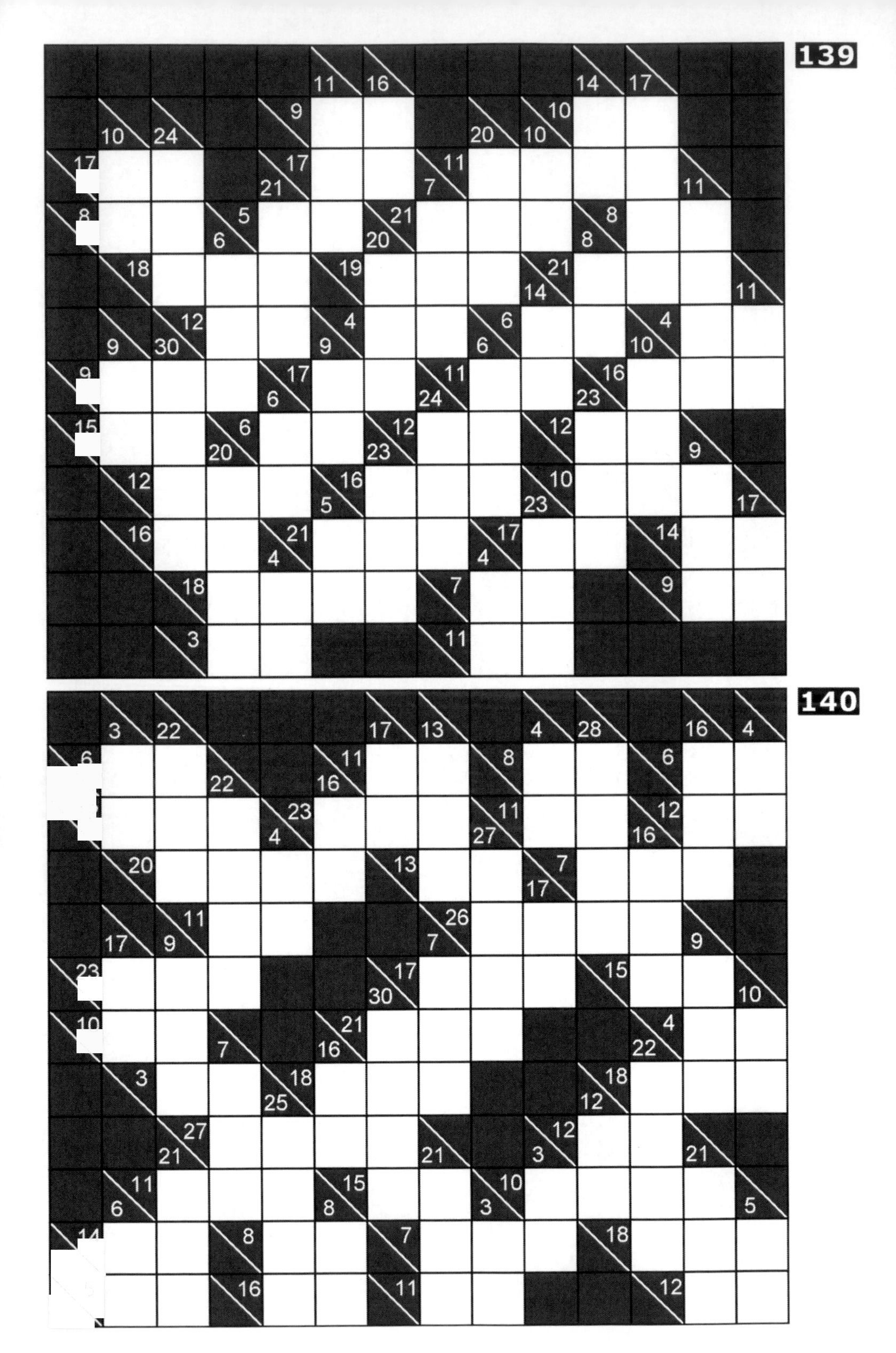
139
140

141

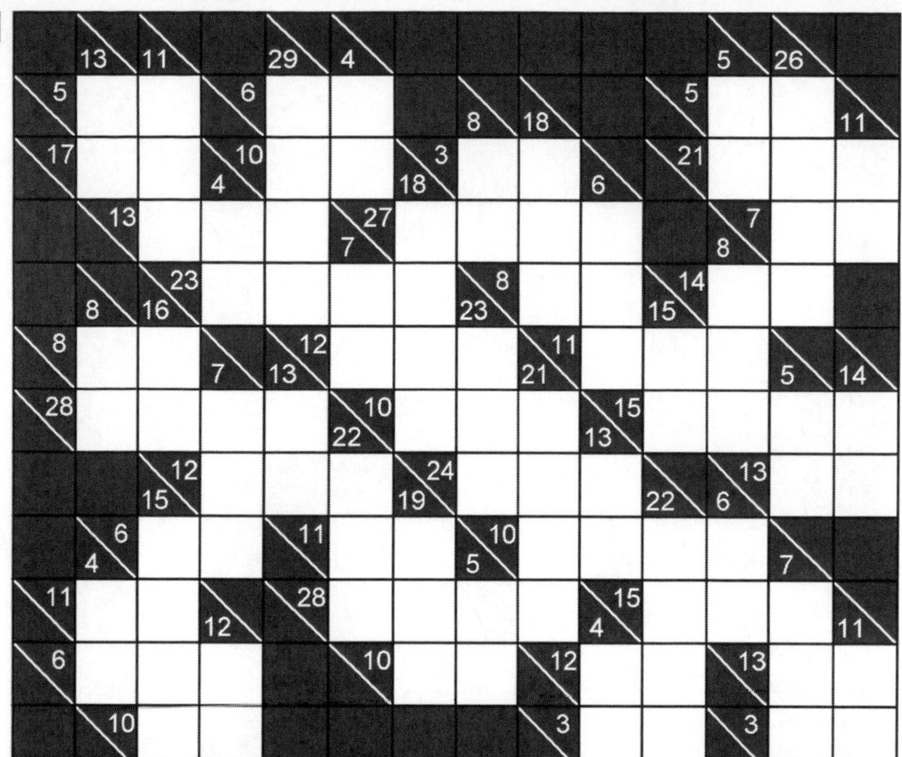

142

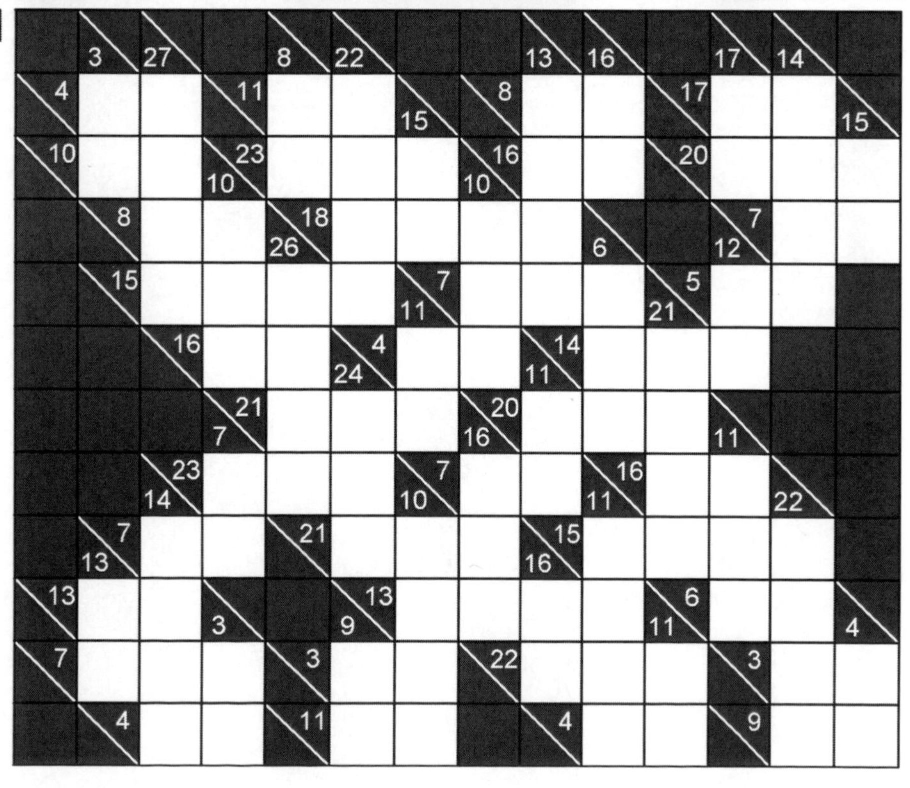

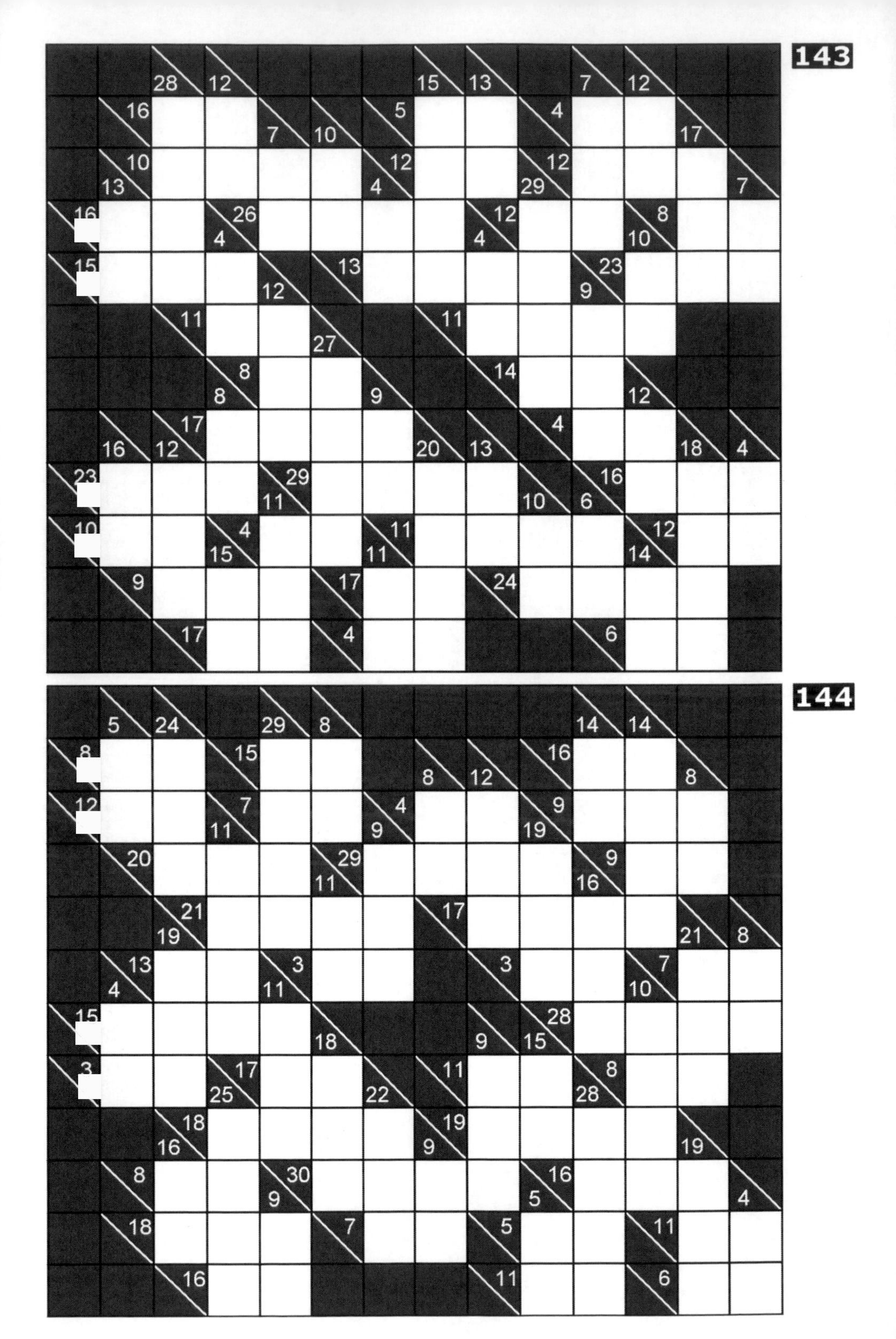
143
144

145

146

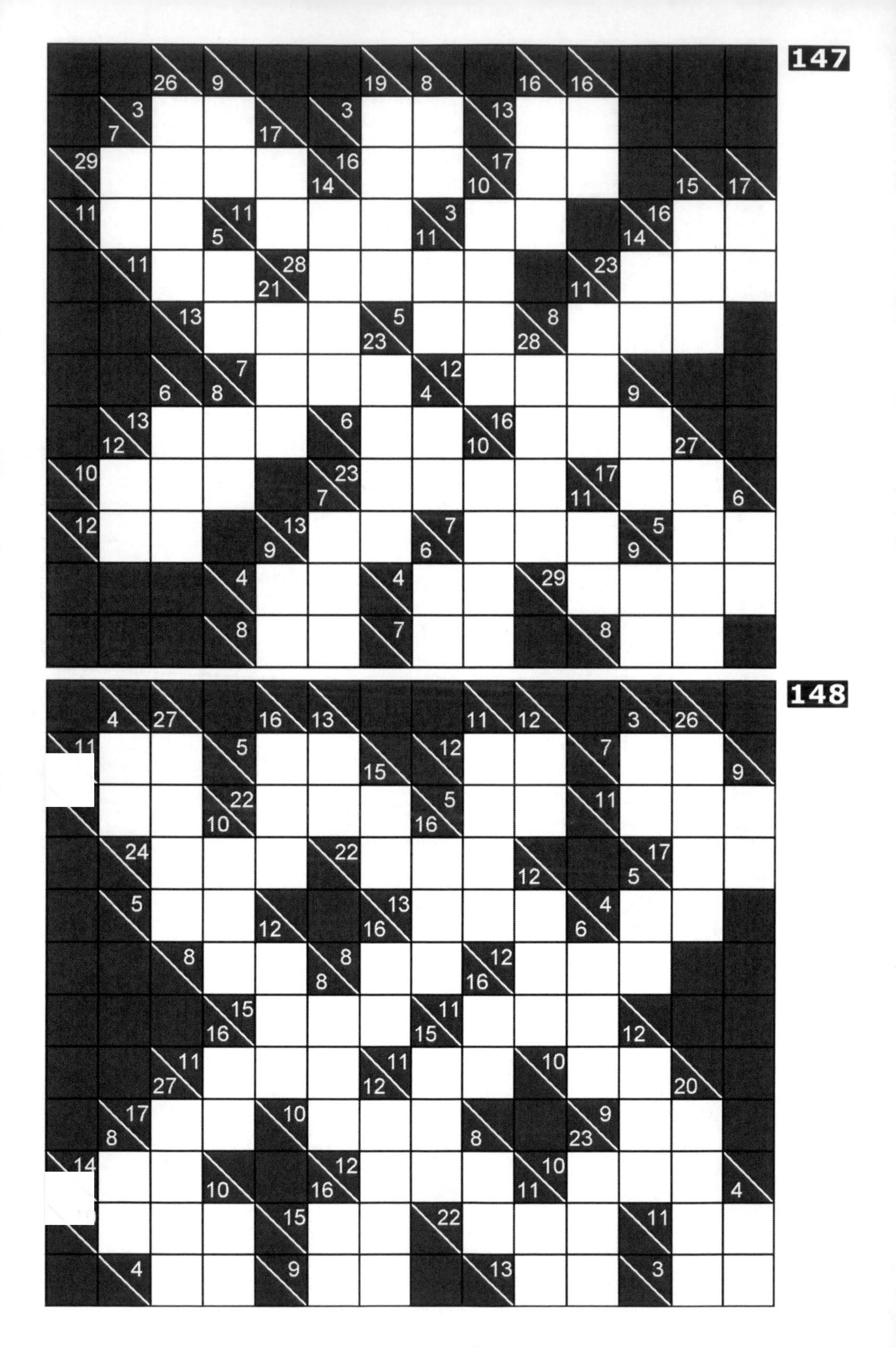
147
148

149

150

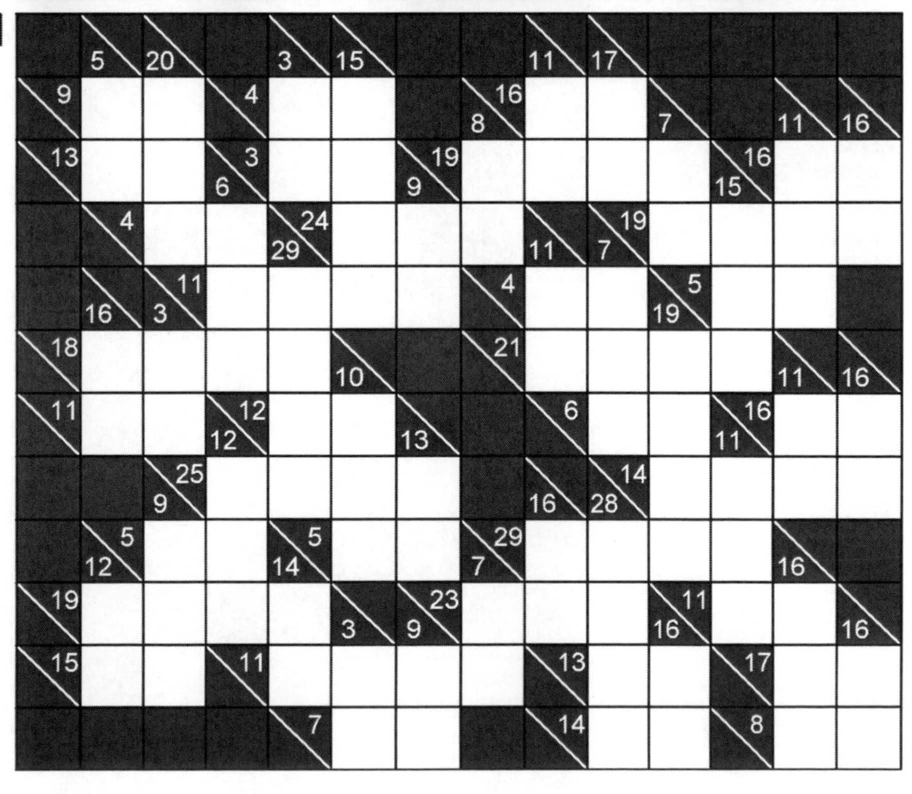

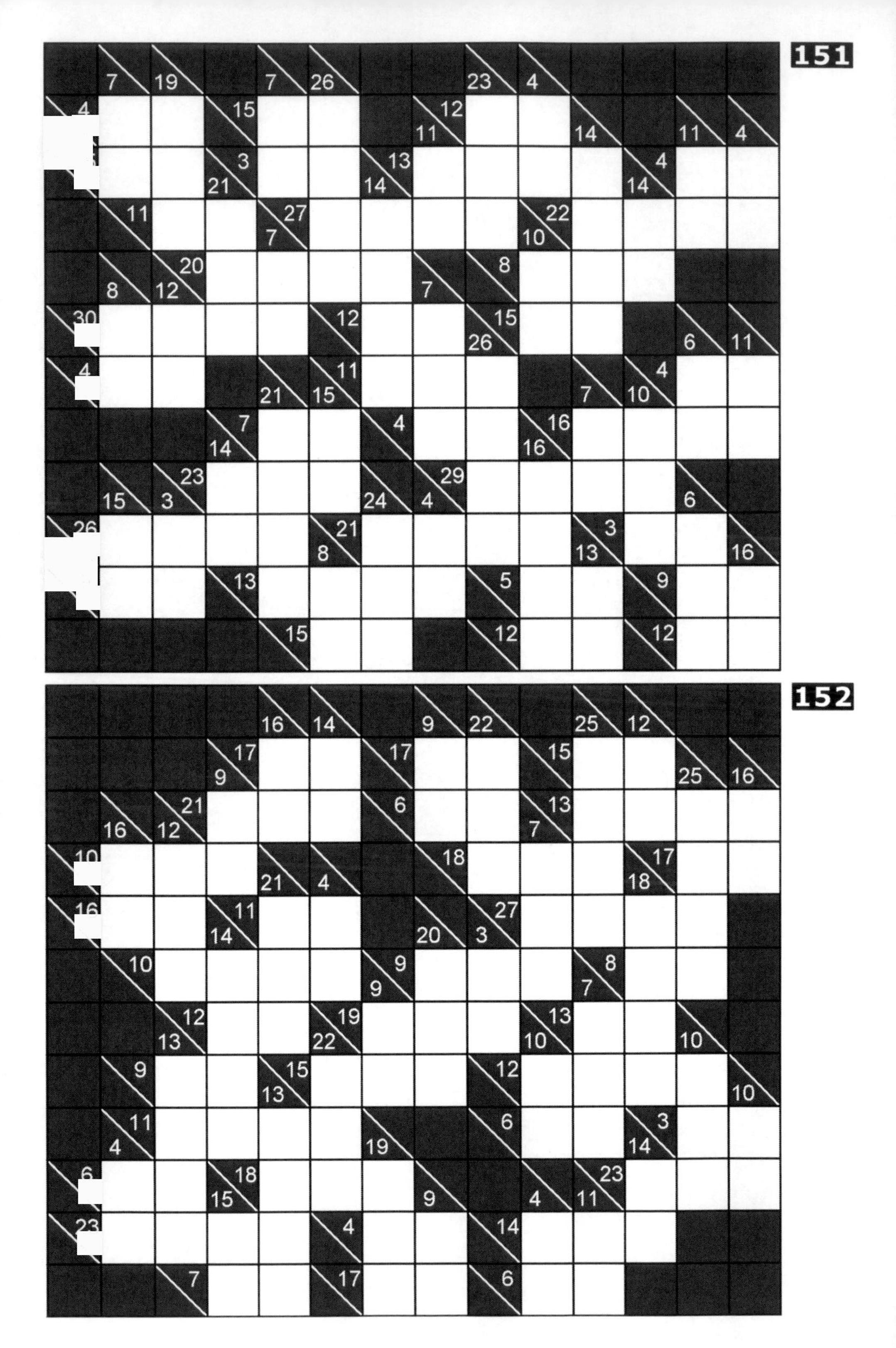
151
152

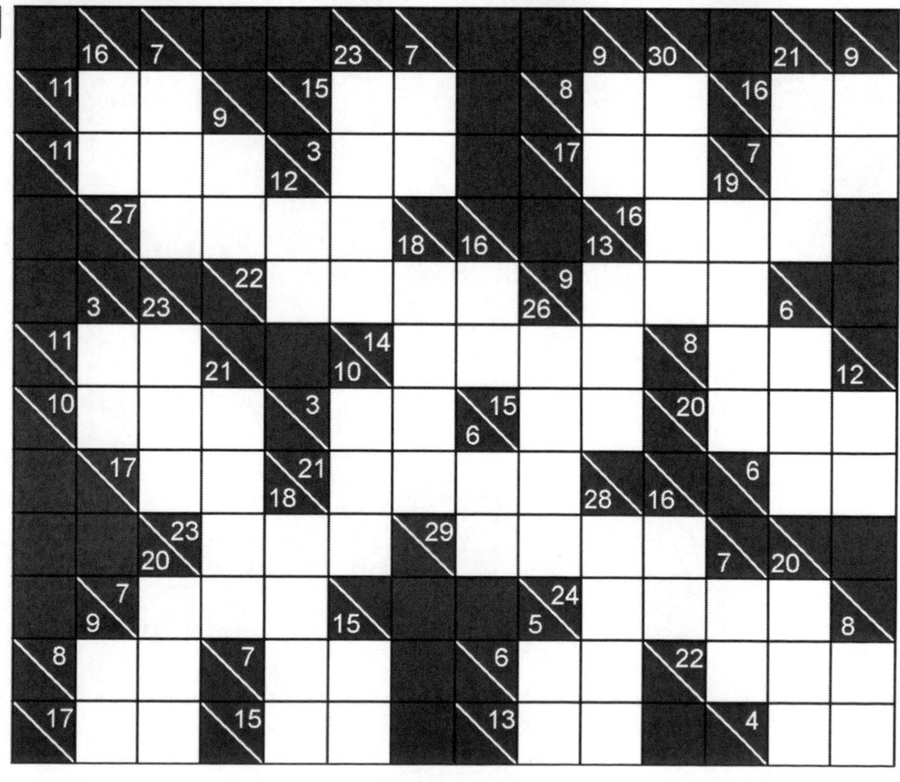

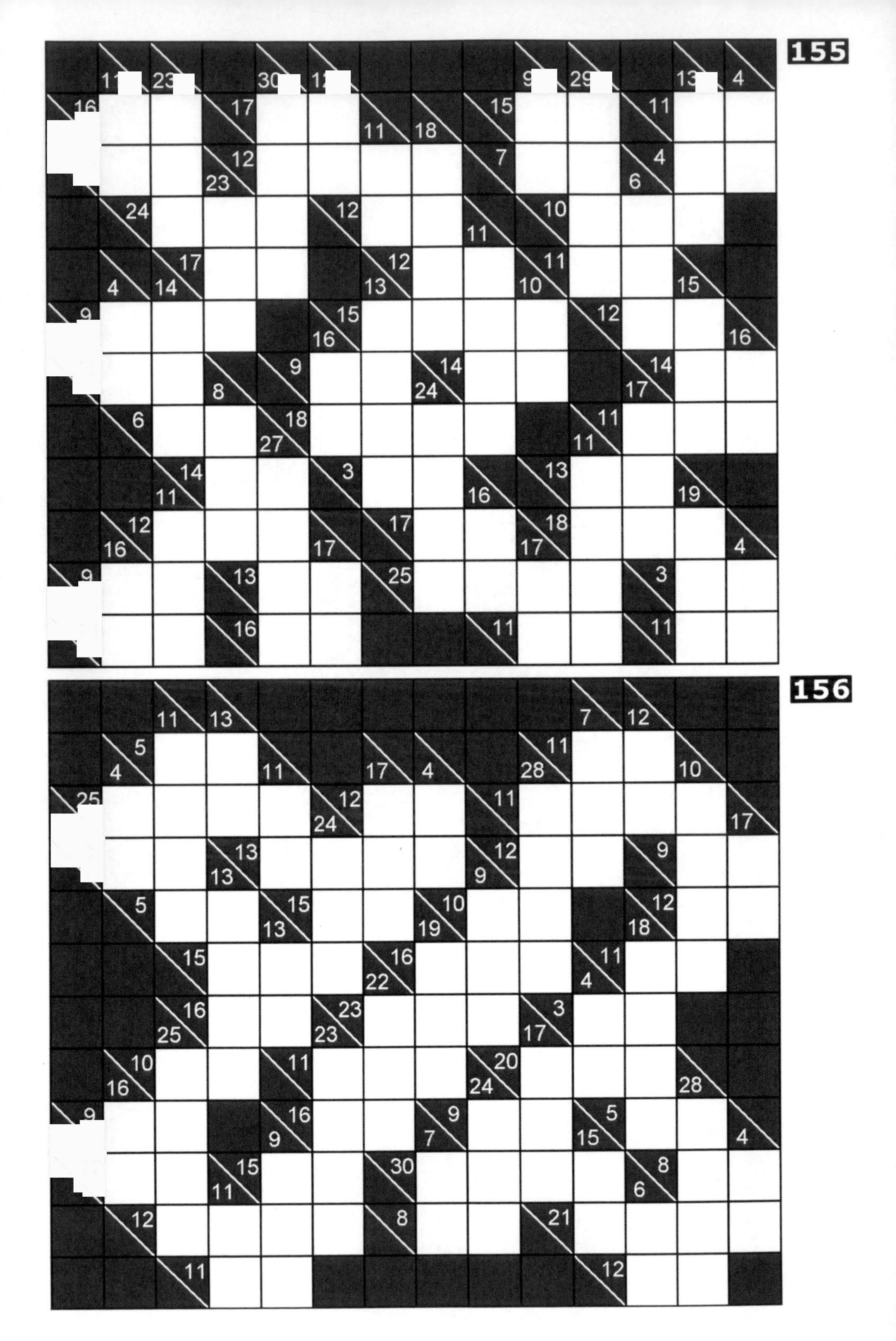
155
156

157

158

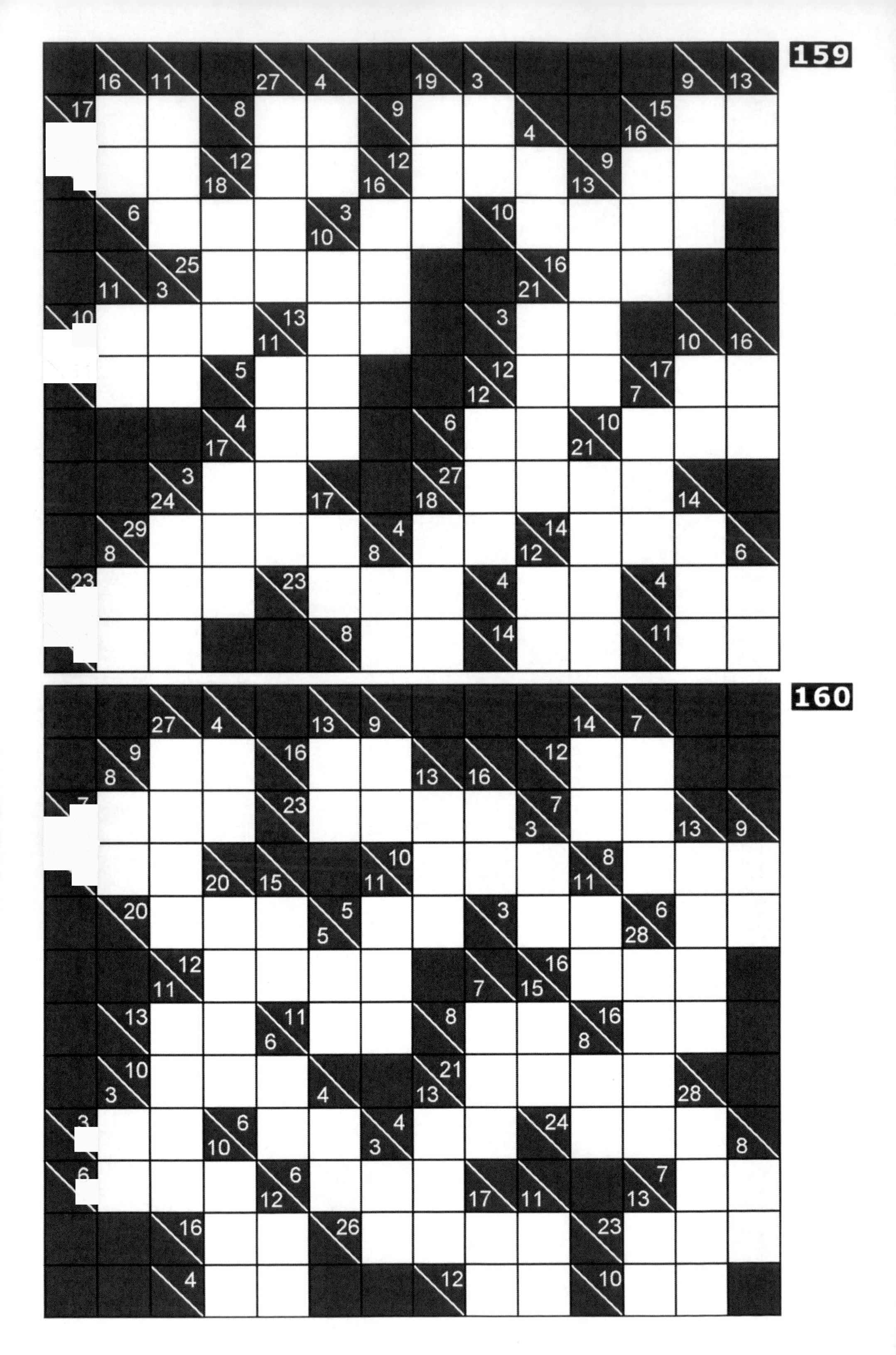
159
160

161

162

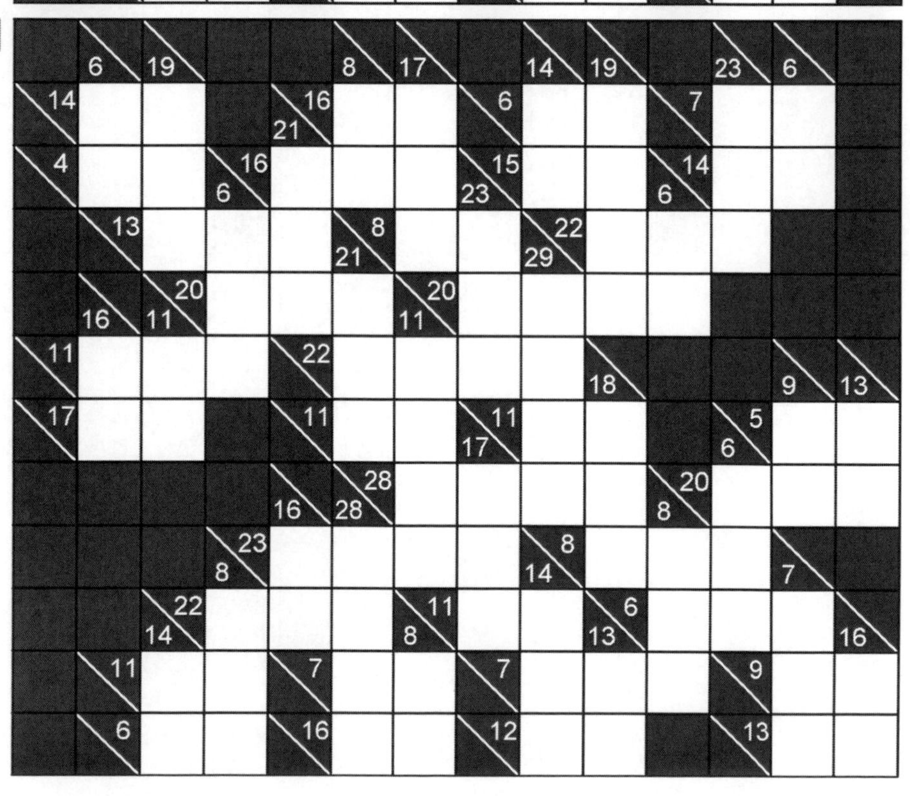

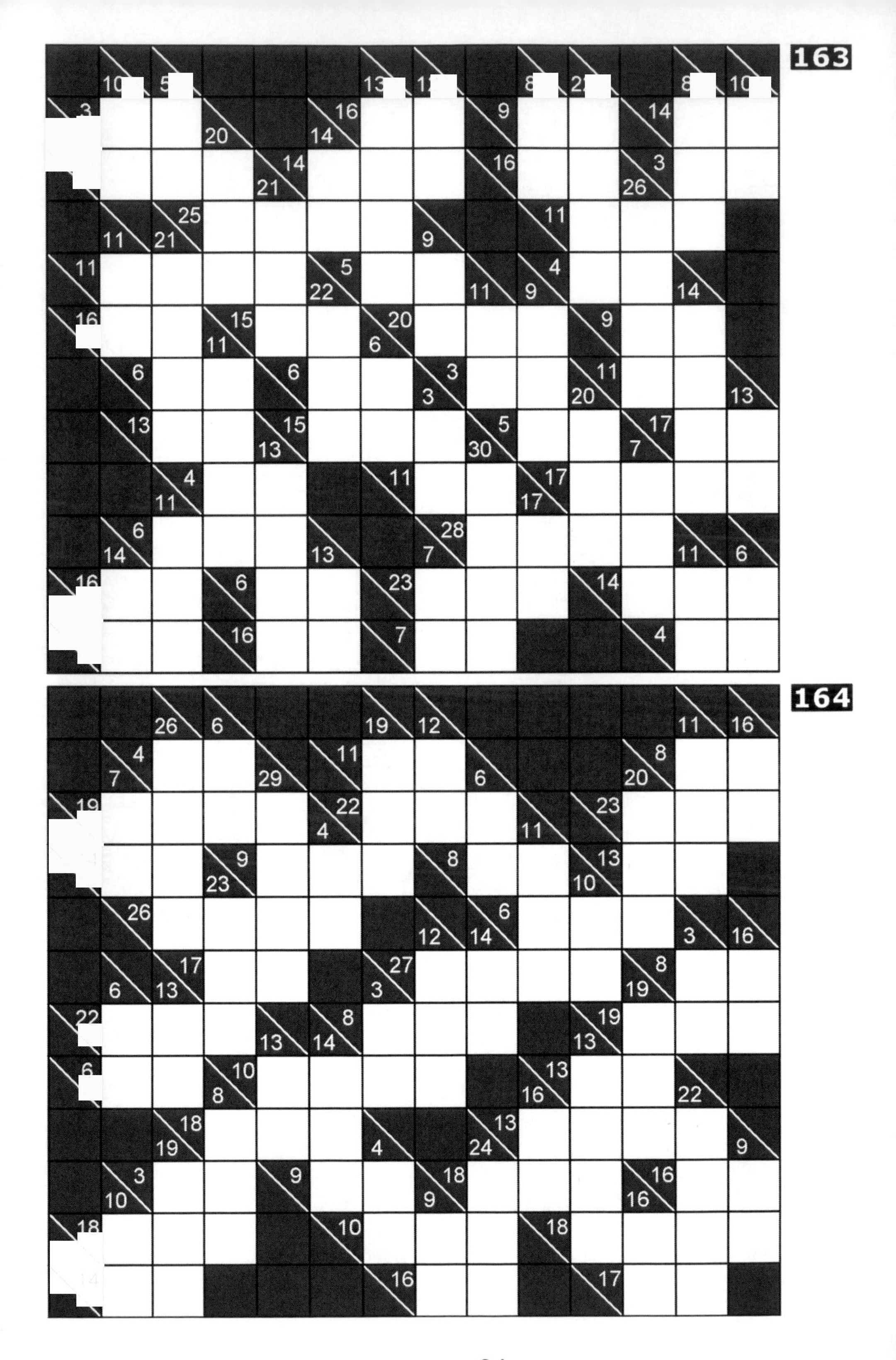
163
164

165

166

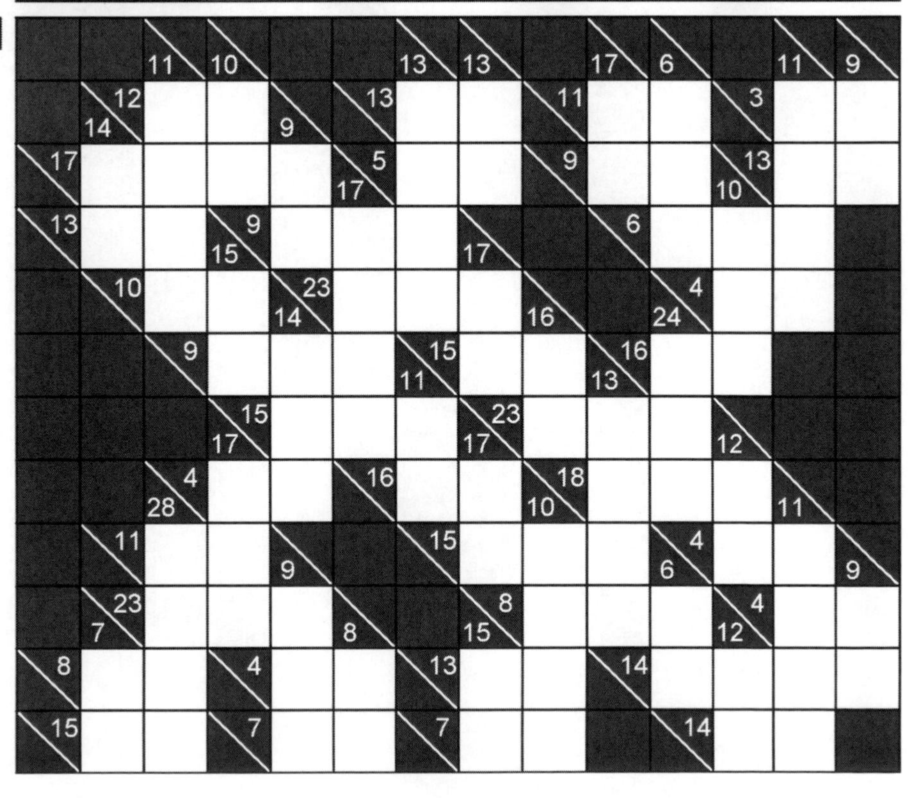

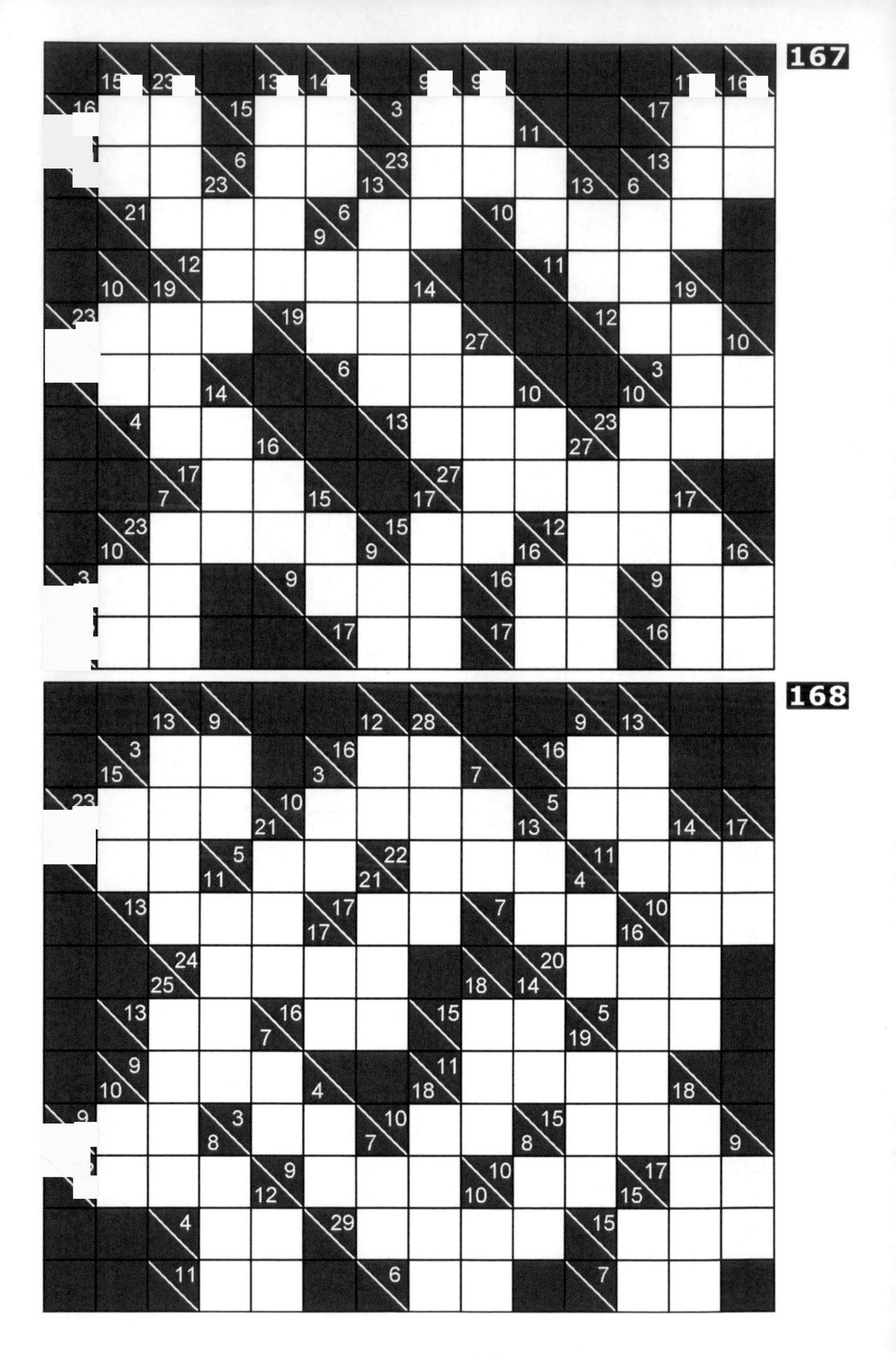
167
168

169

170

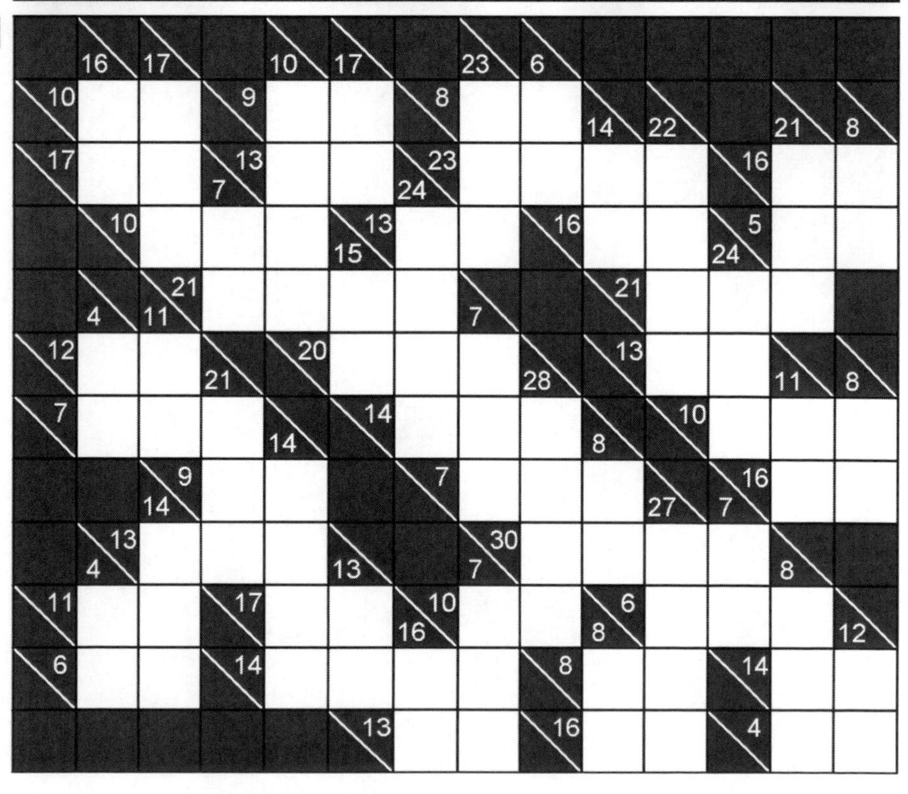

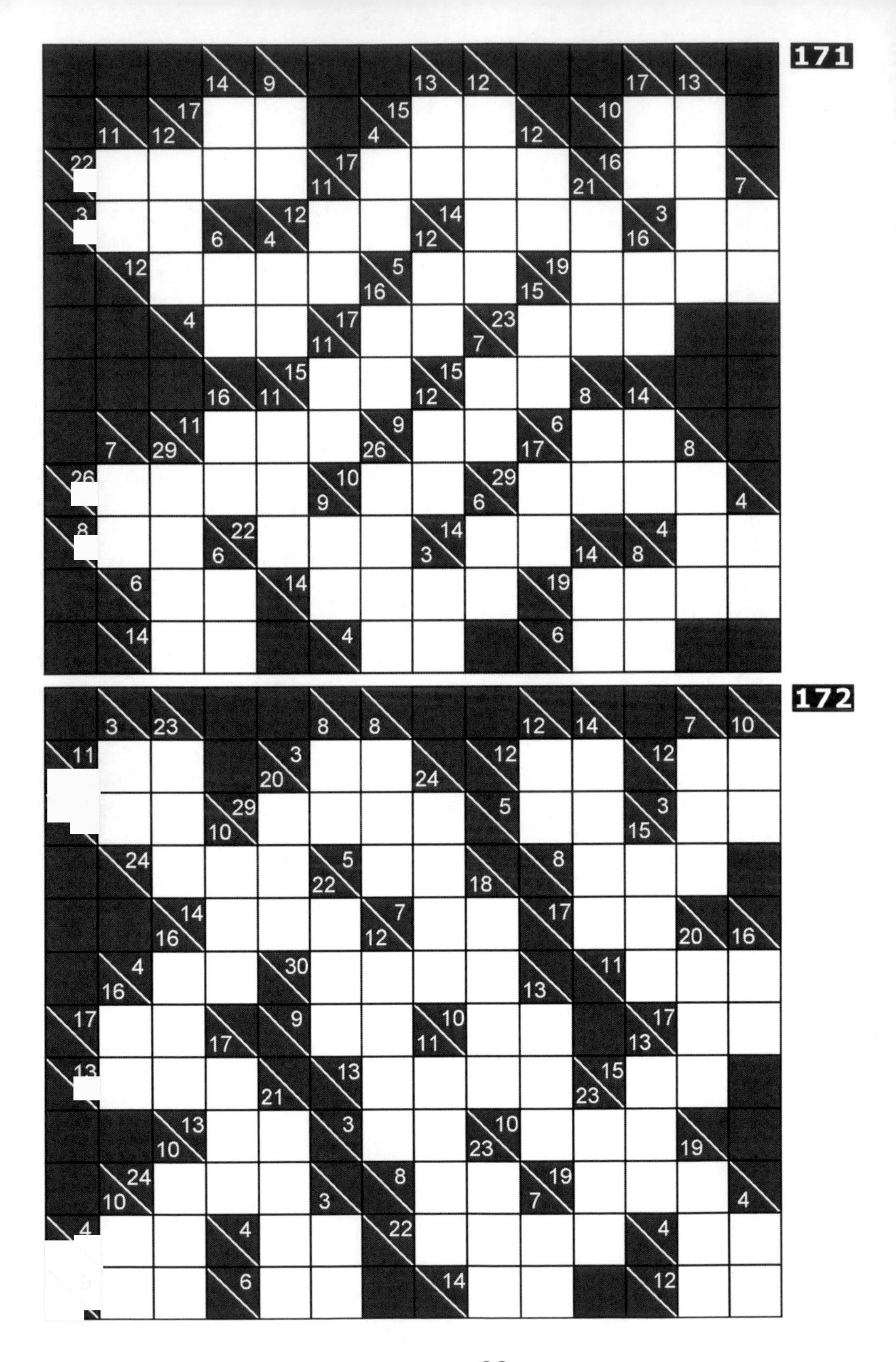
171
172

173

174

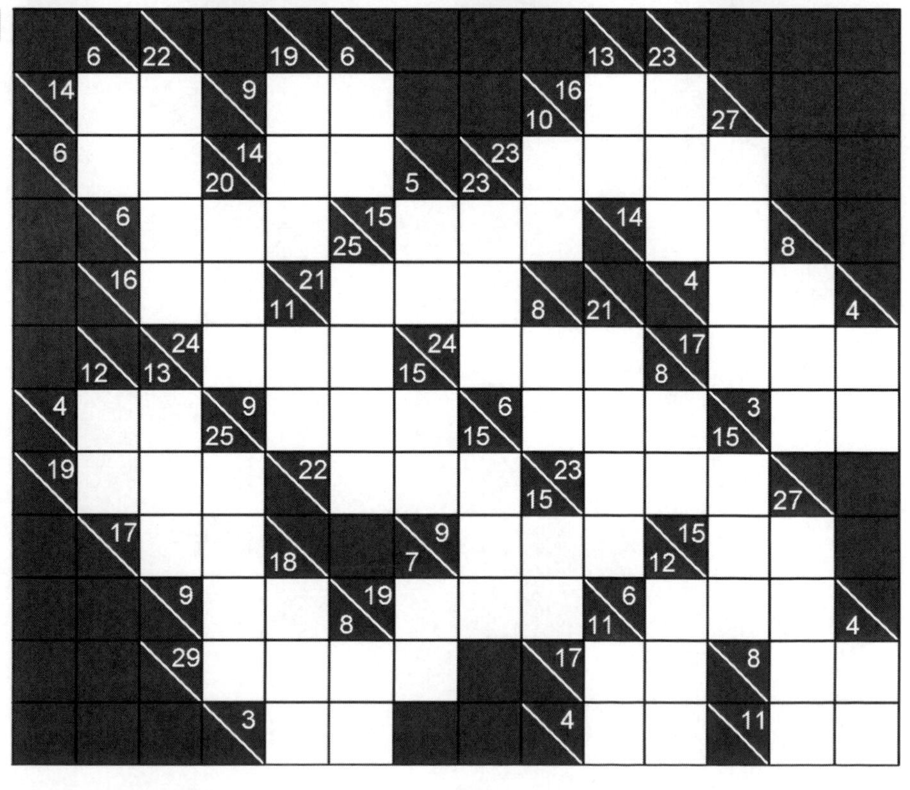

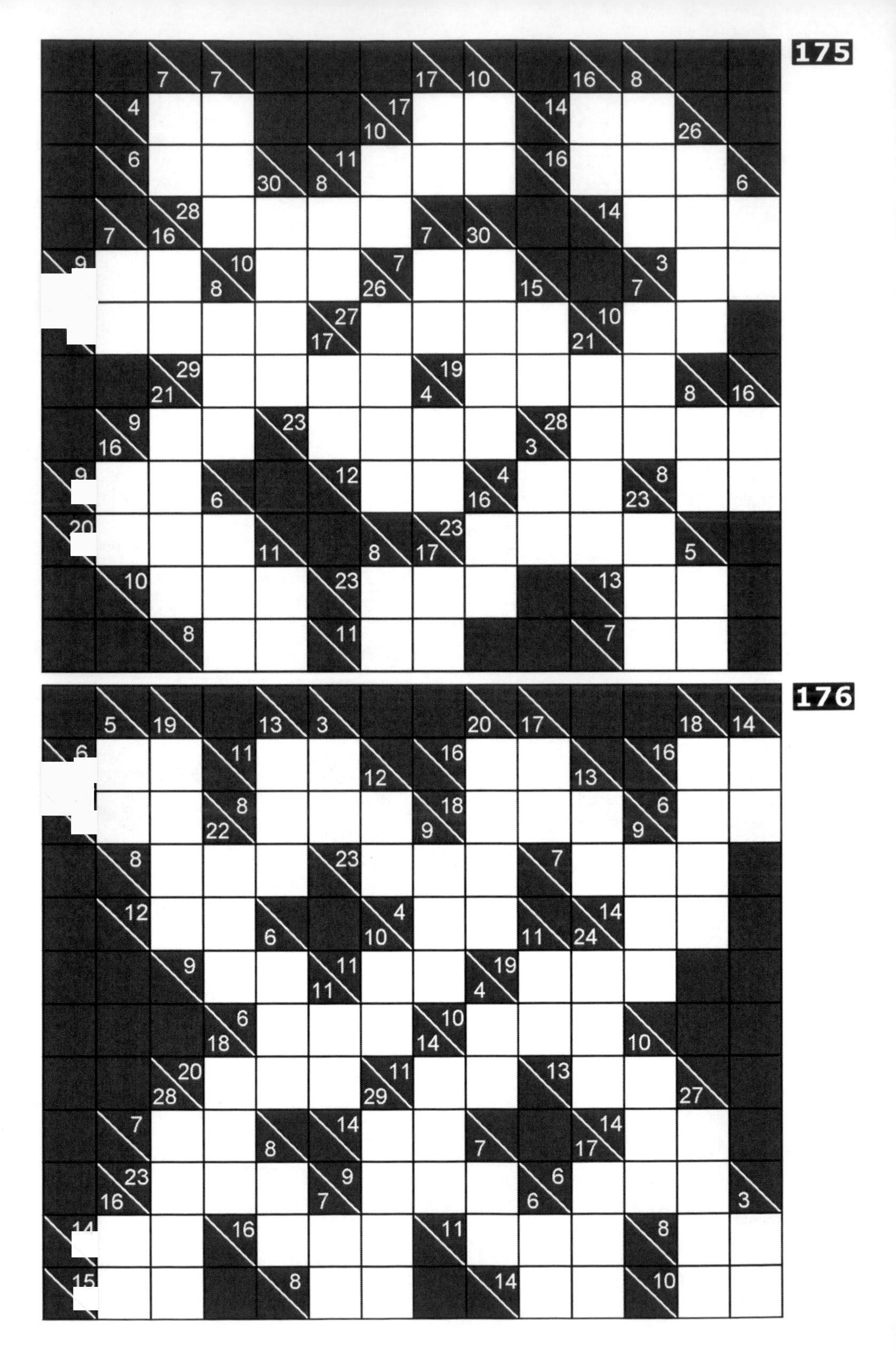
175
176

177

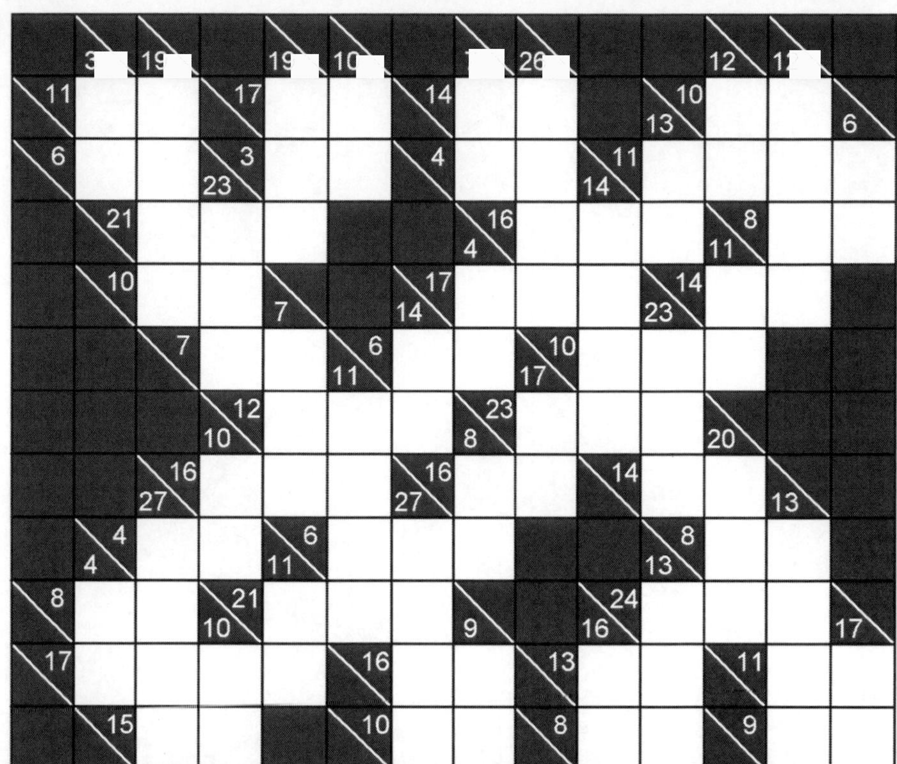

178

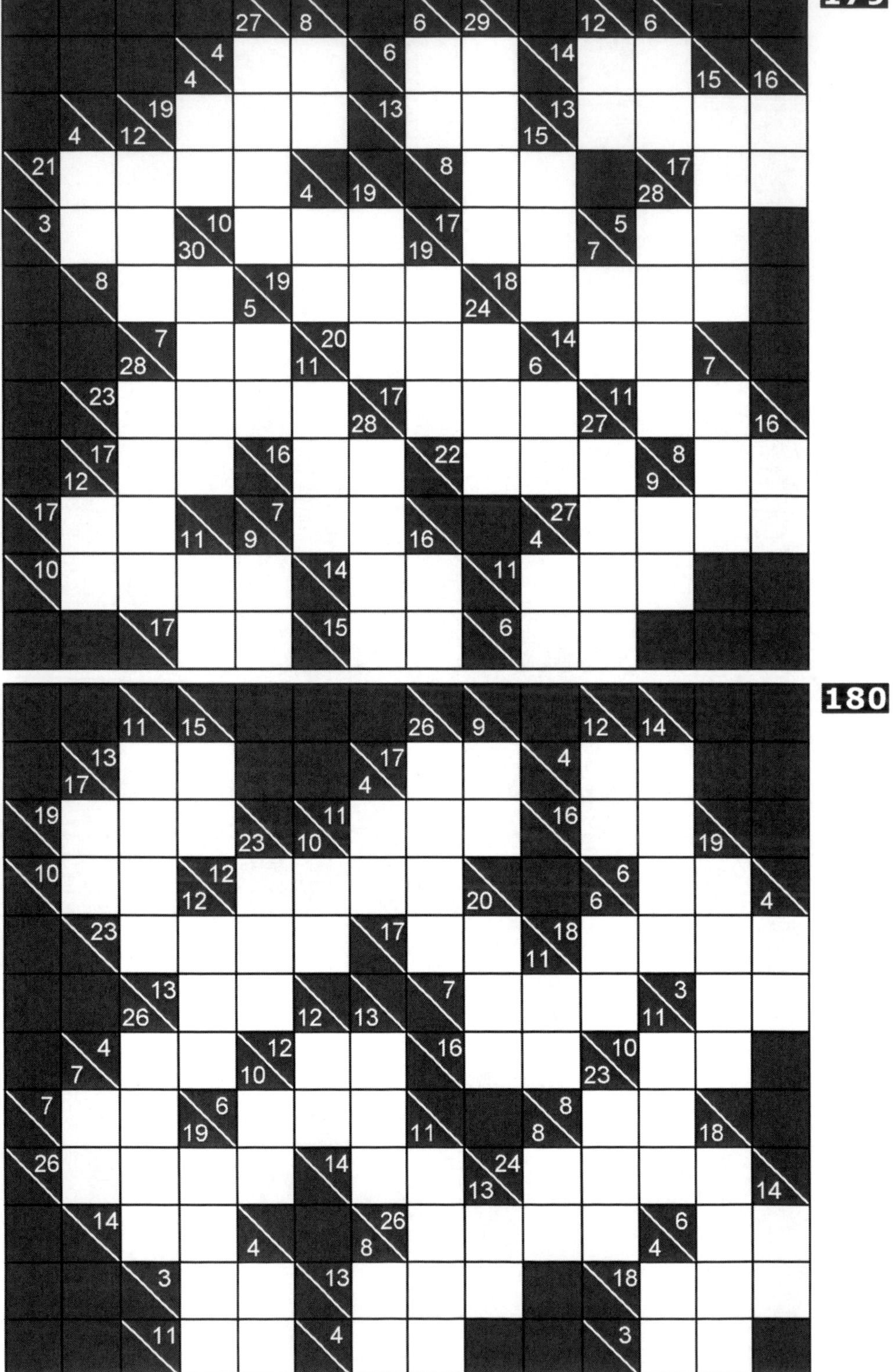

181

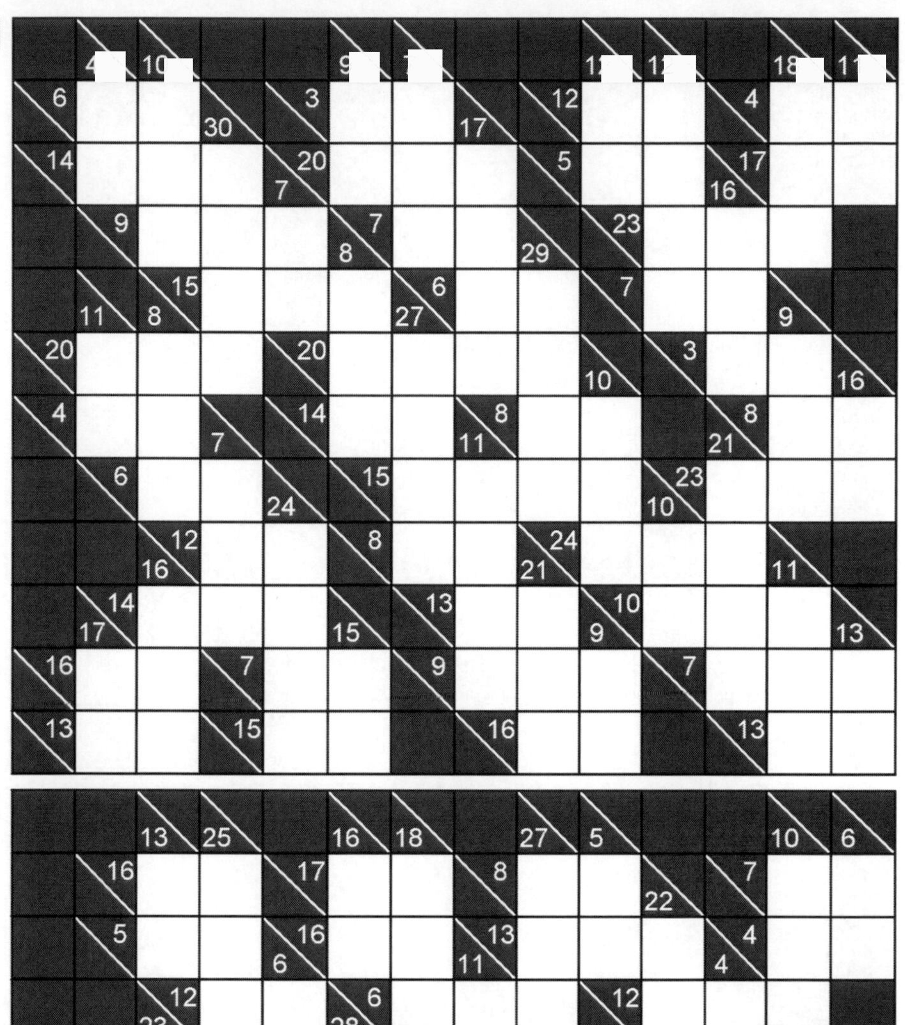

182

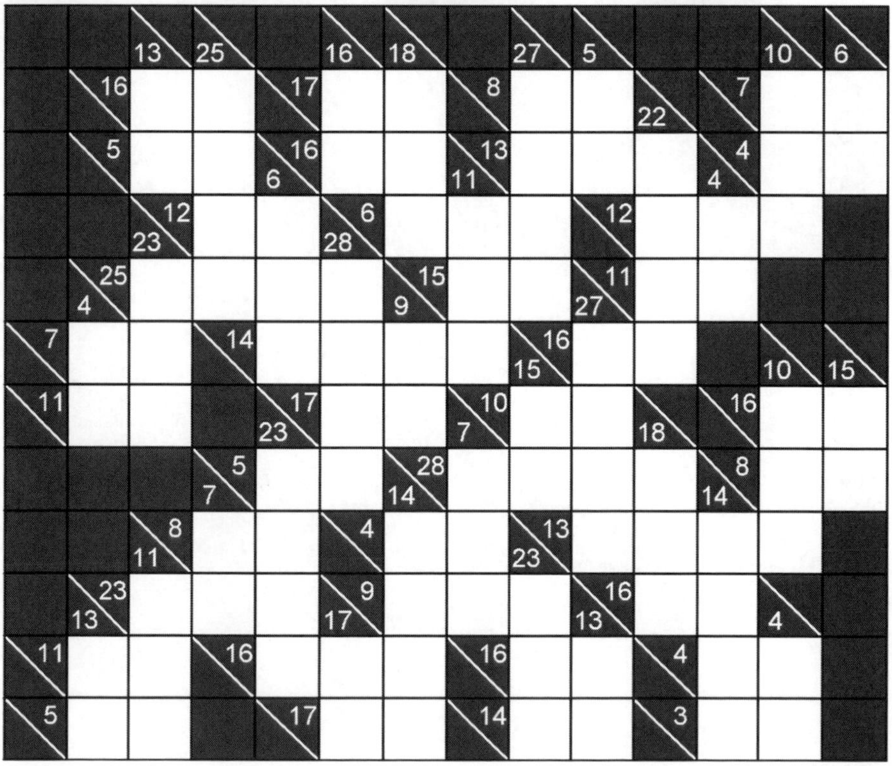

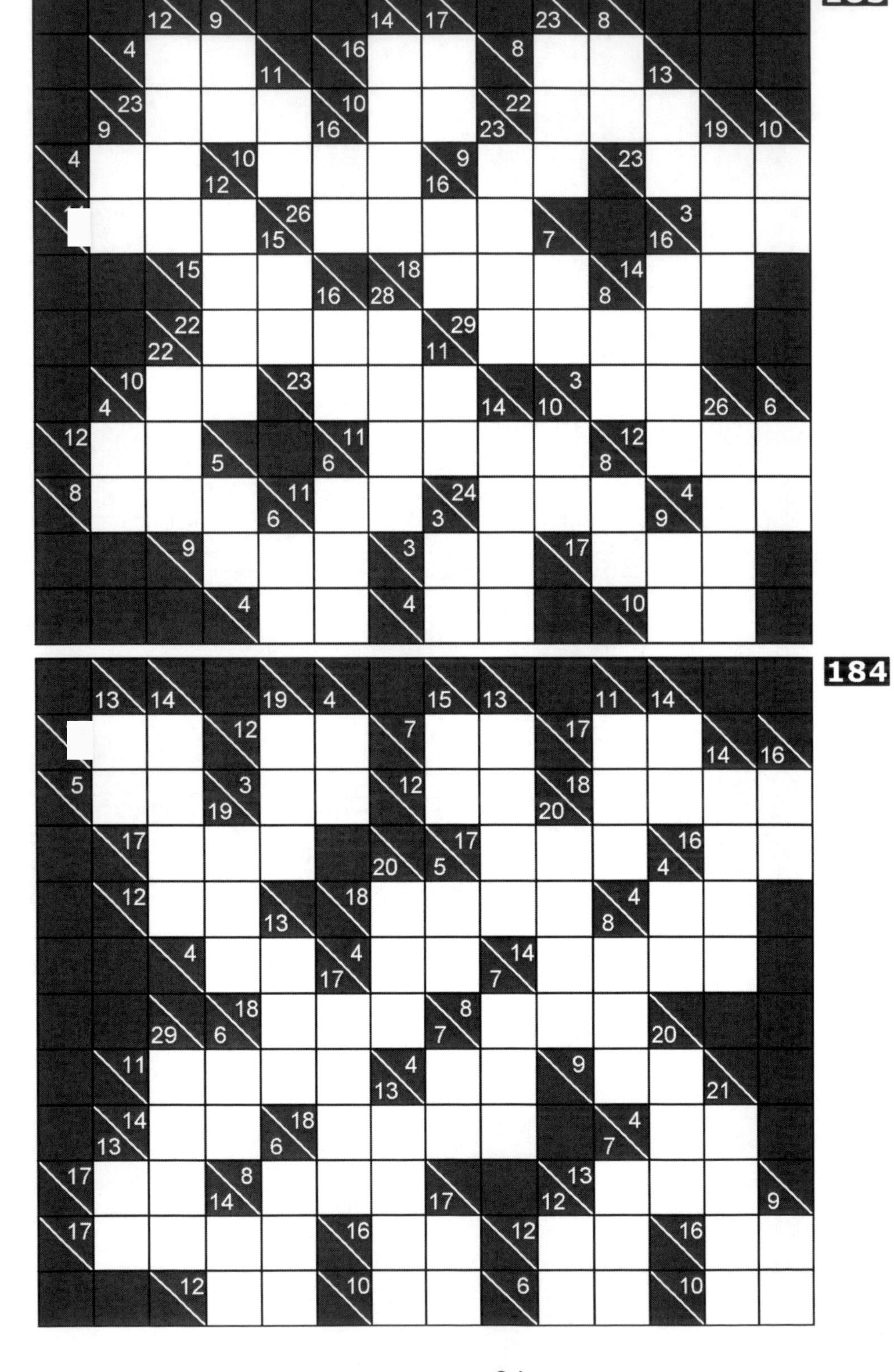

184

185

186

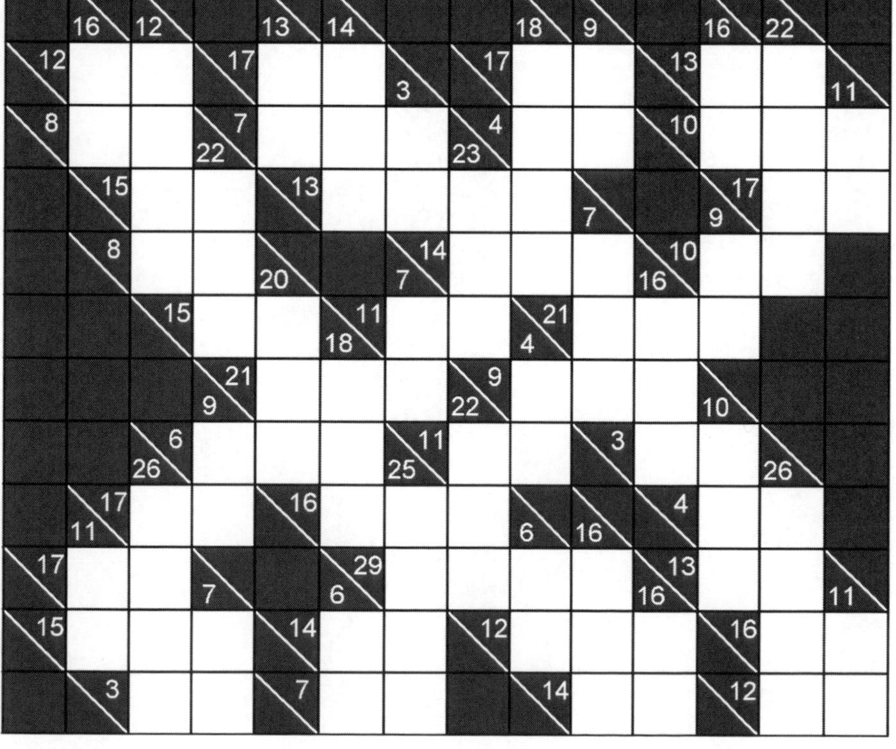

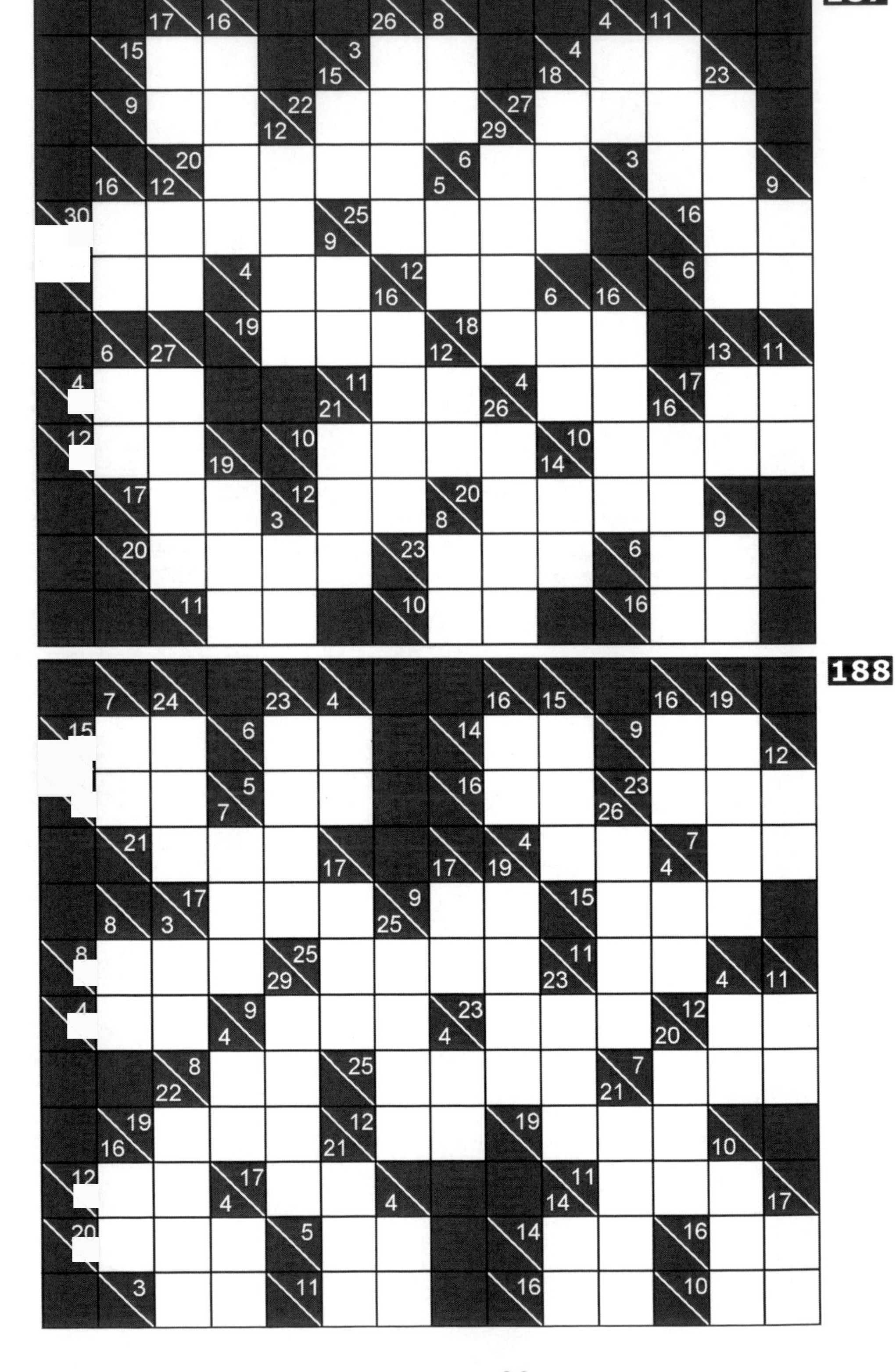

188

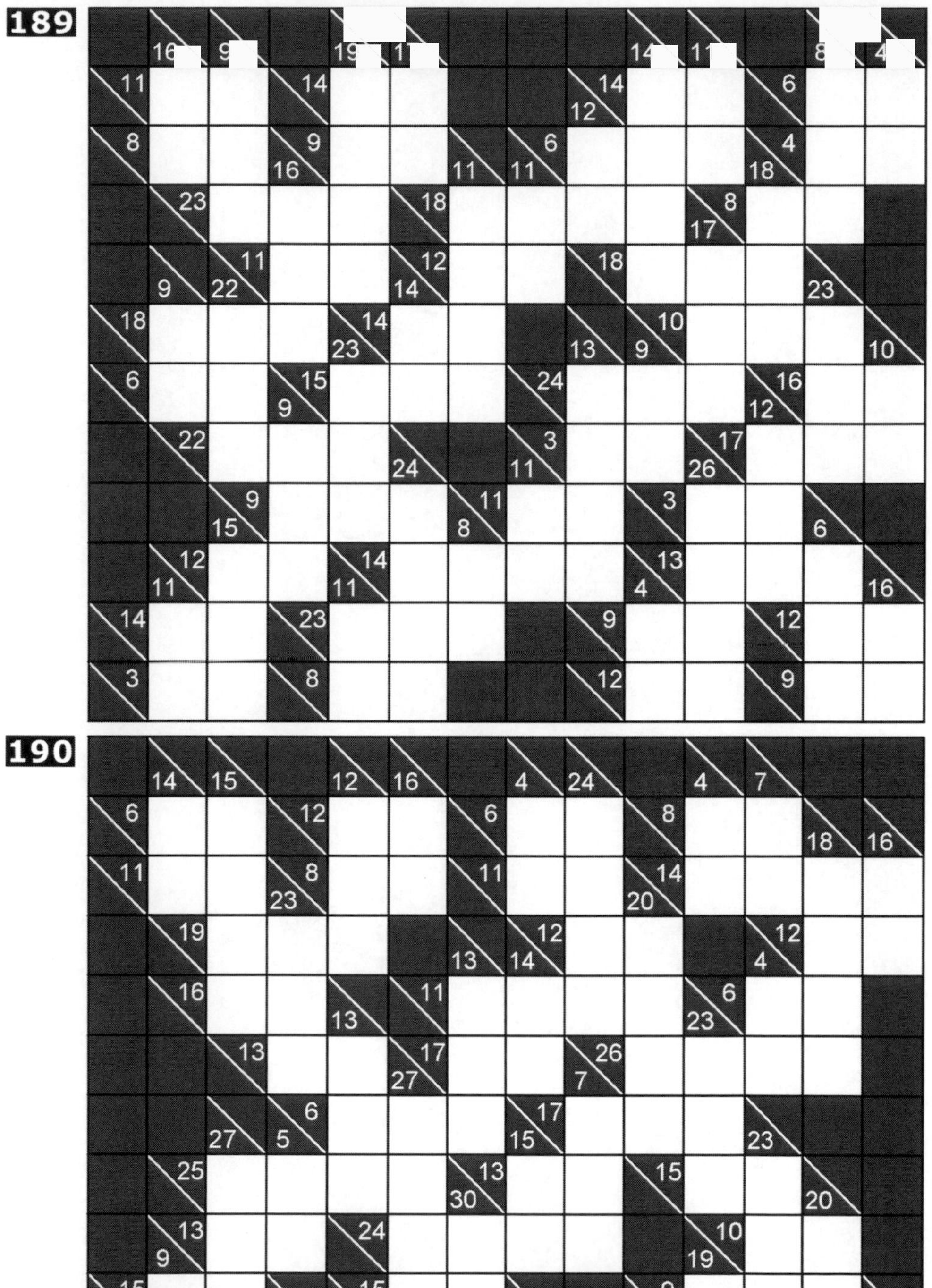
189
190

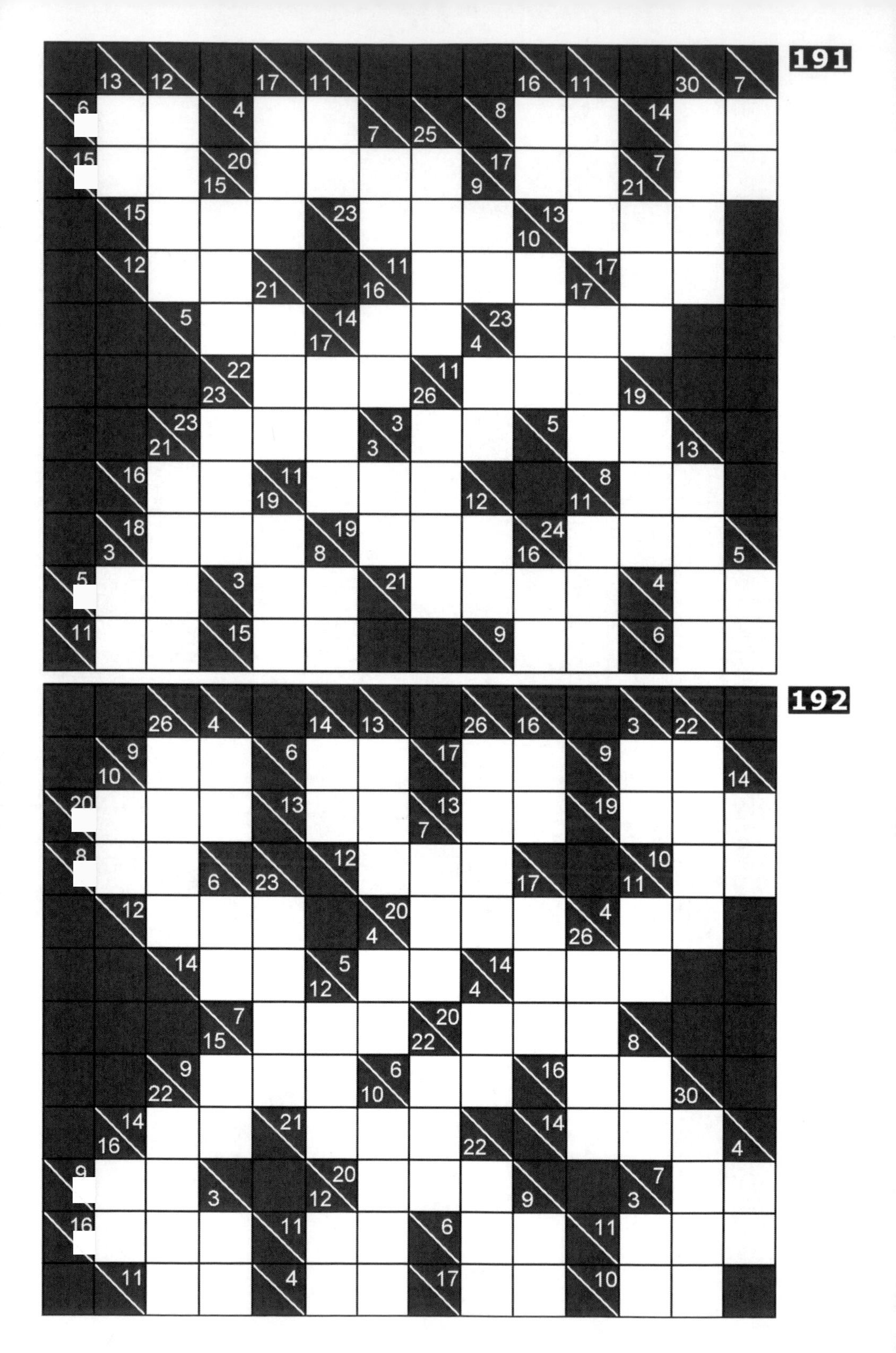

193

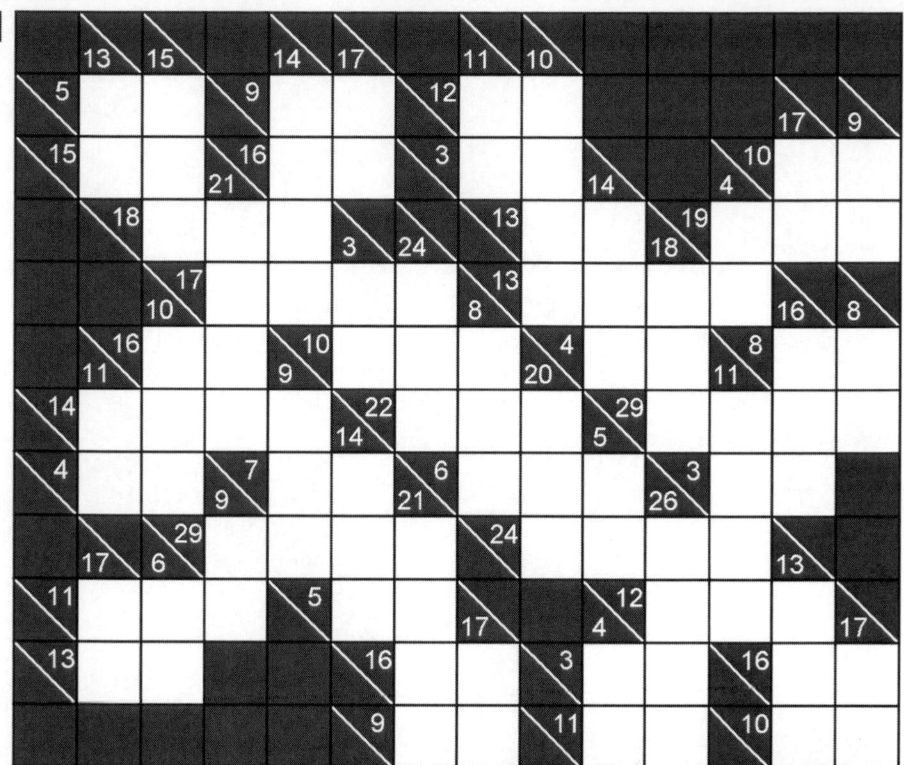

194

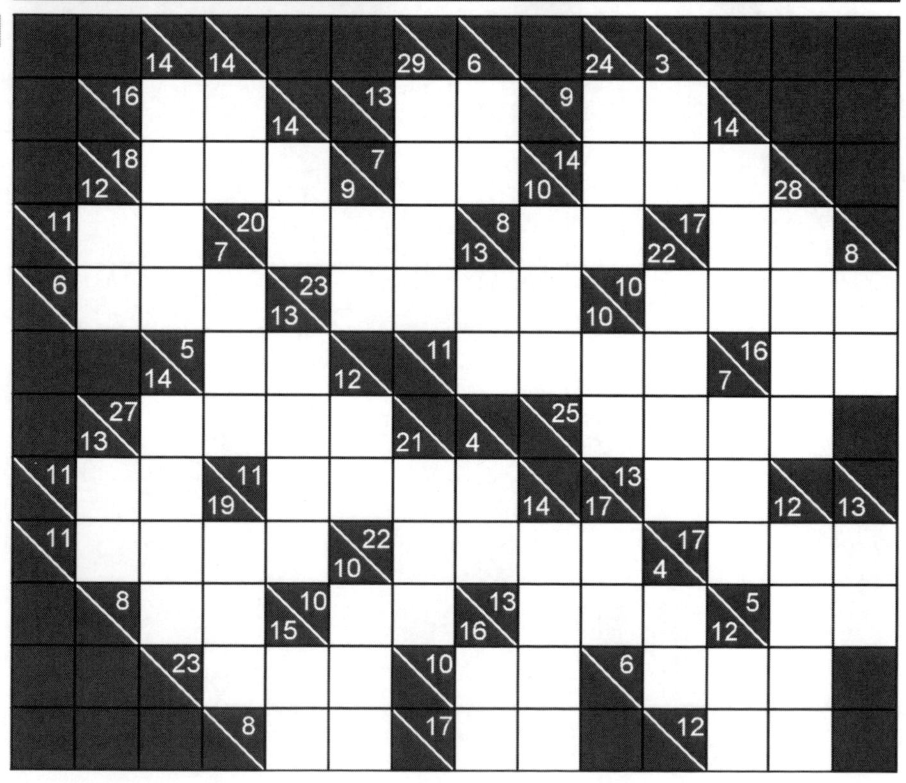

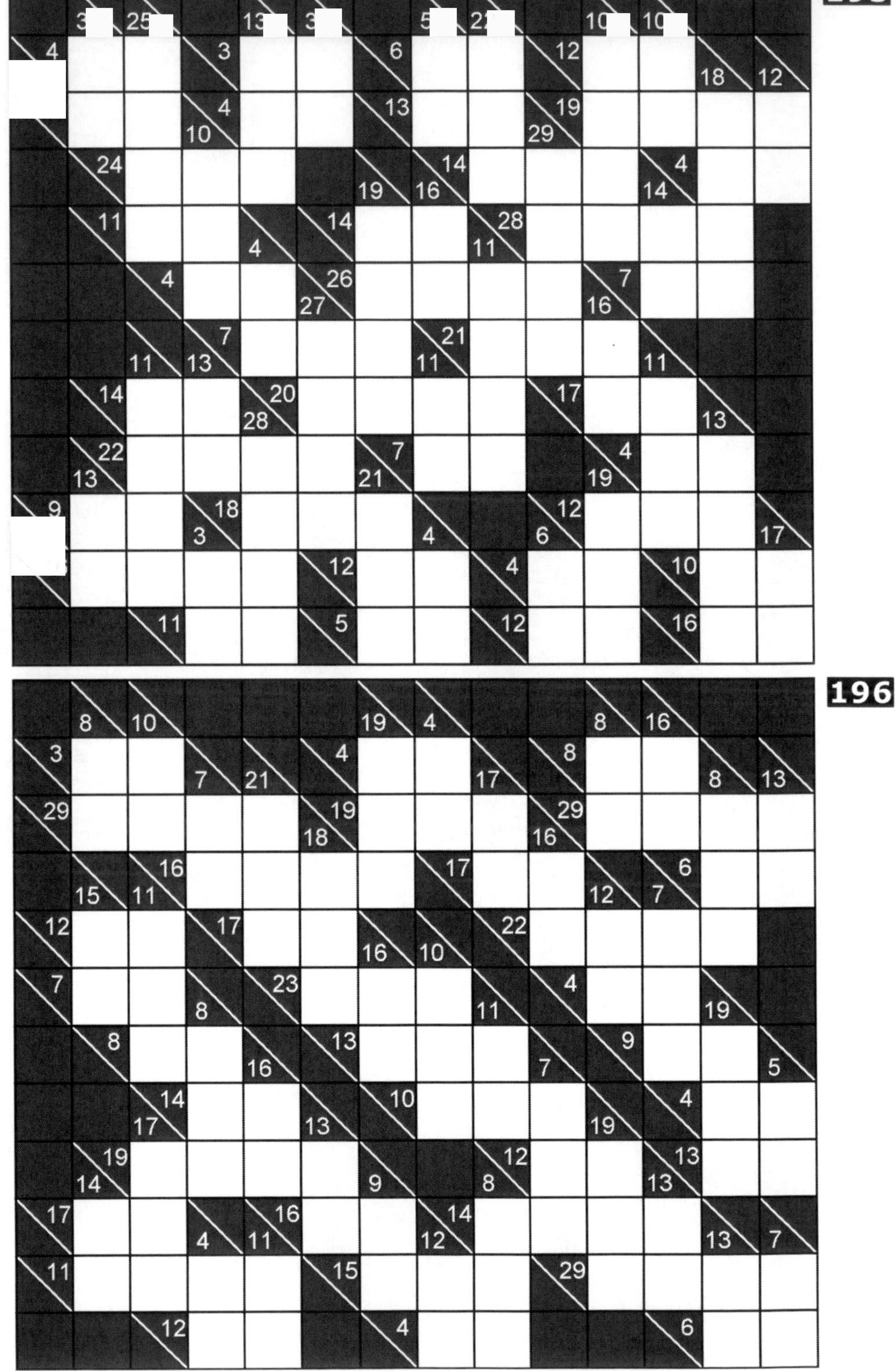

197

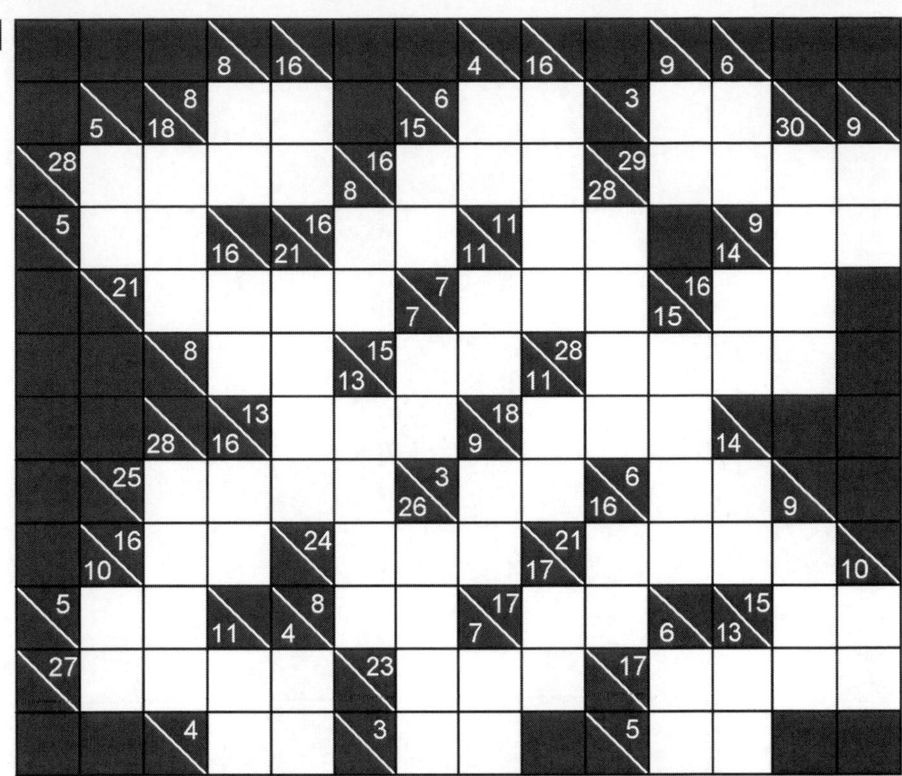

198

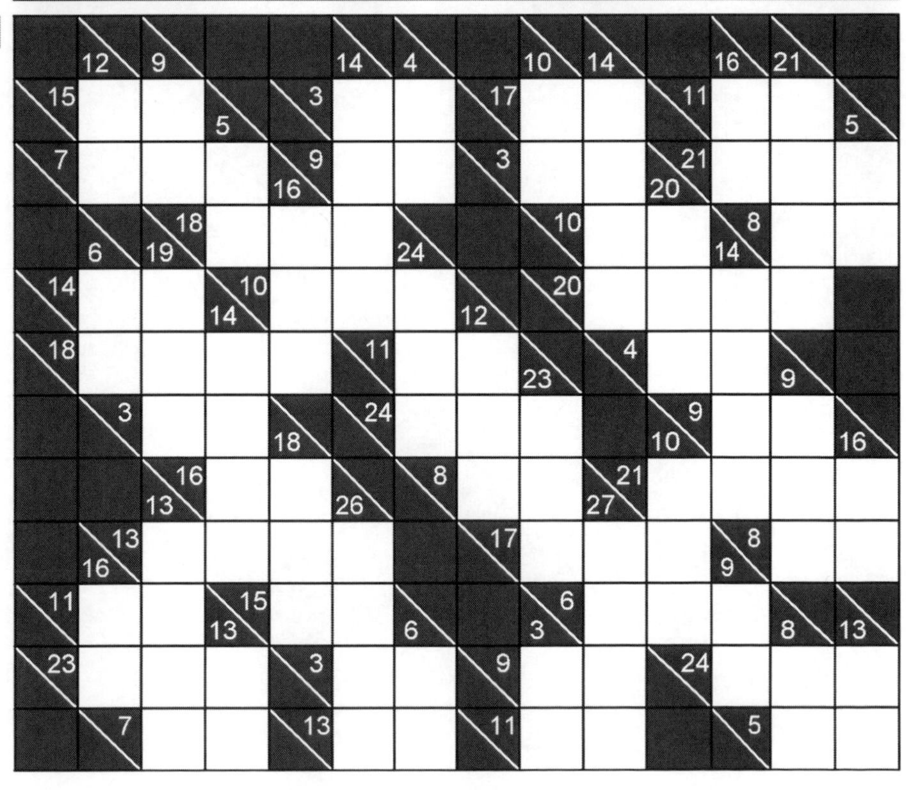

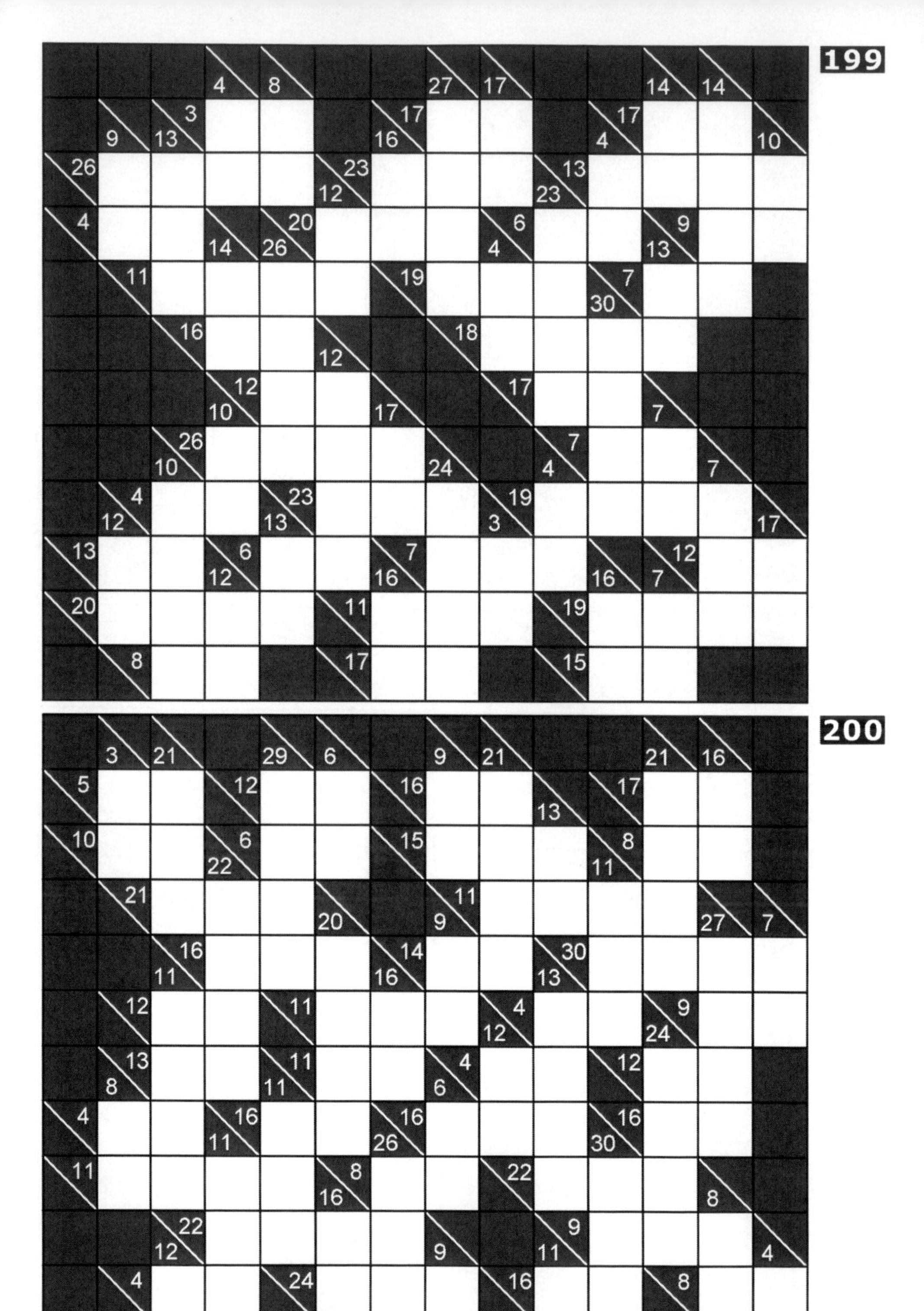

201

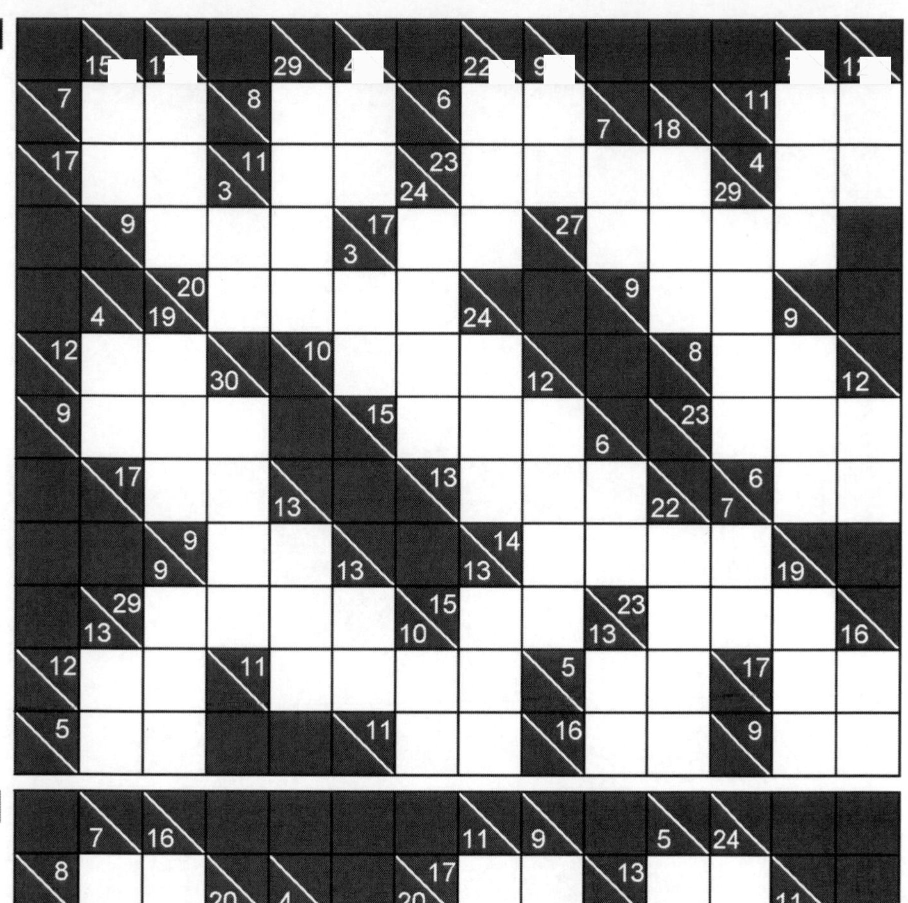

202

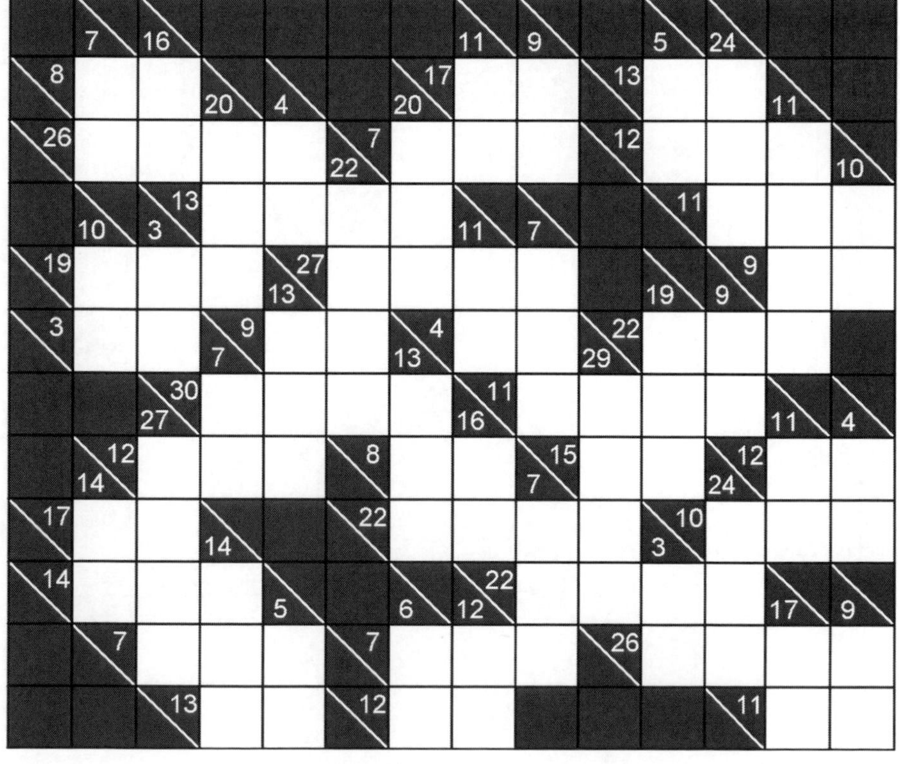

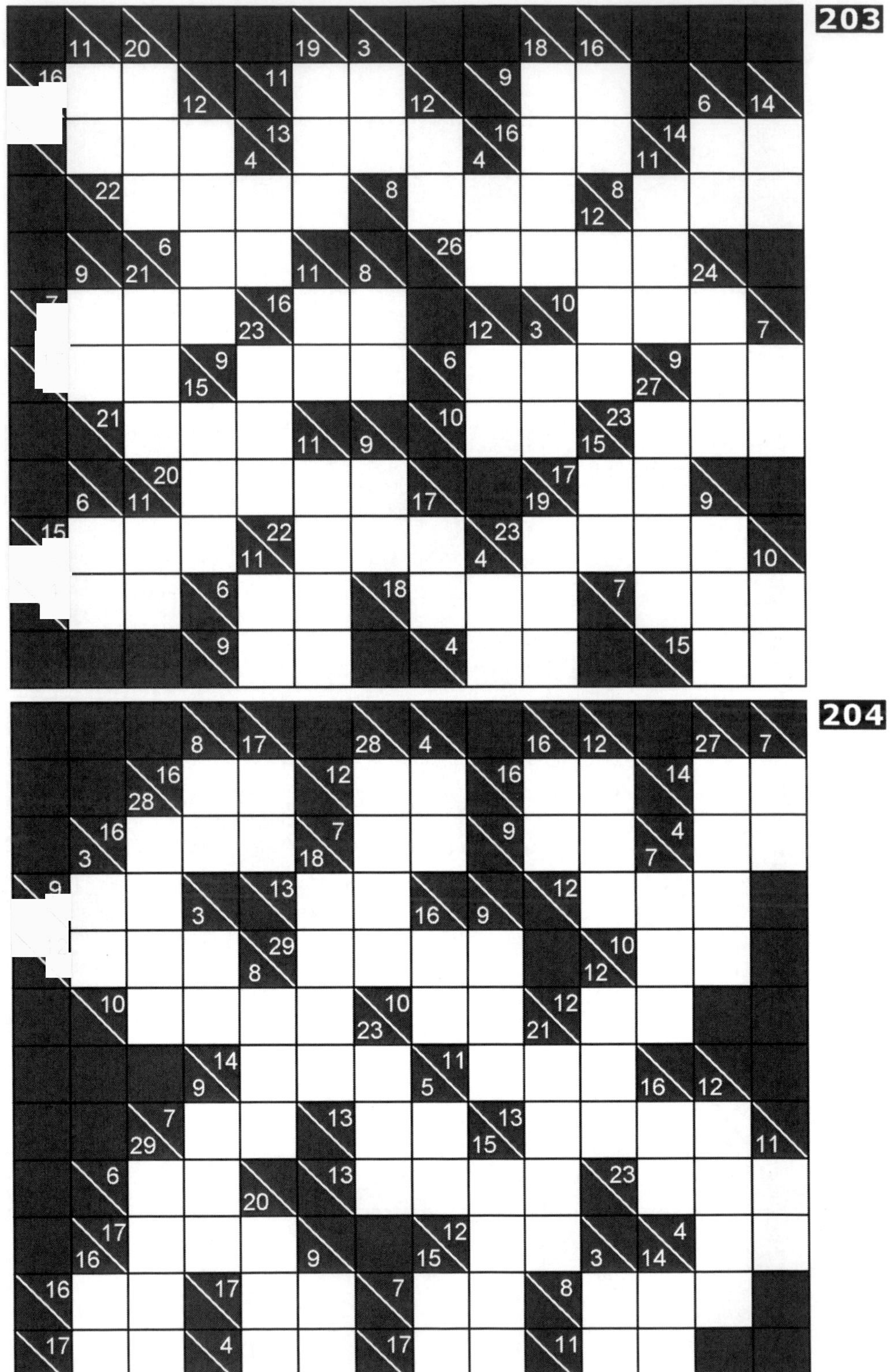
203
204

205

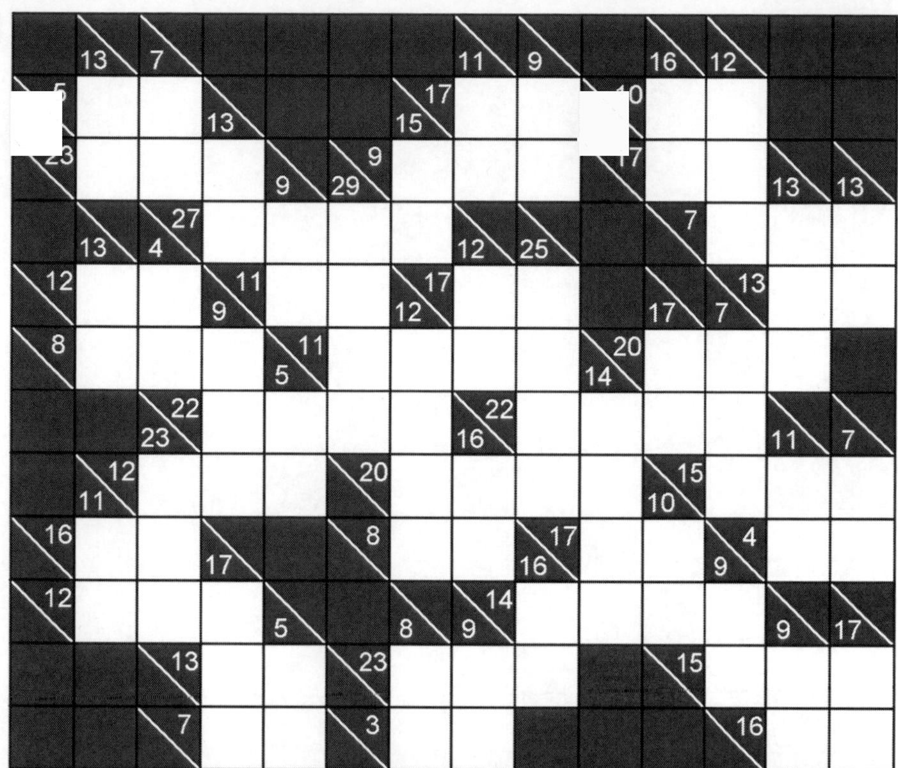

206

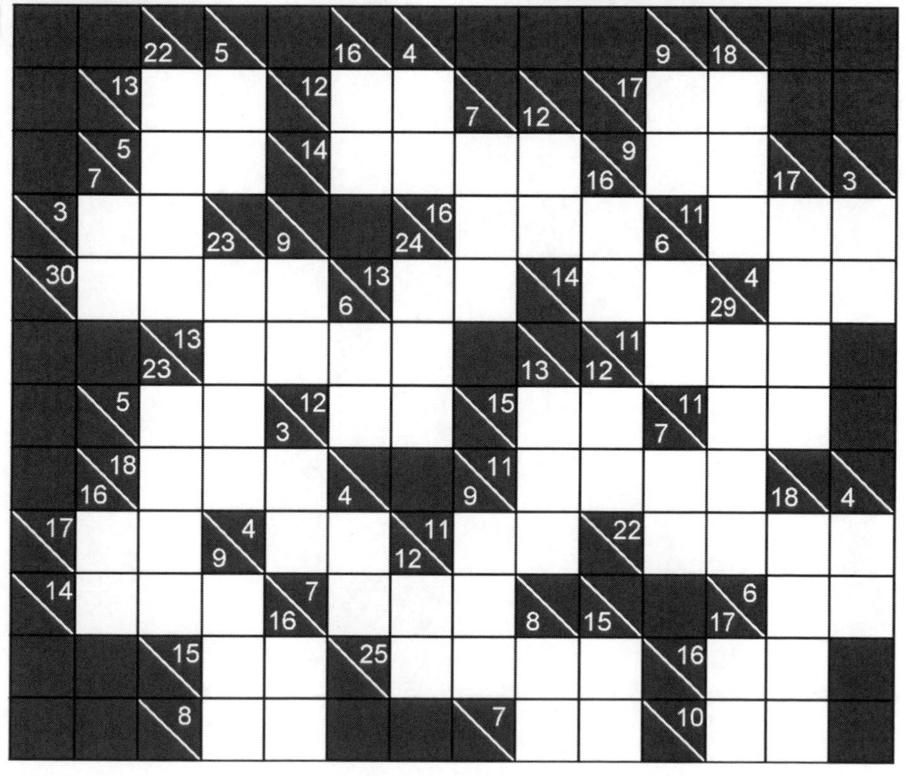

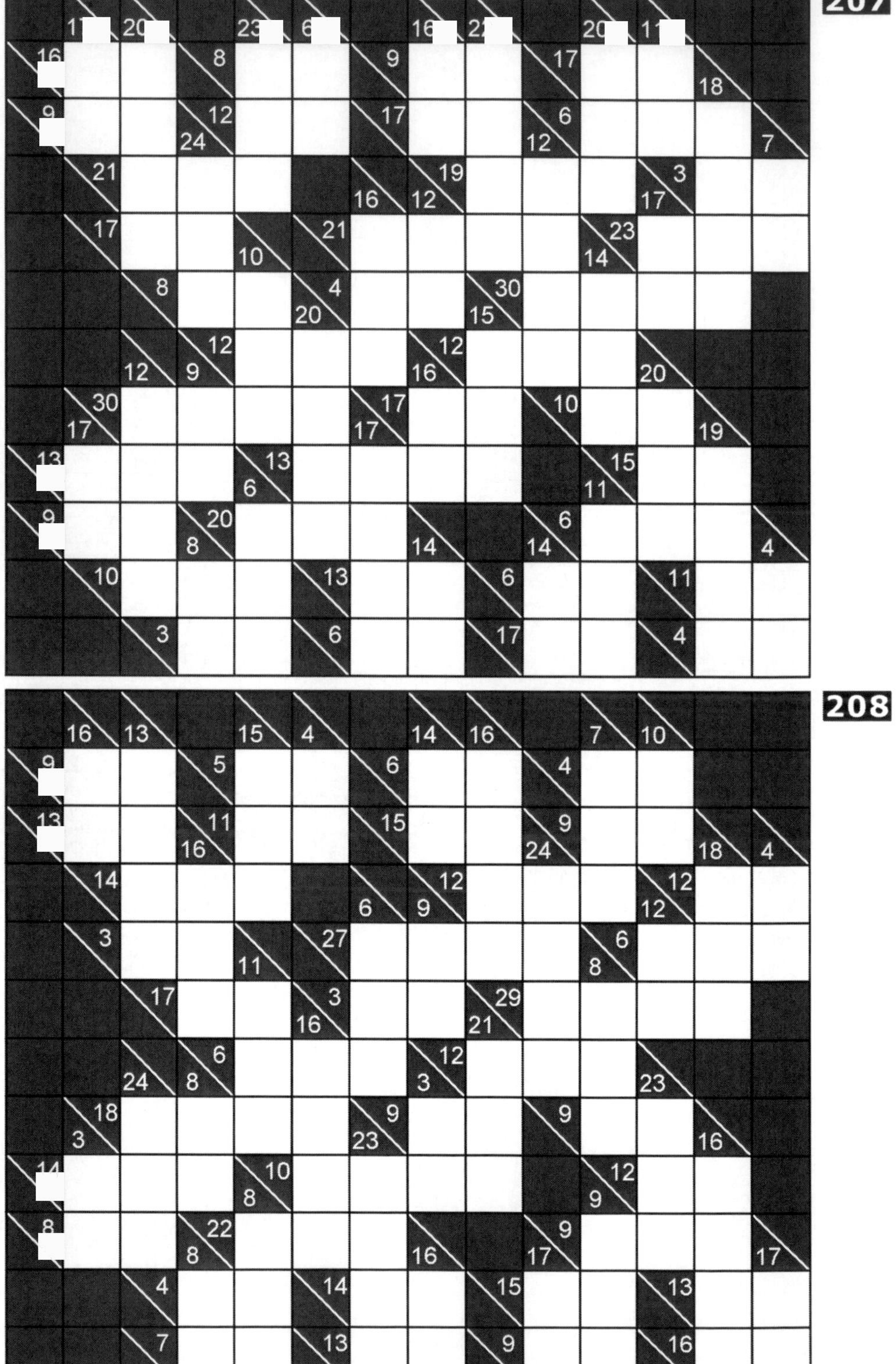
207
208

209

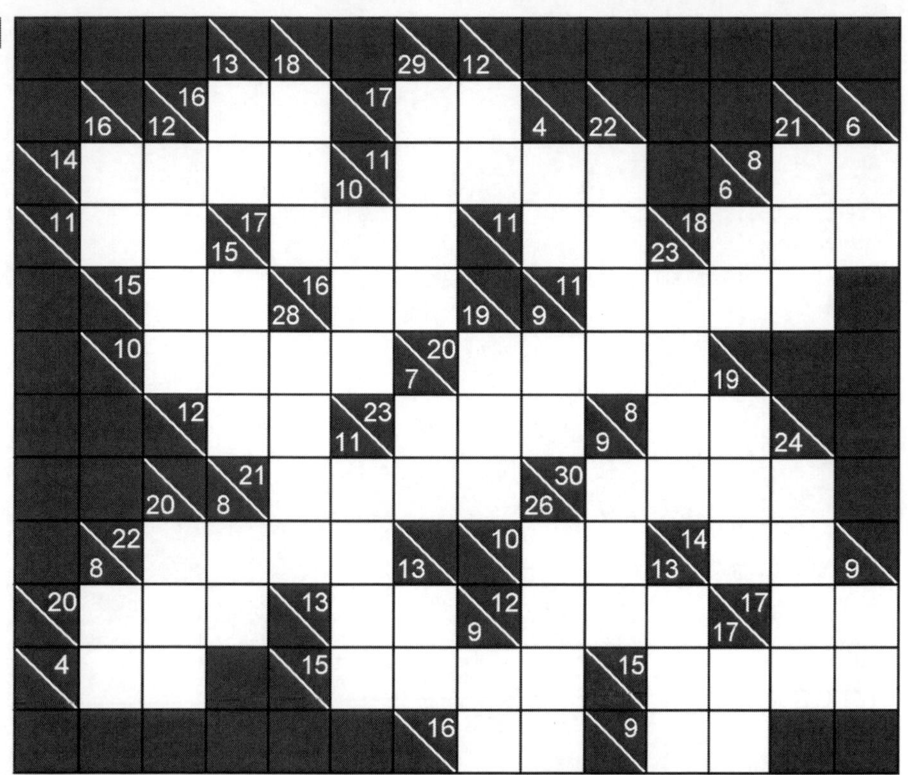

210

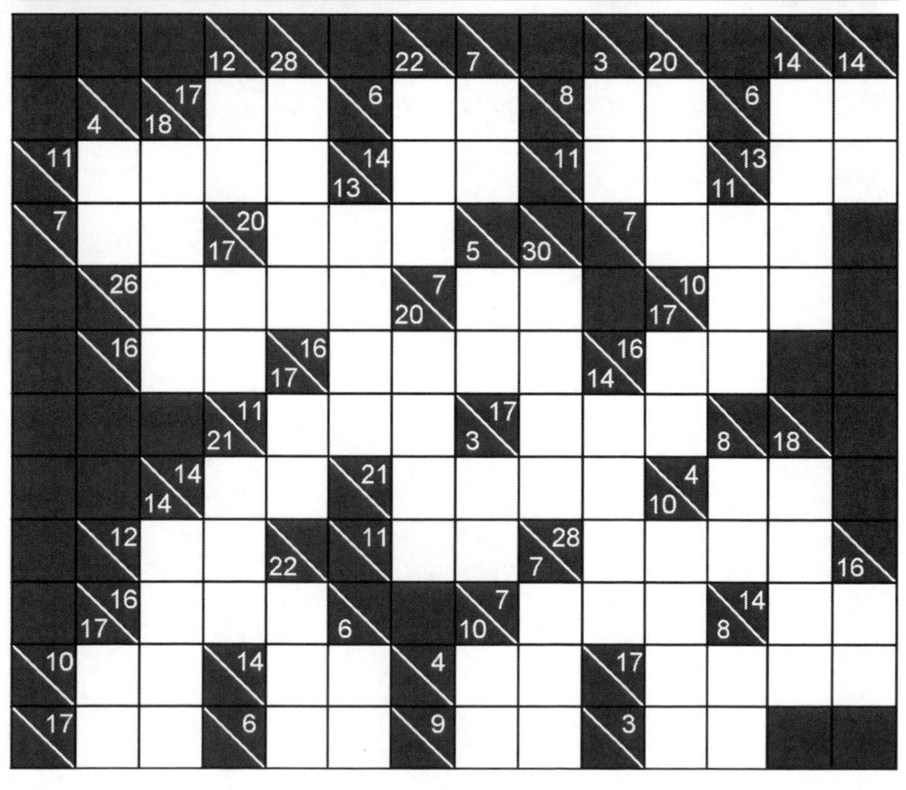

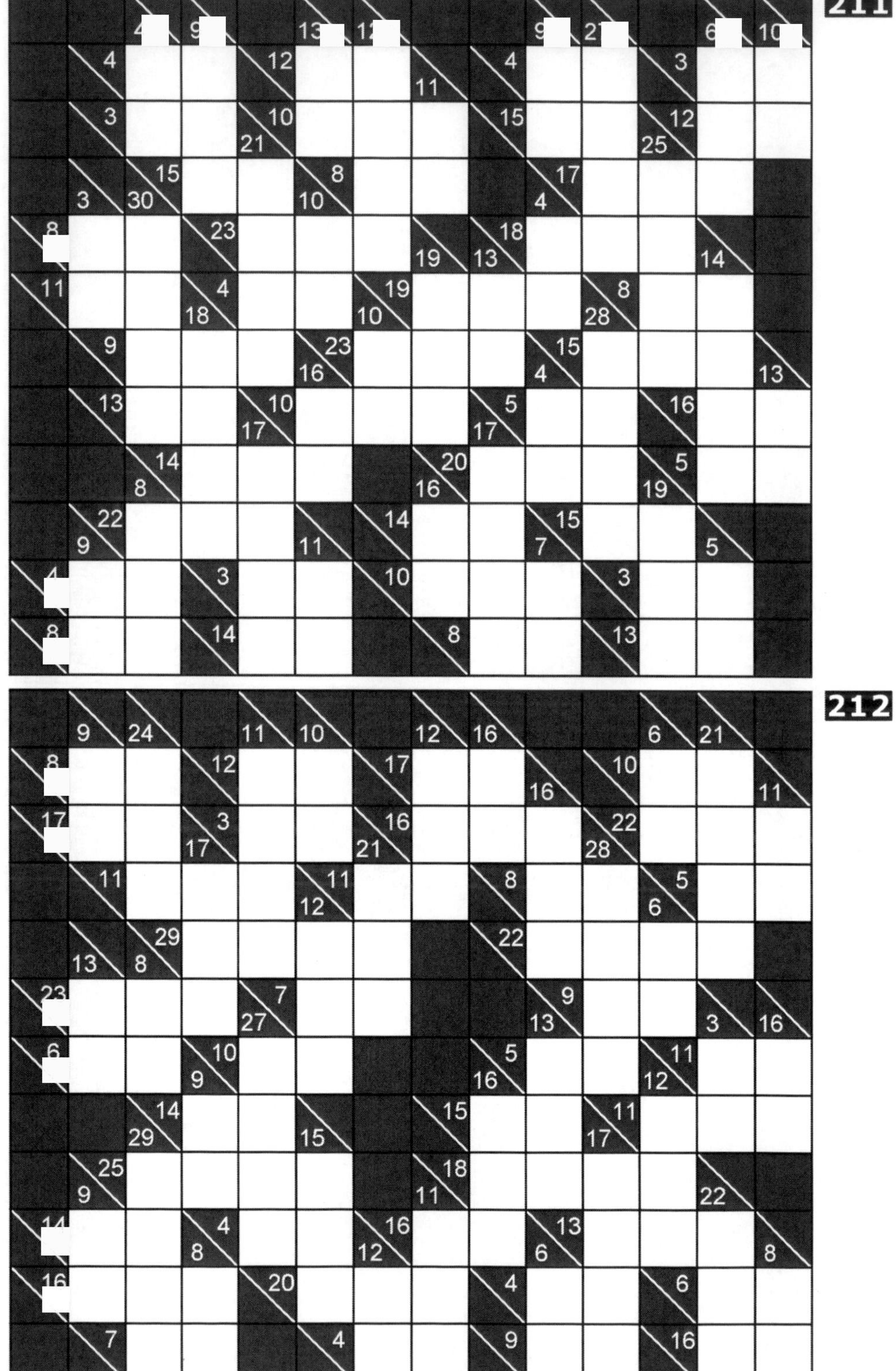
211
212

213

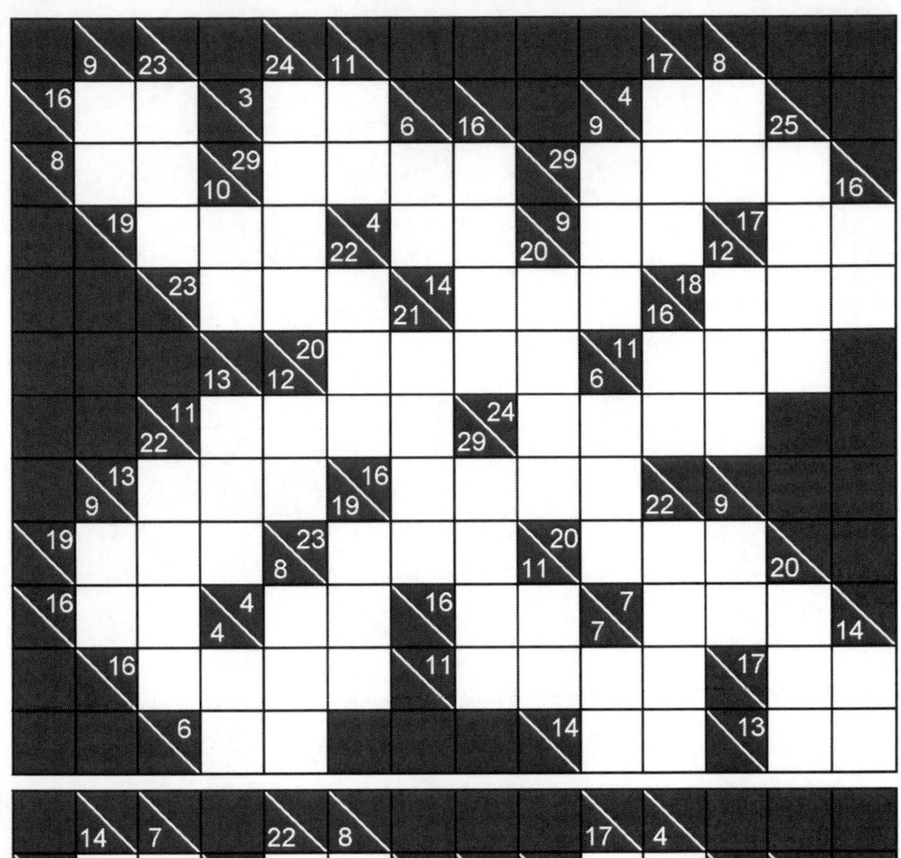

214

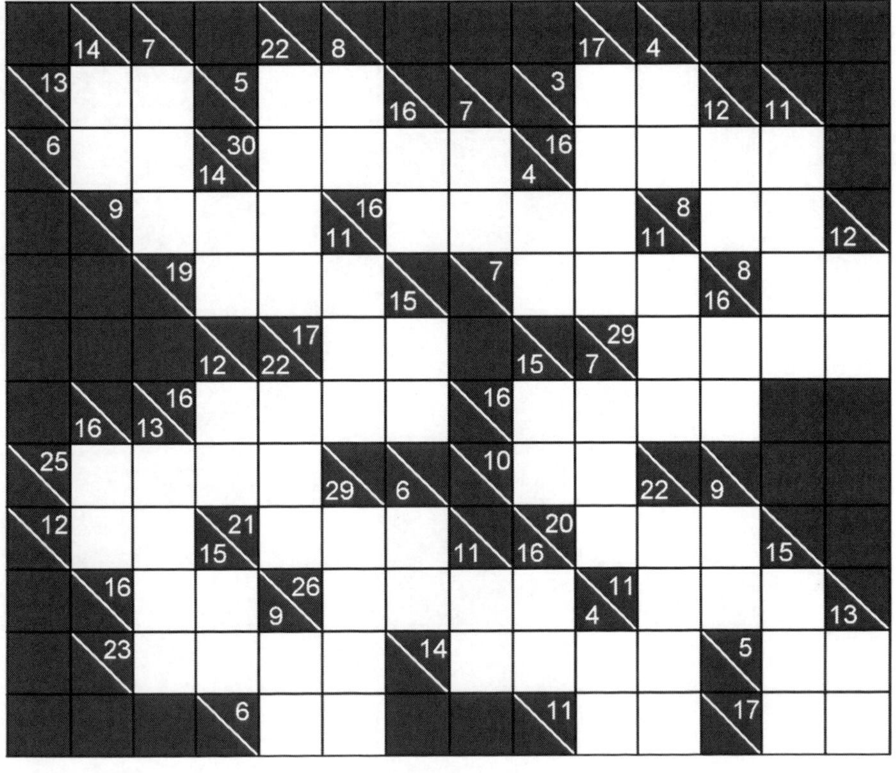

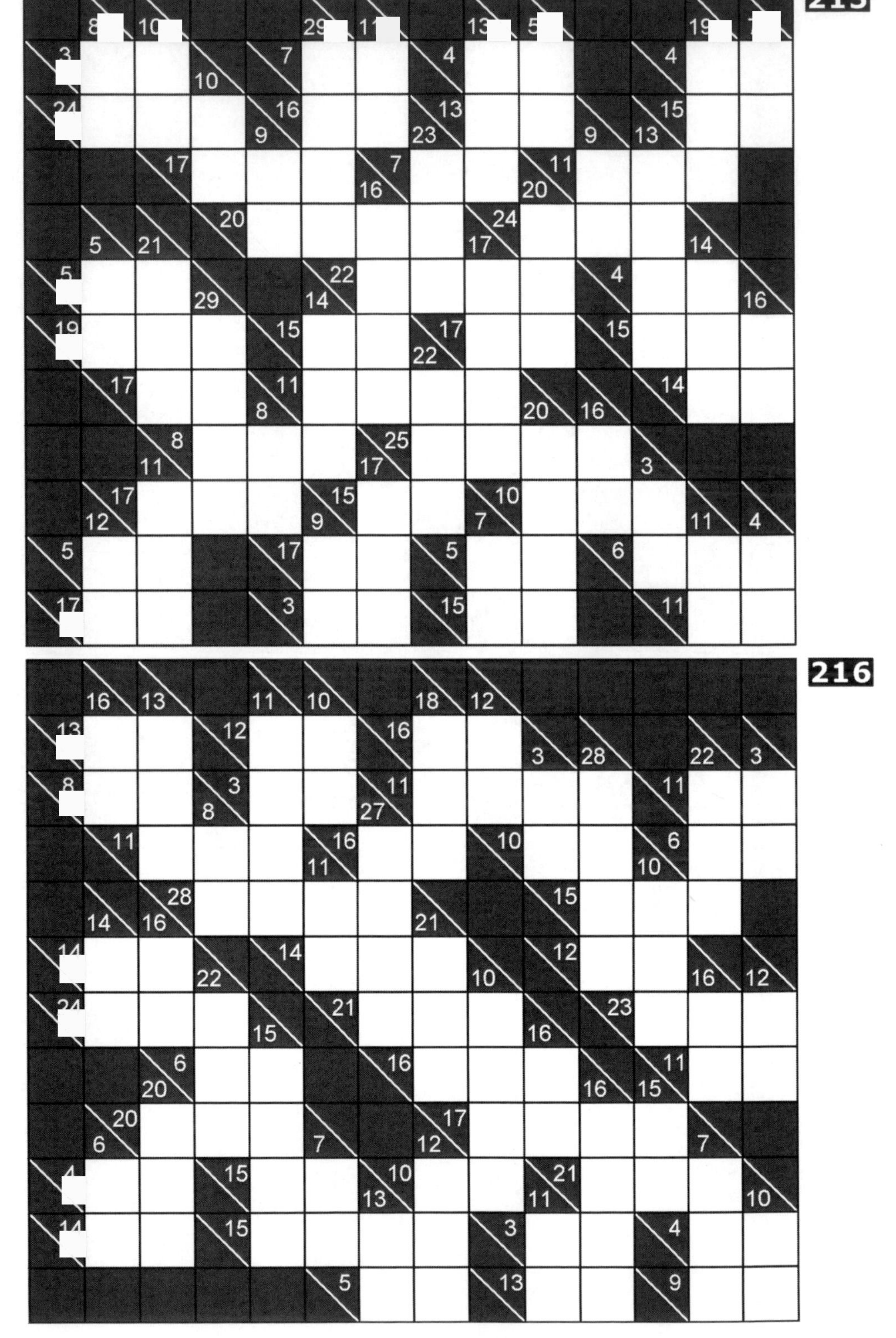
215
216

217

218

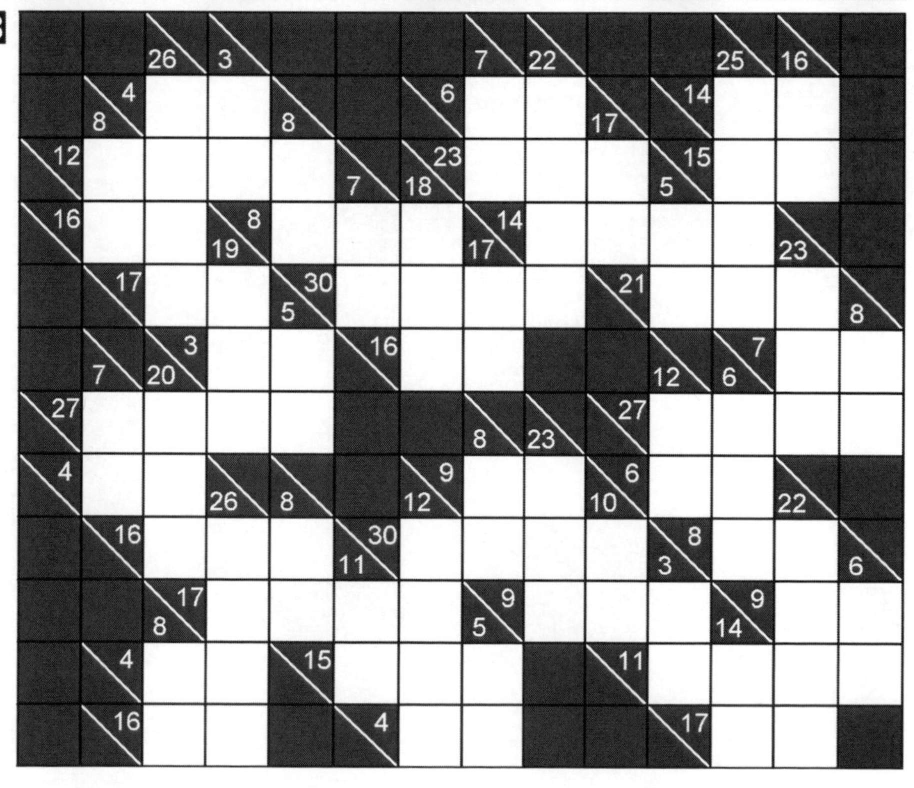

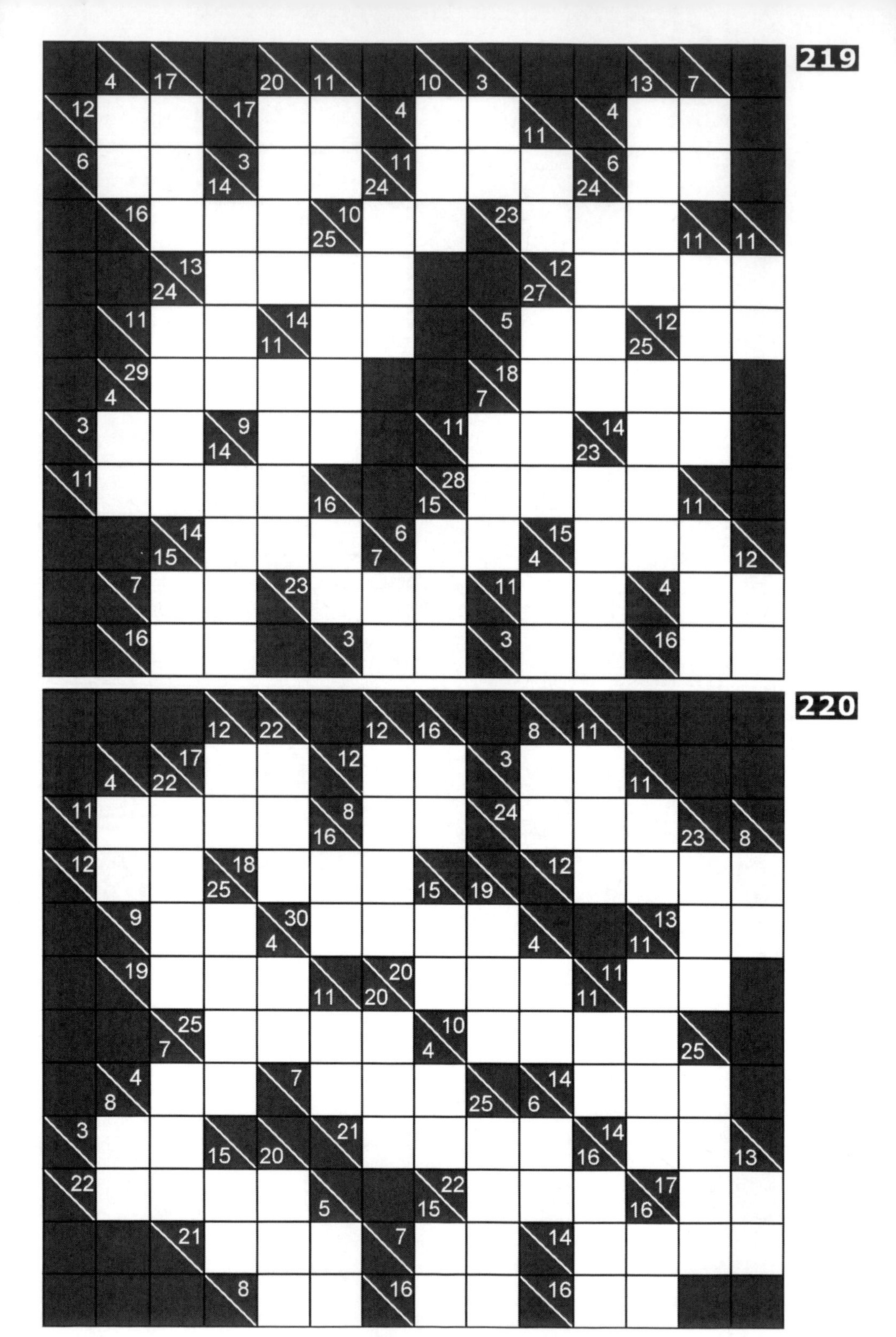
219
220

221

222

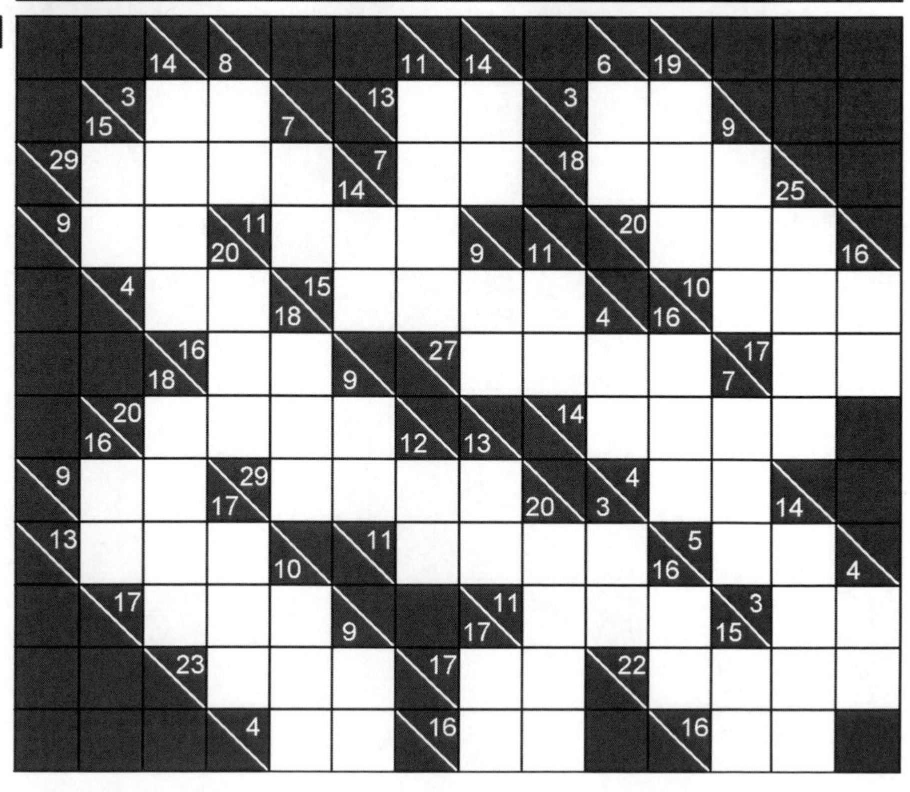

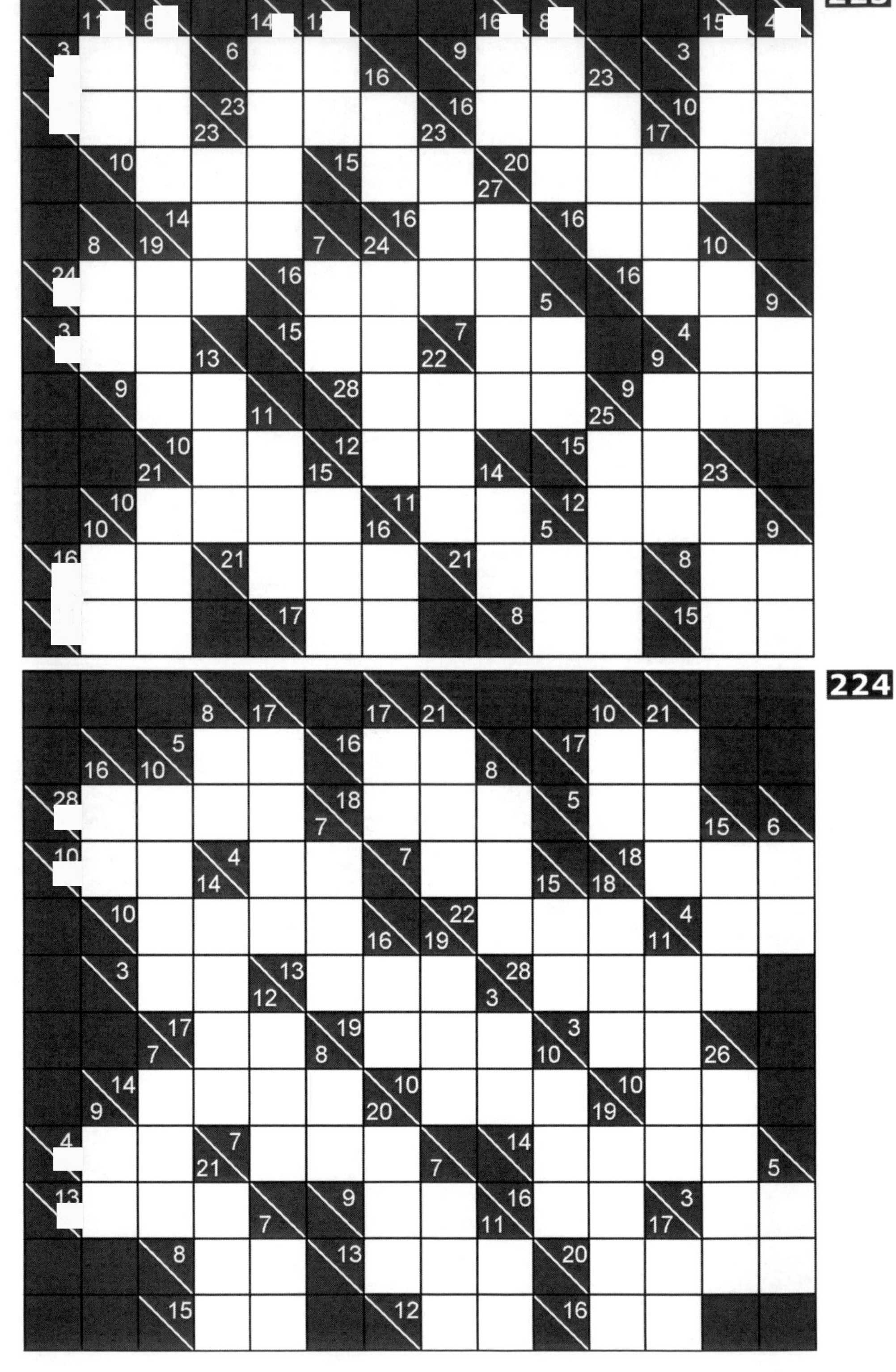
223
224

225

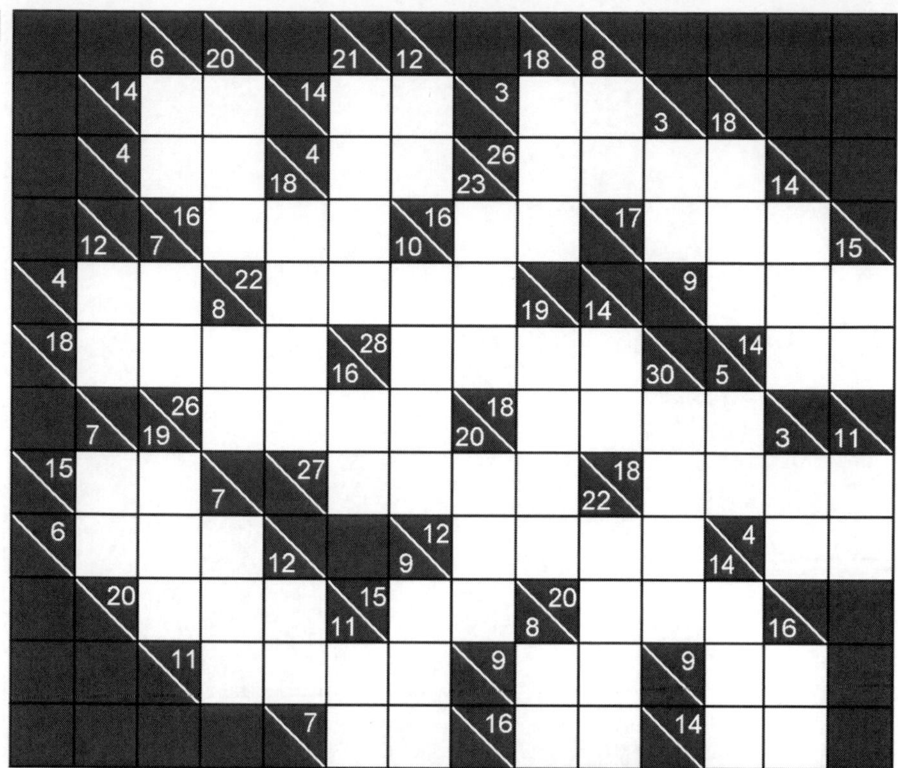

226

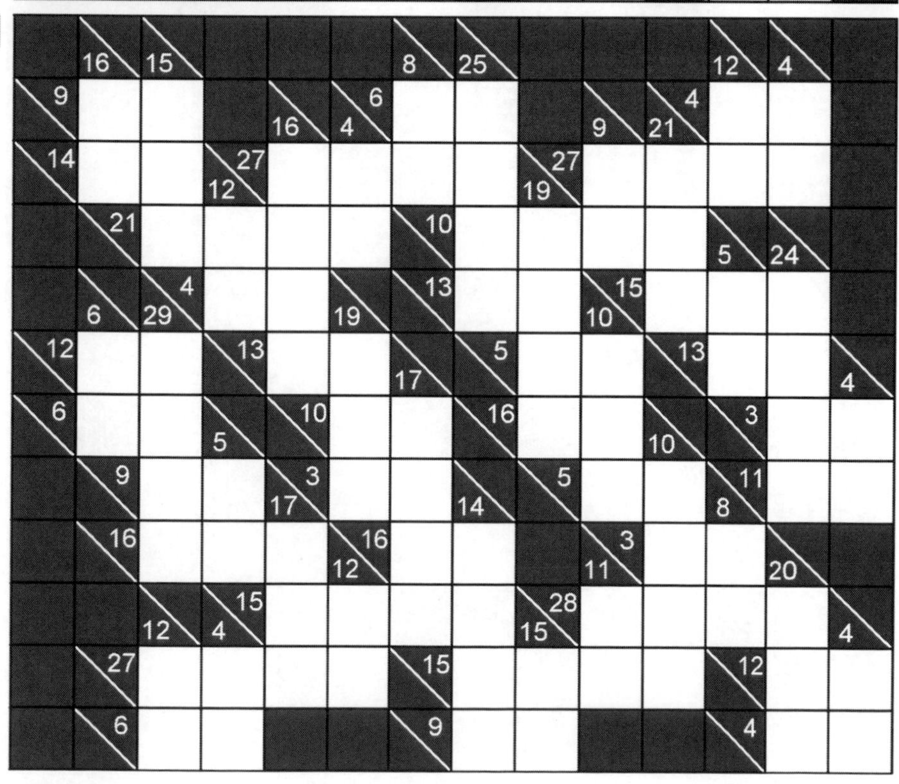

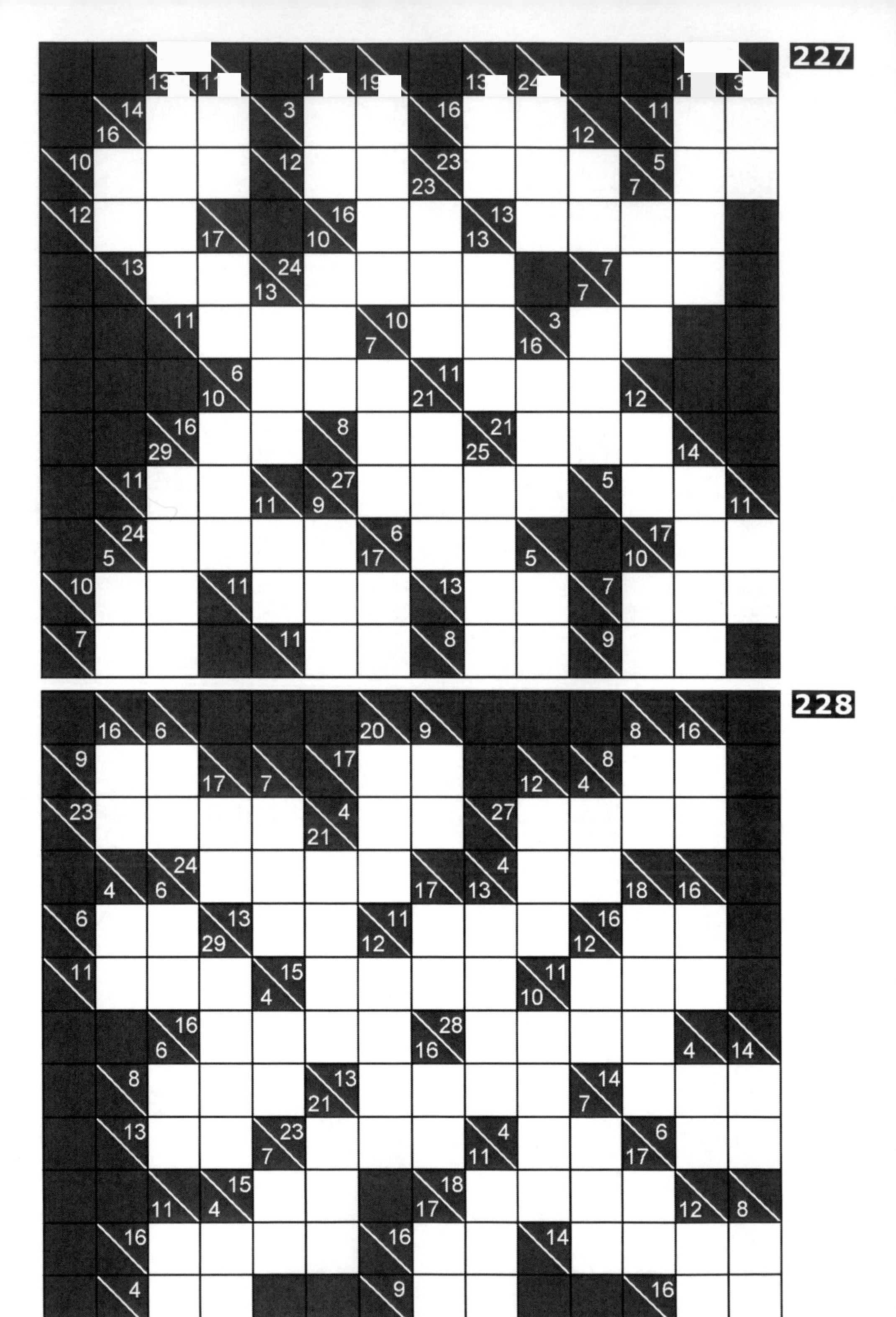

229

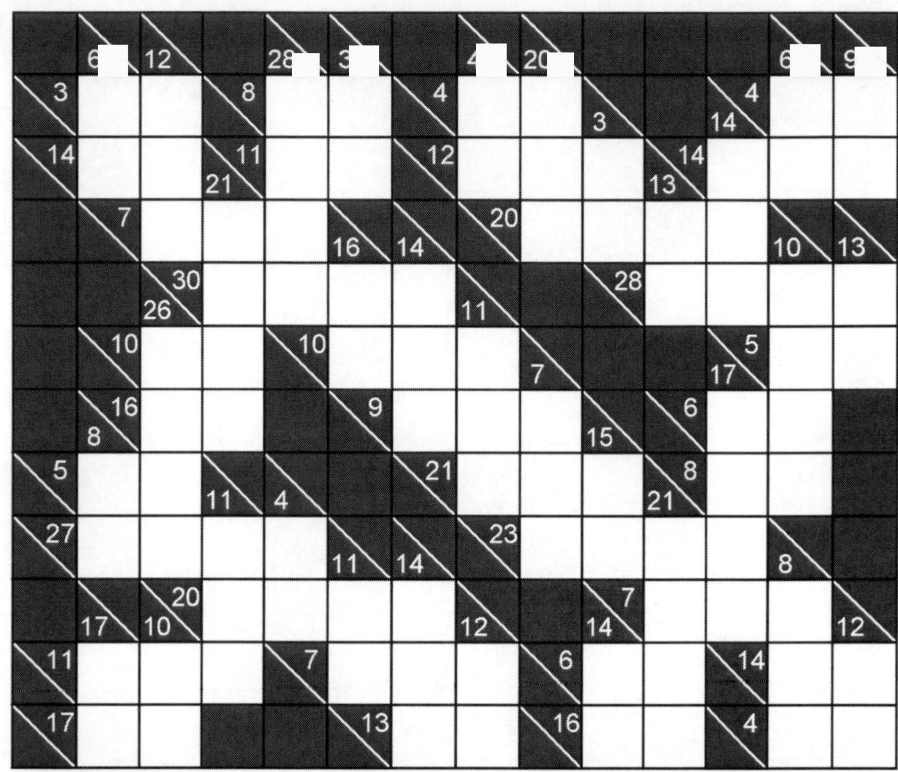

230

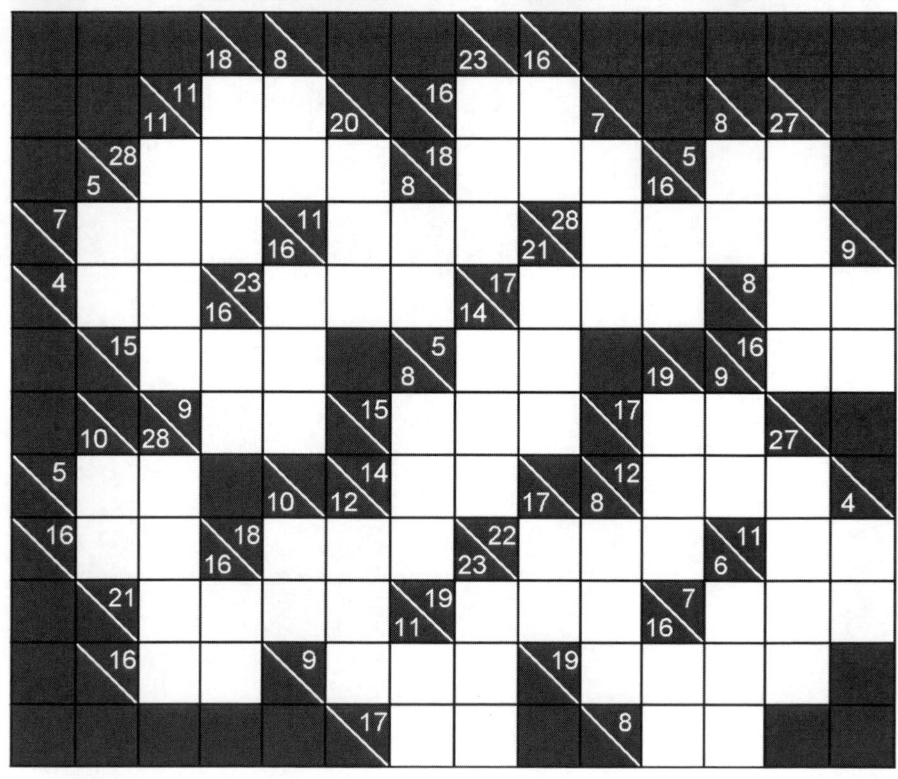

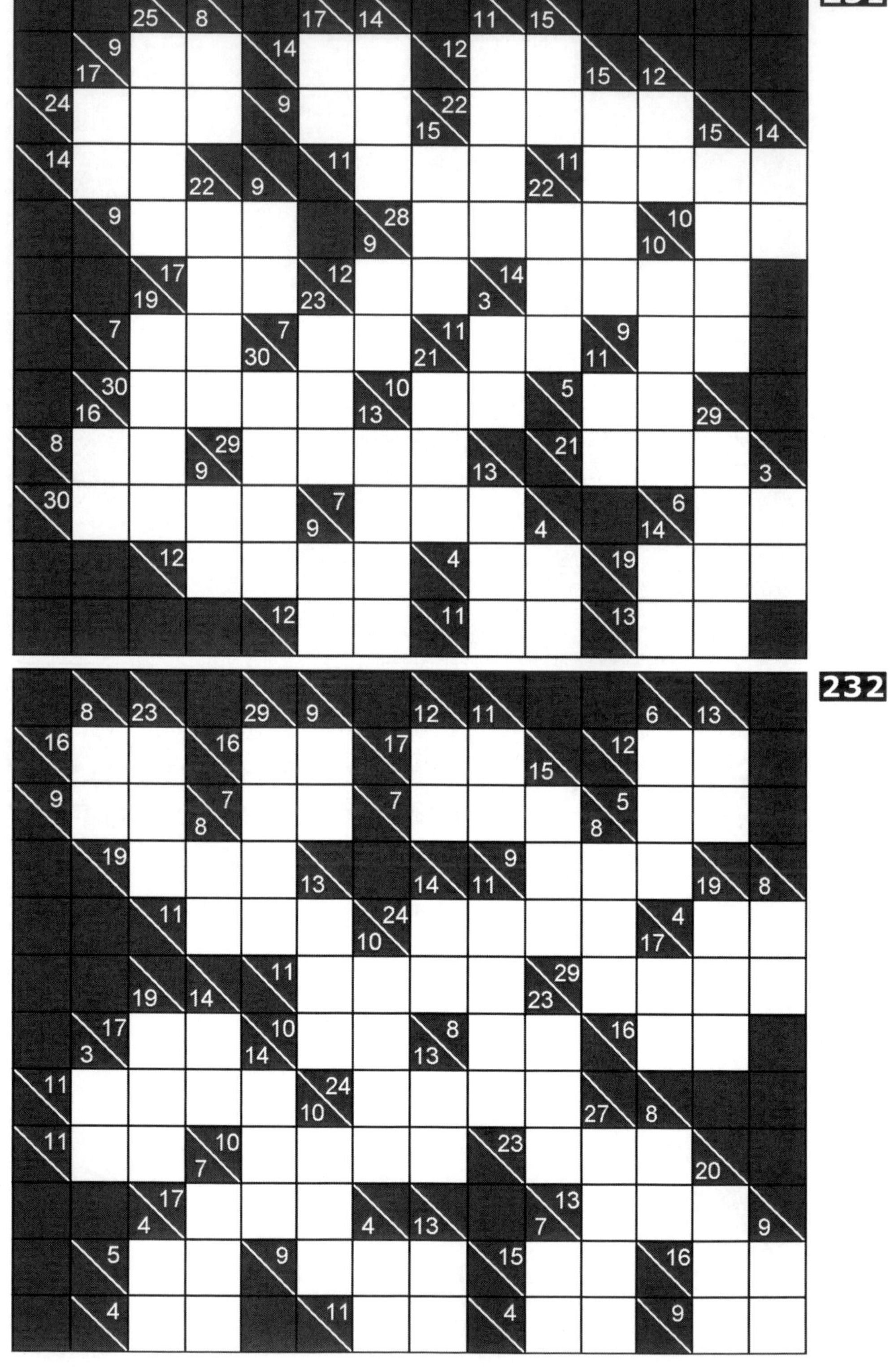

232

233

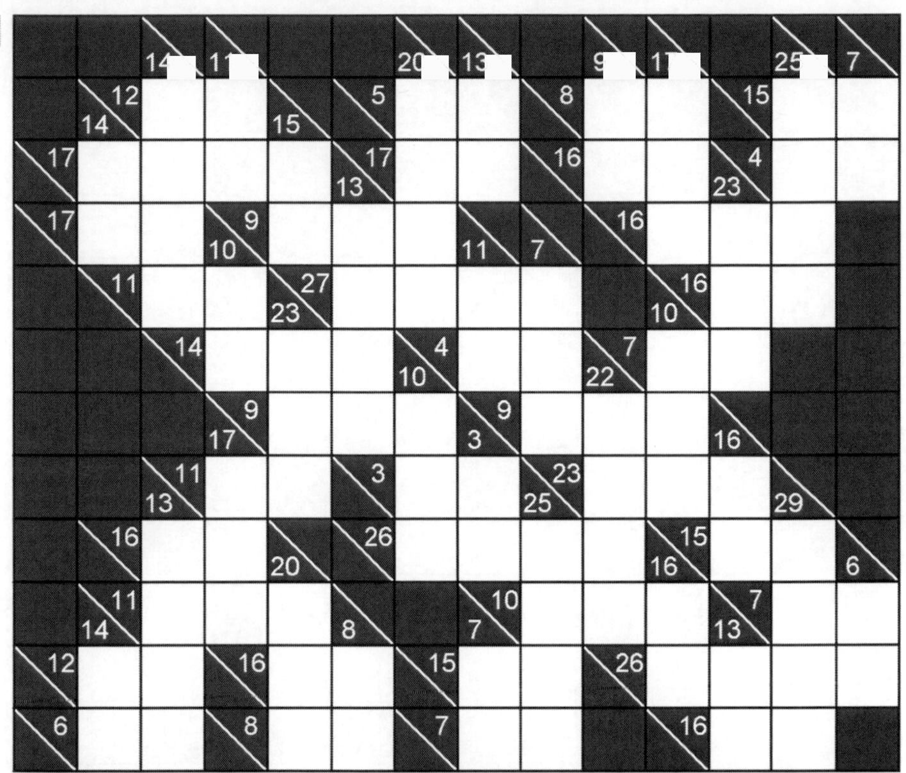

234

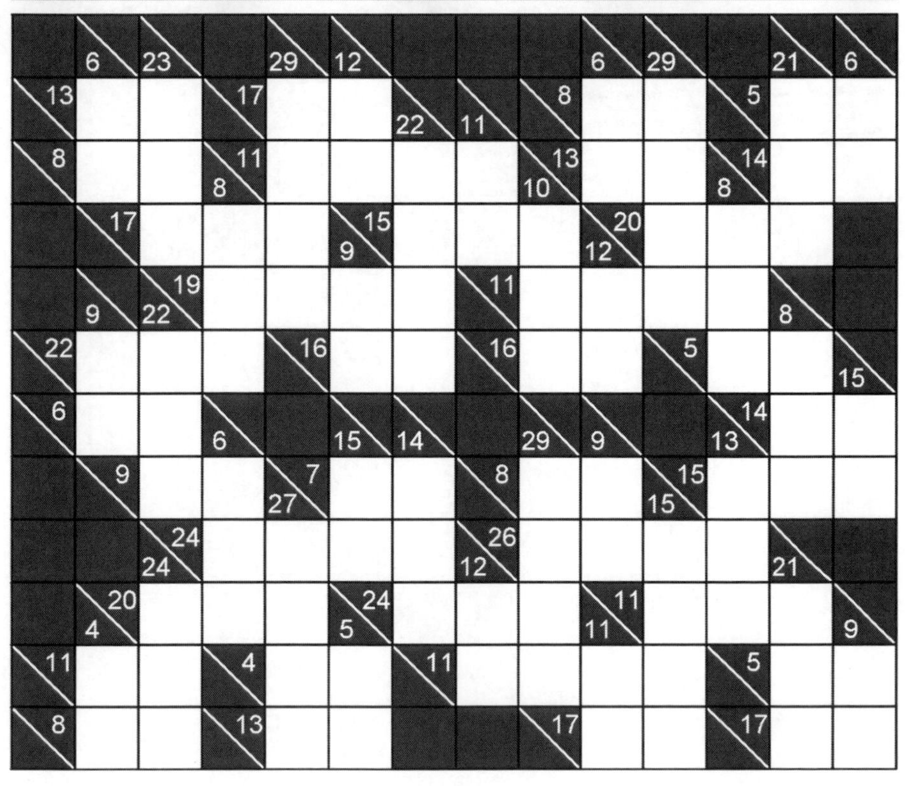

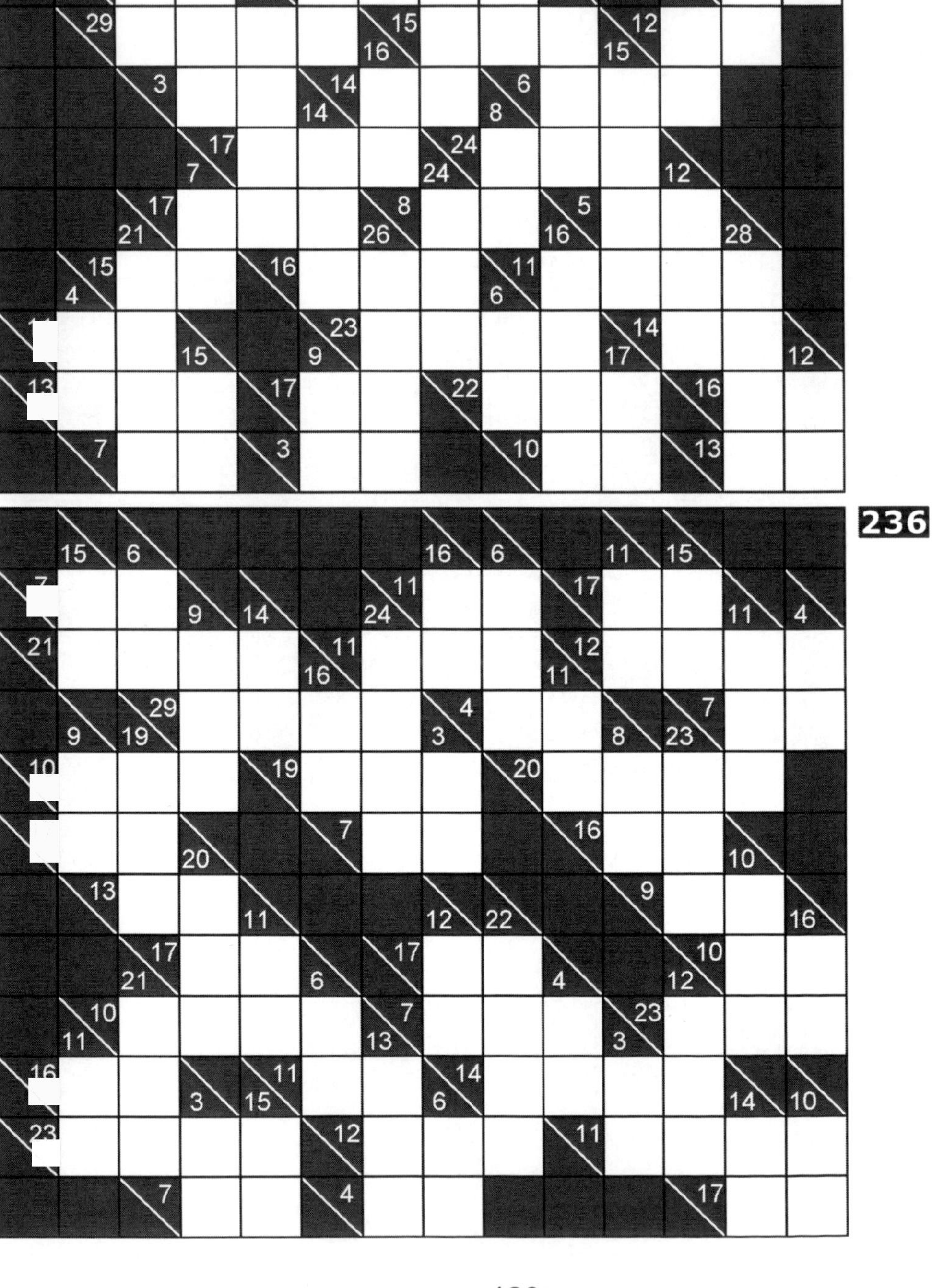

236

237

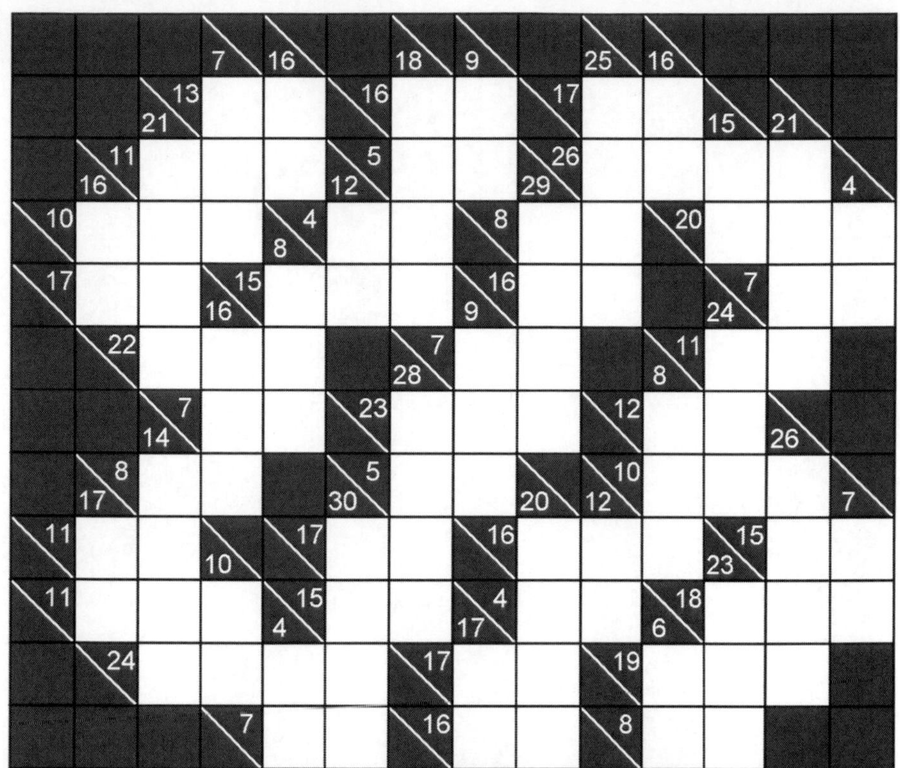

238

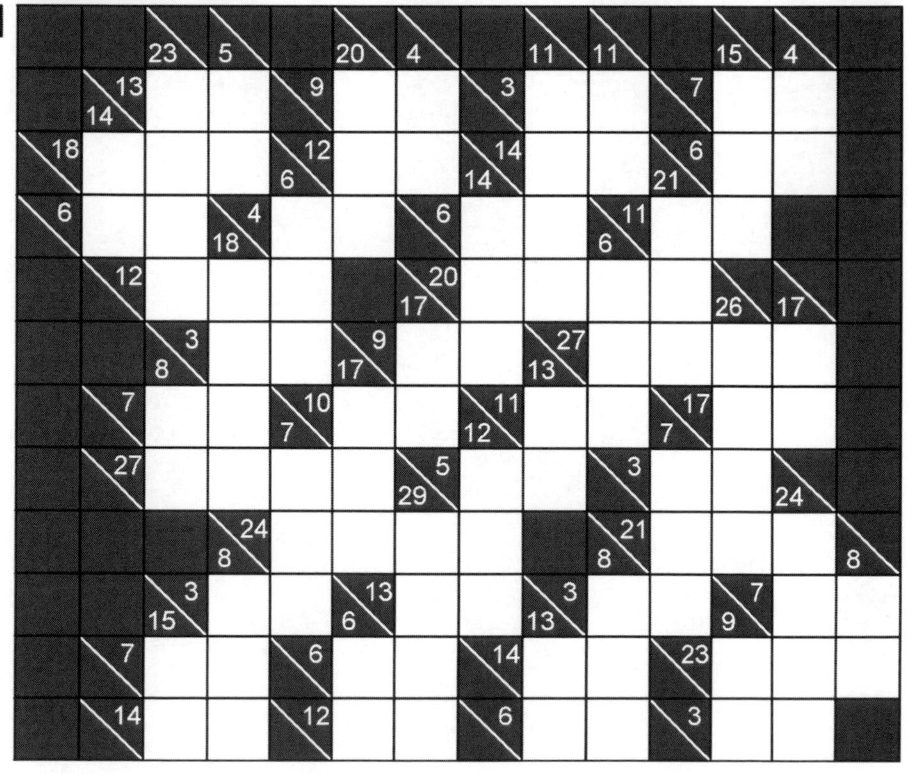

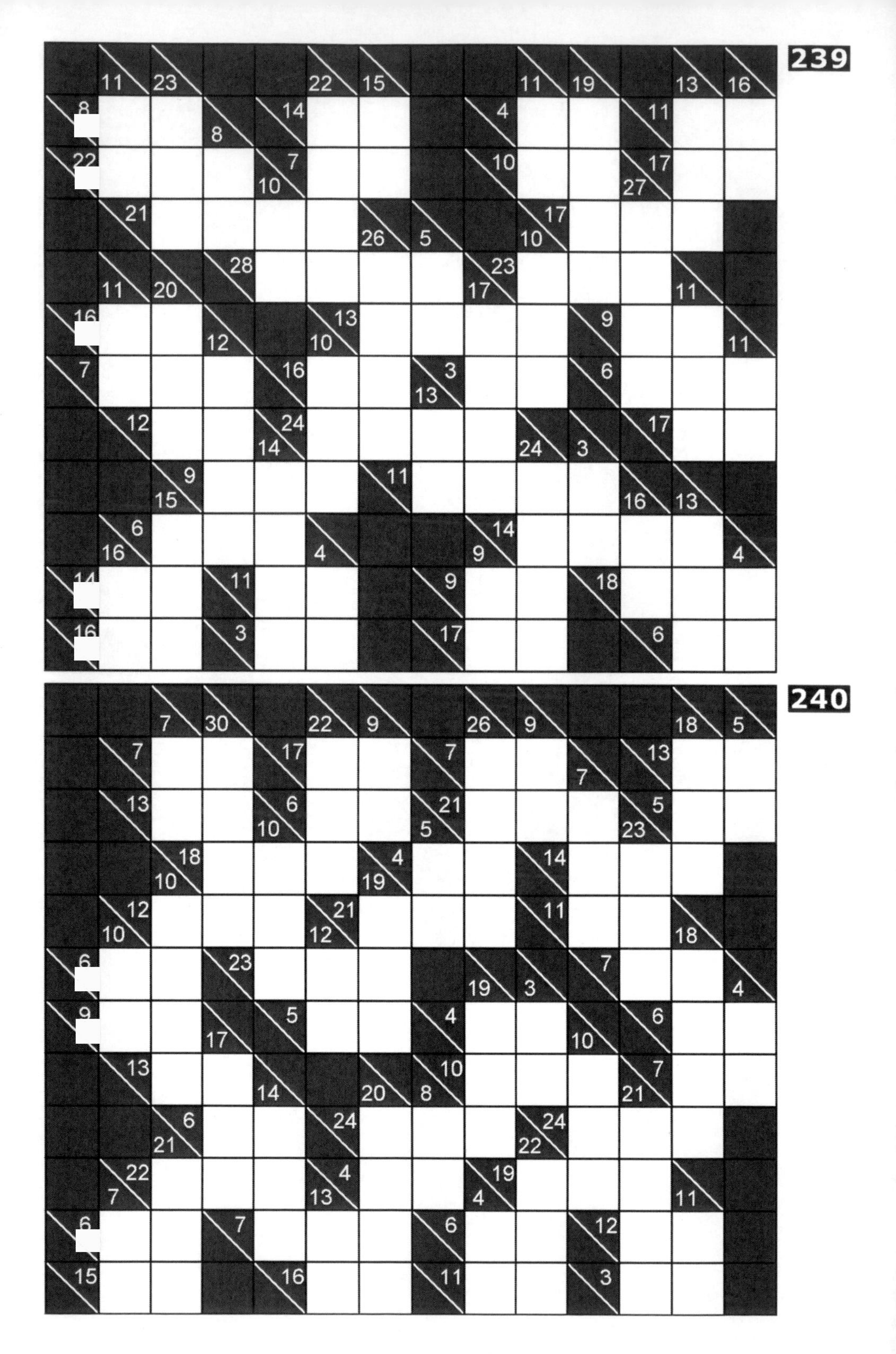
239
240

241

242

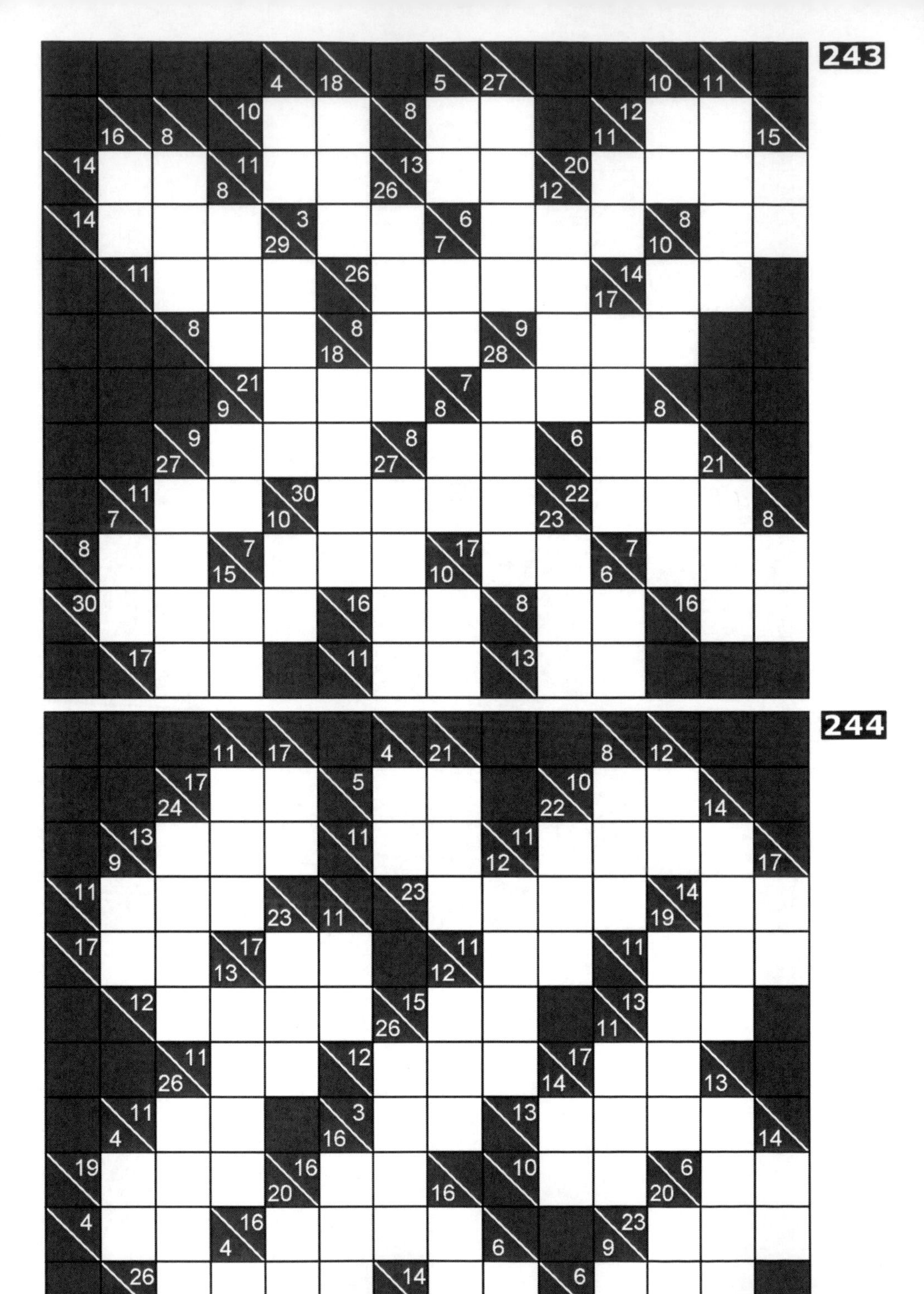

245

246

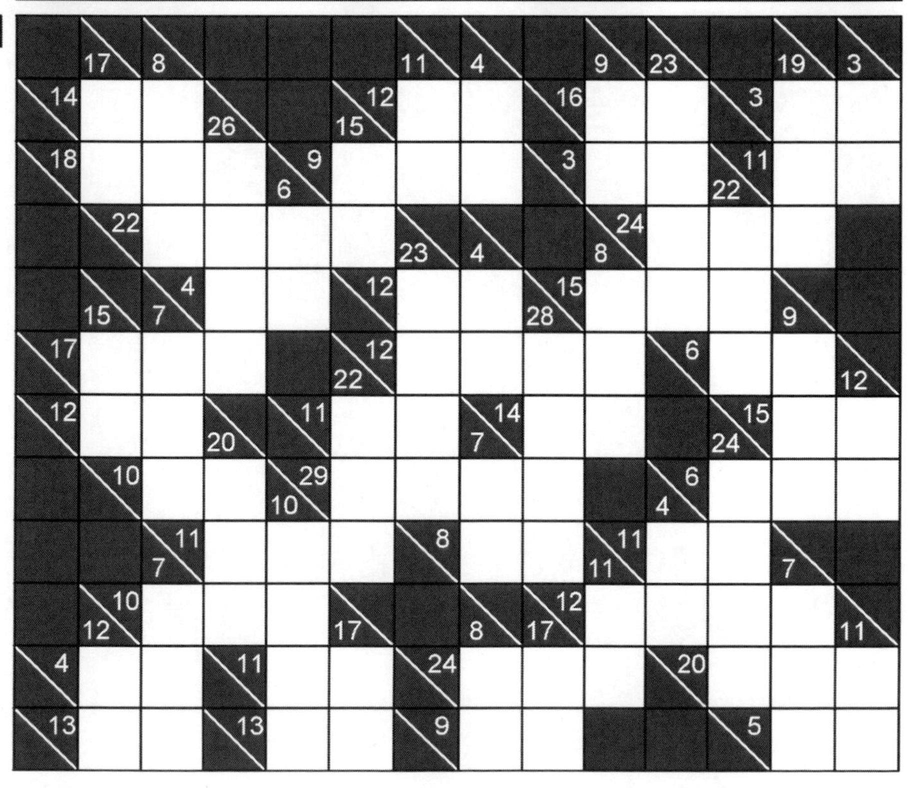

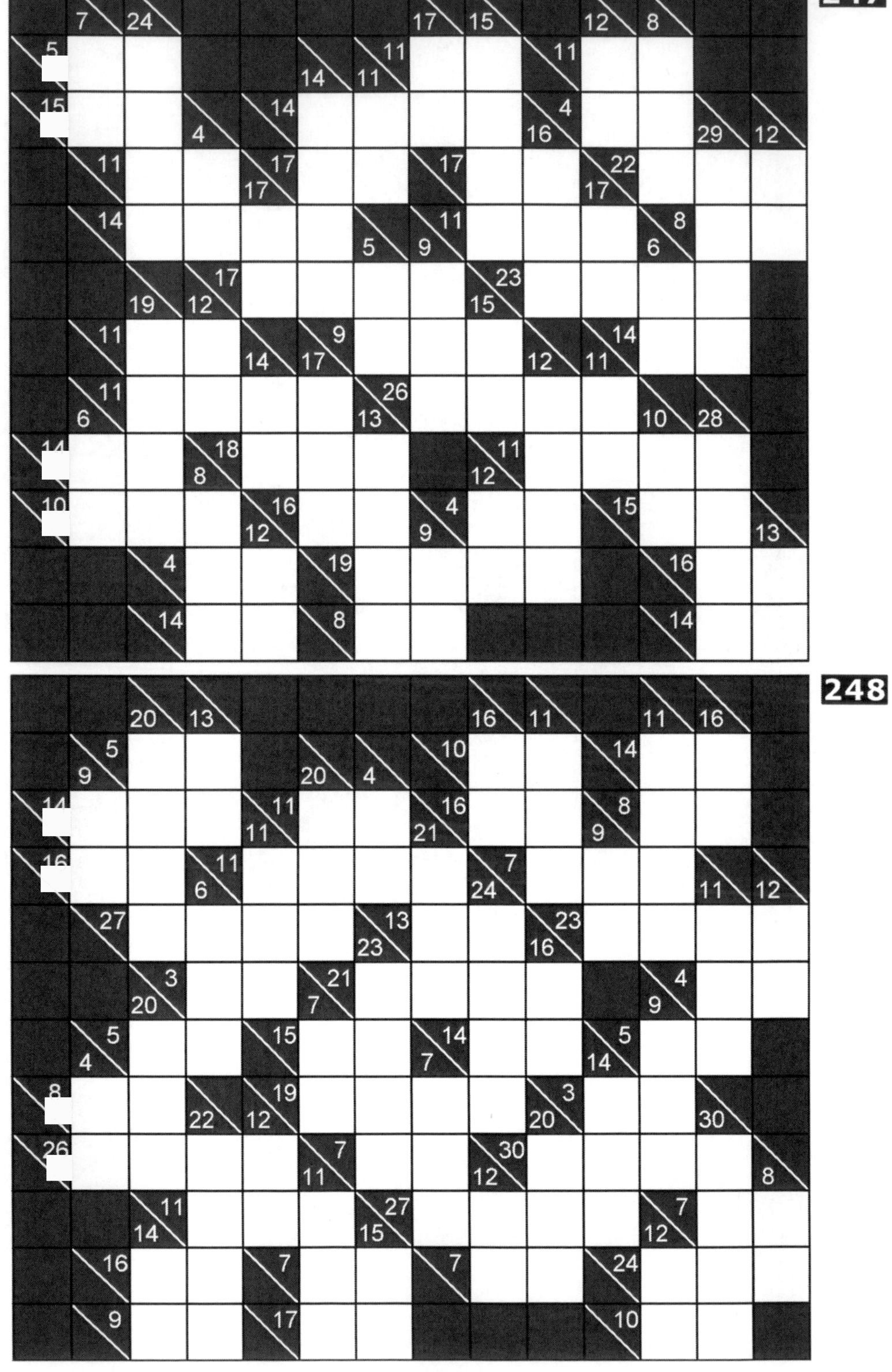

249

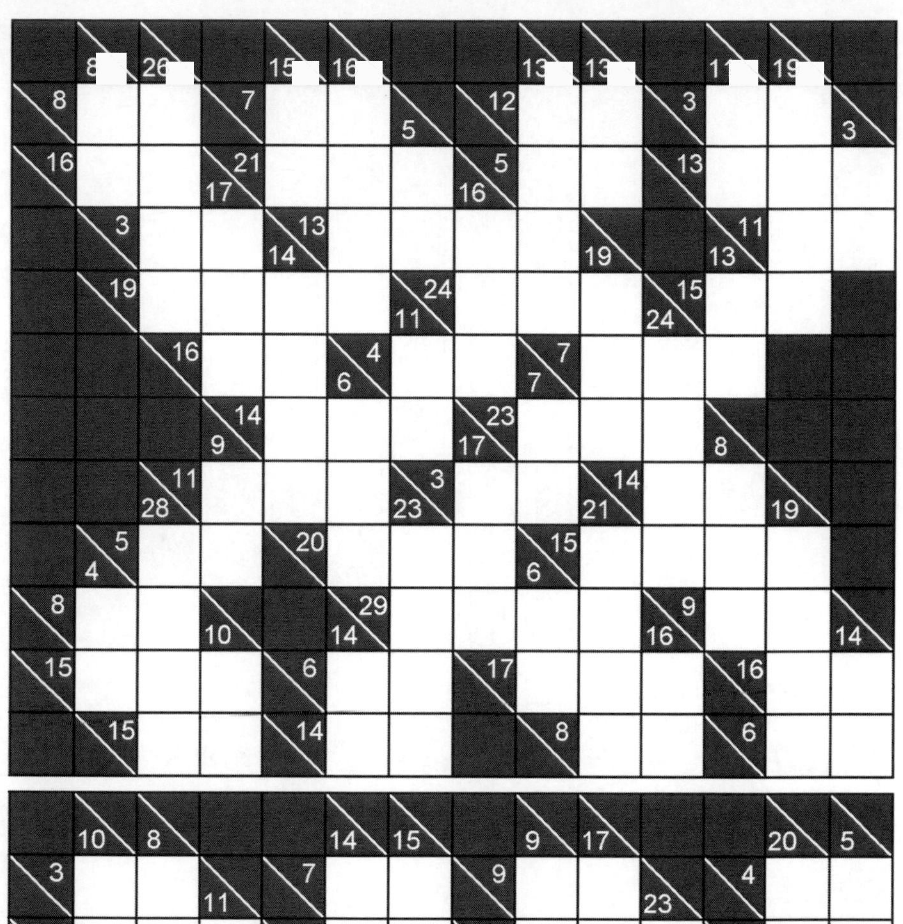

250

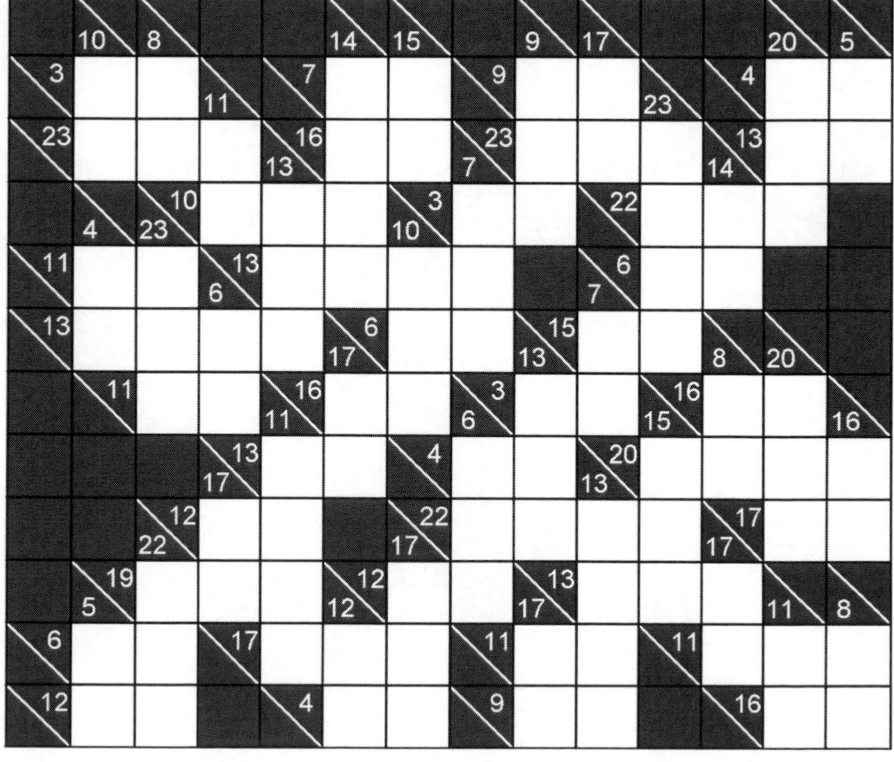

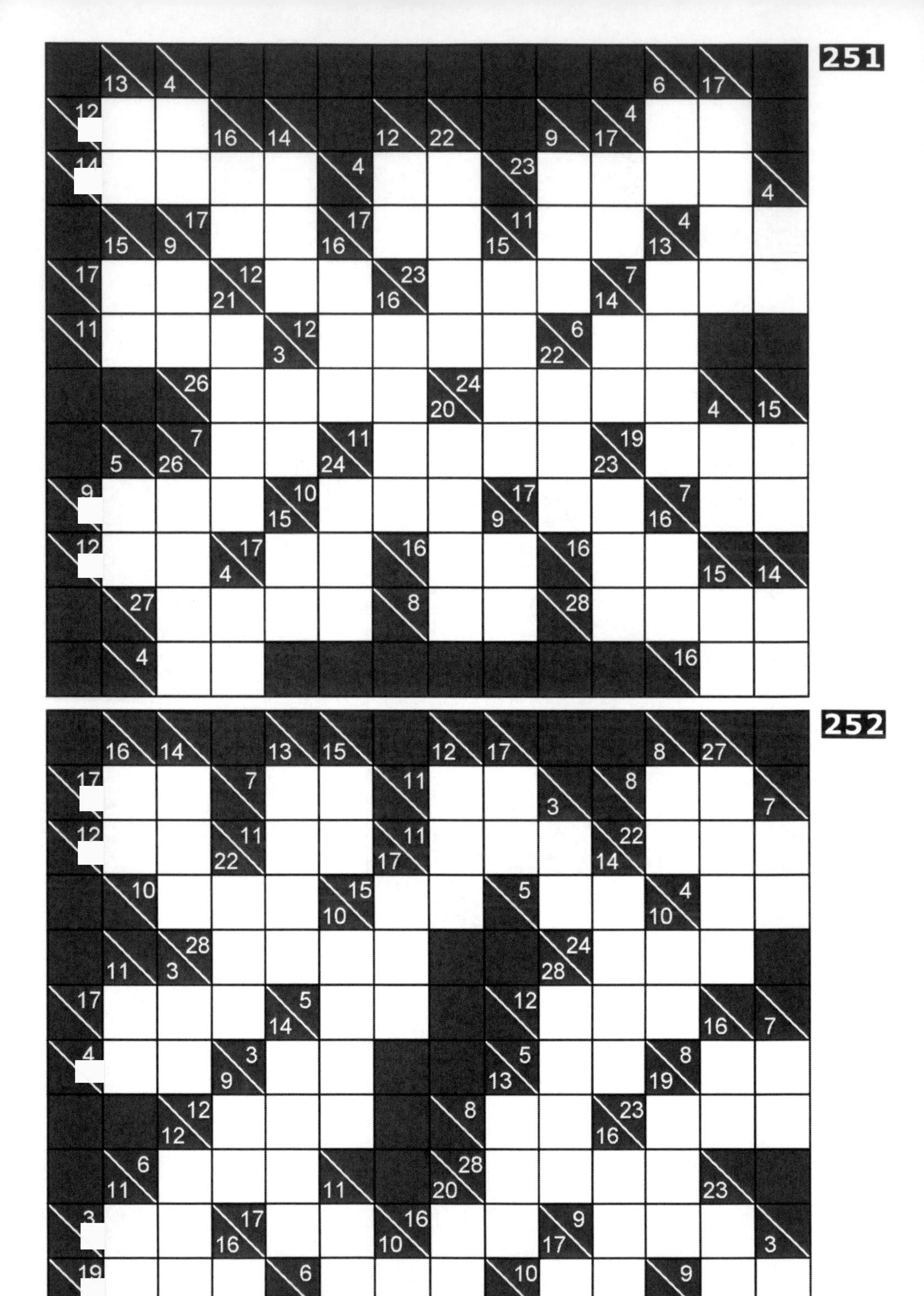
251
252

253

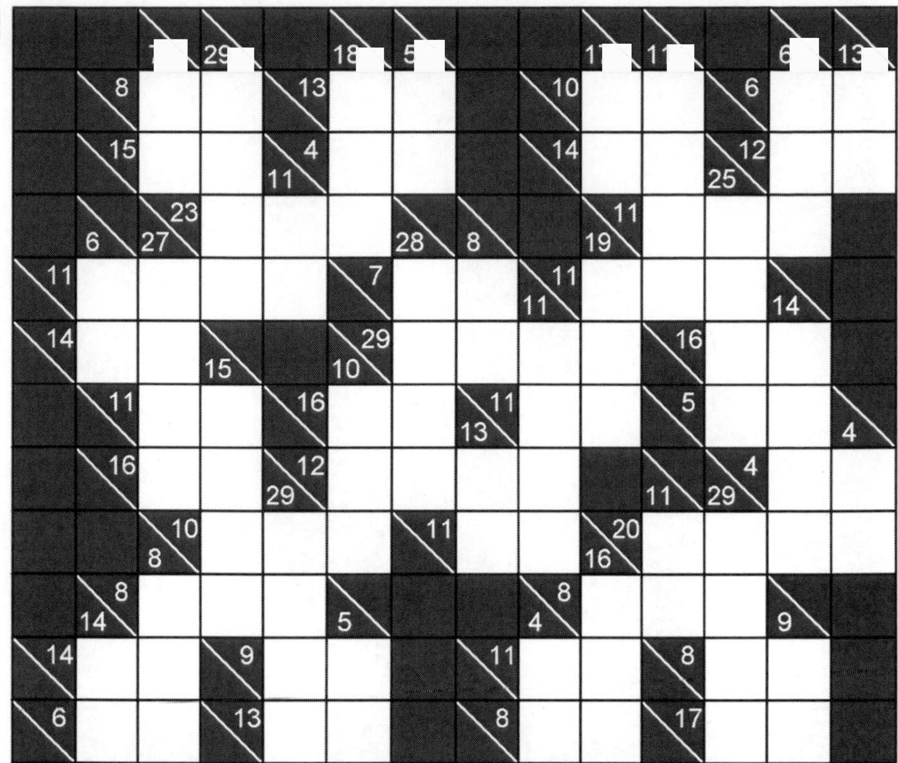

254

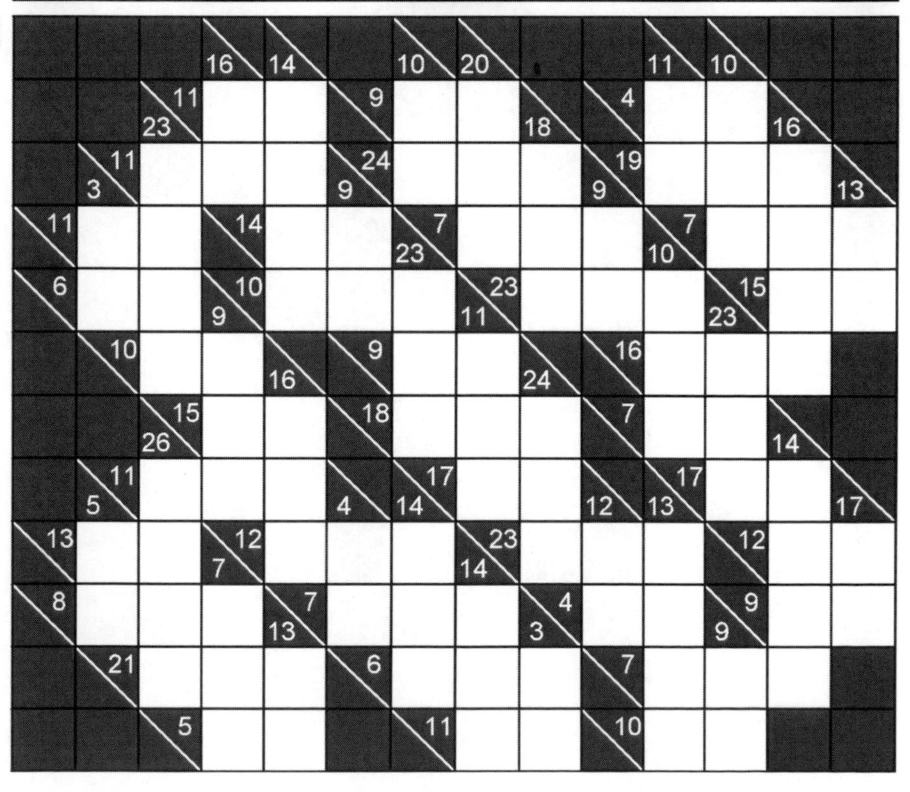

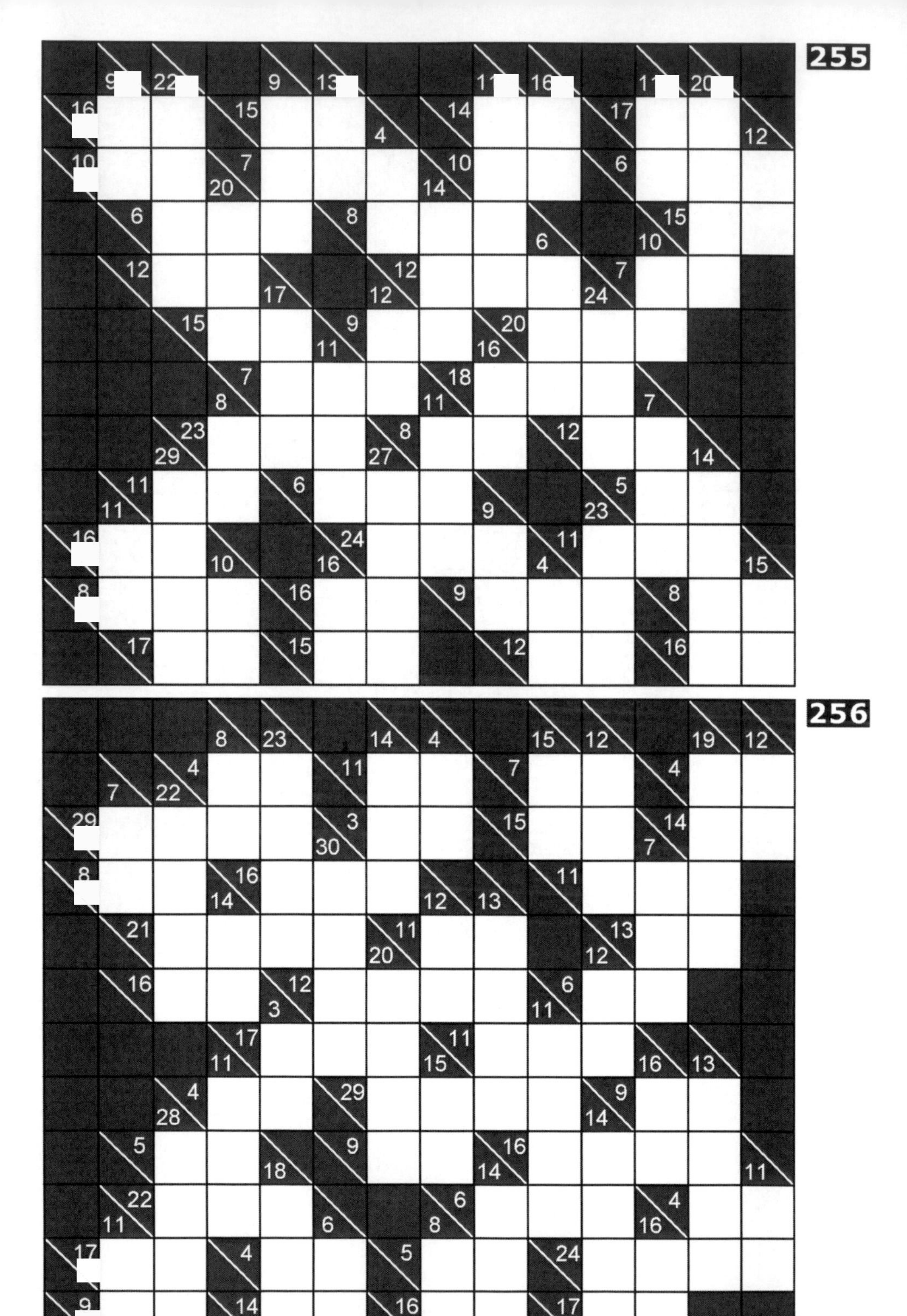
255
256

257

258

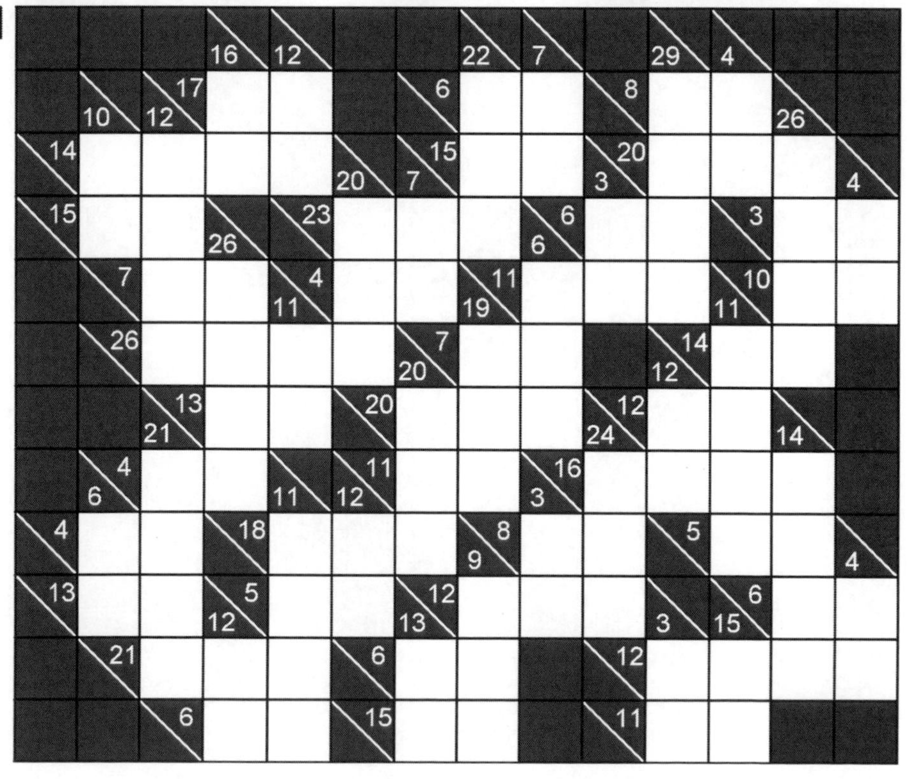

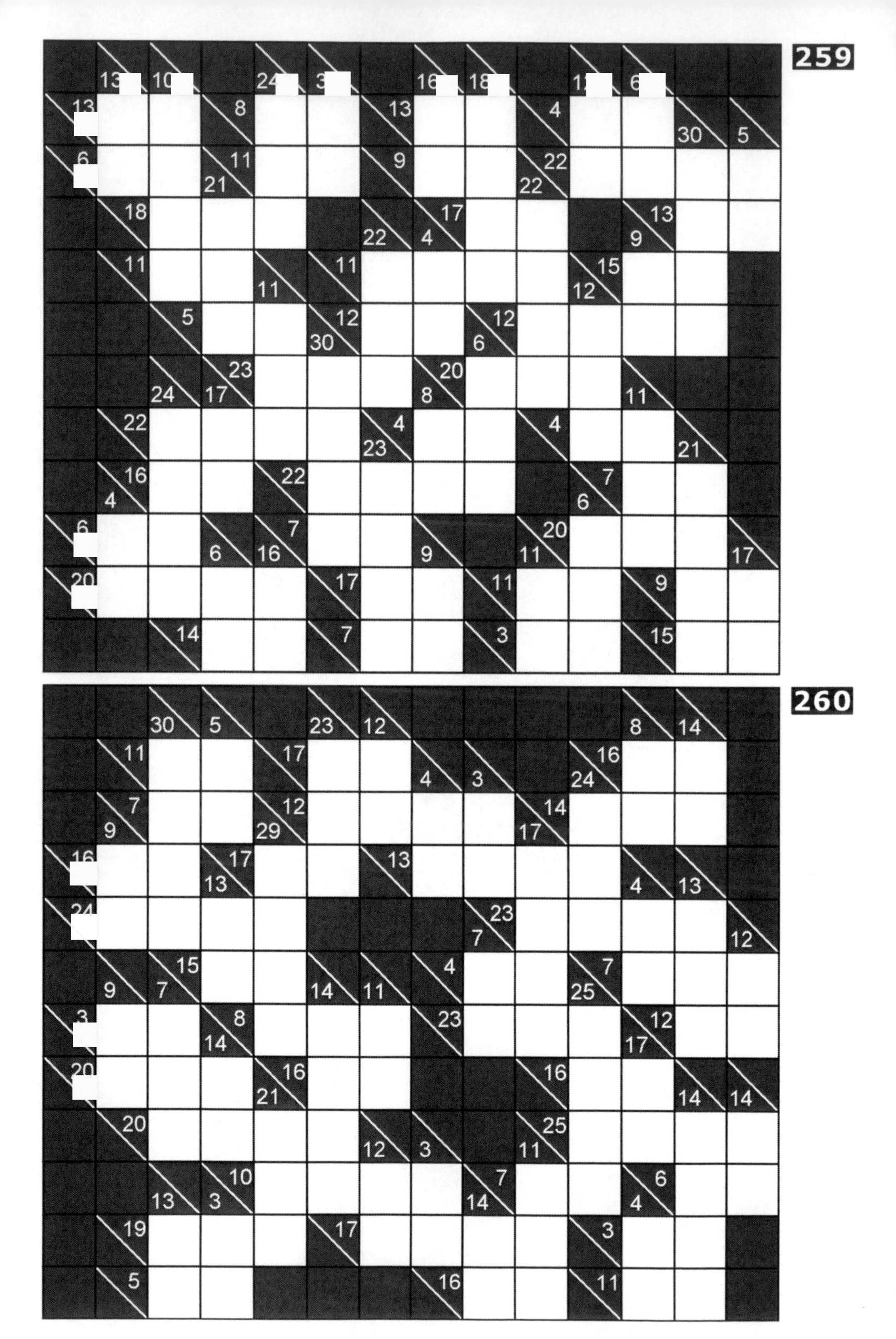
259
260

261

262

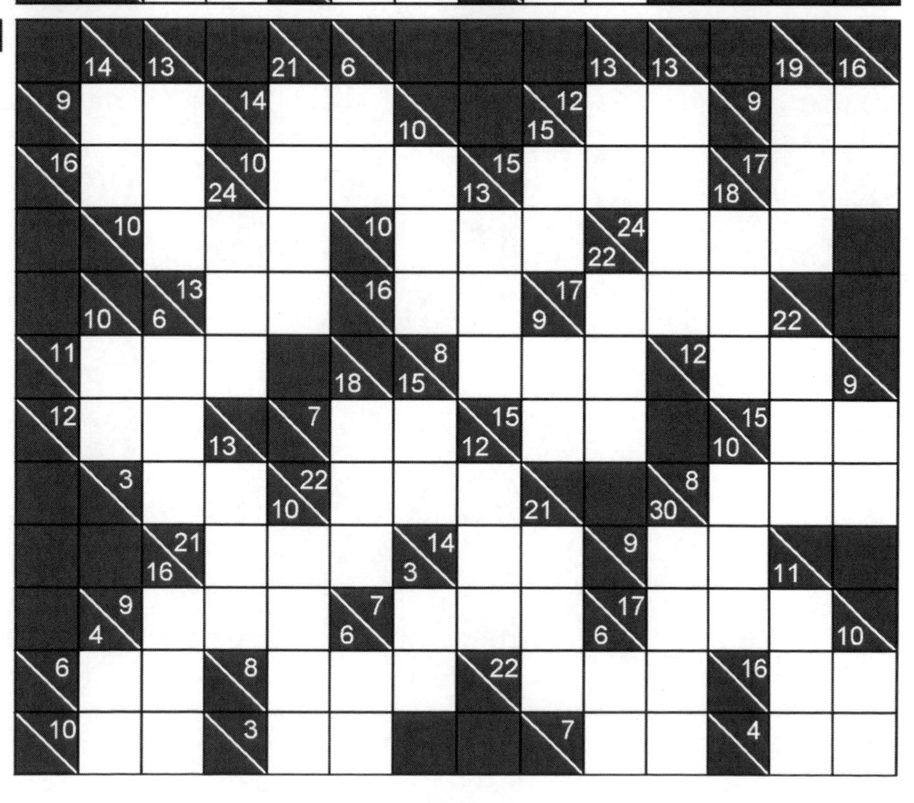

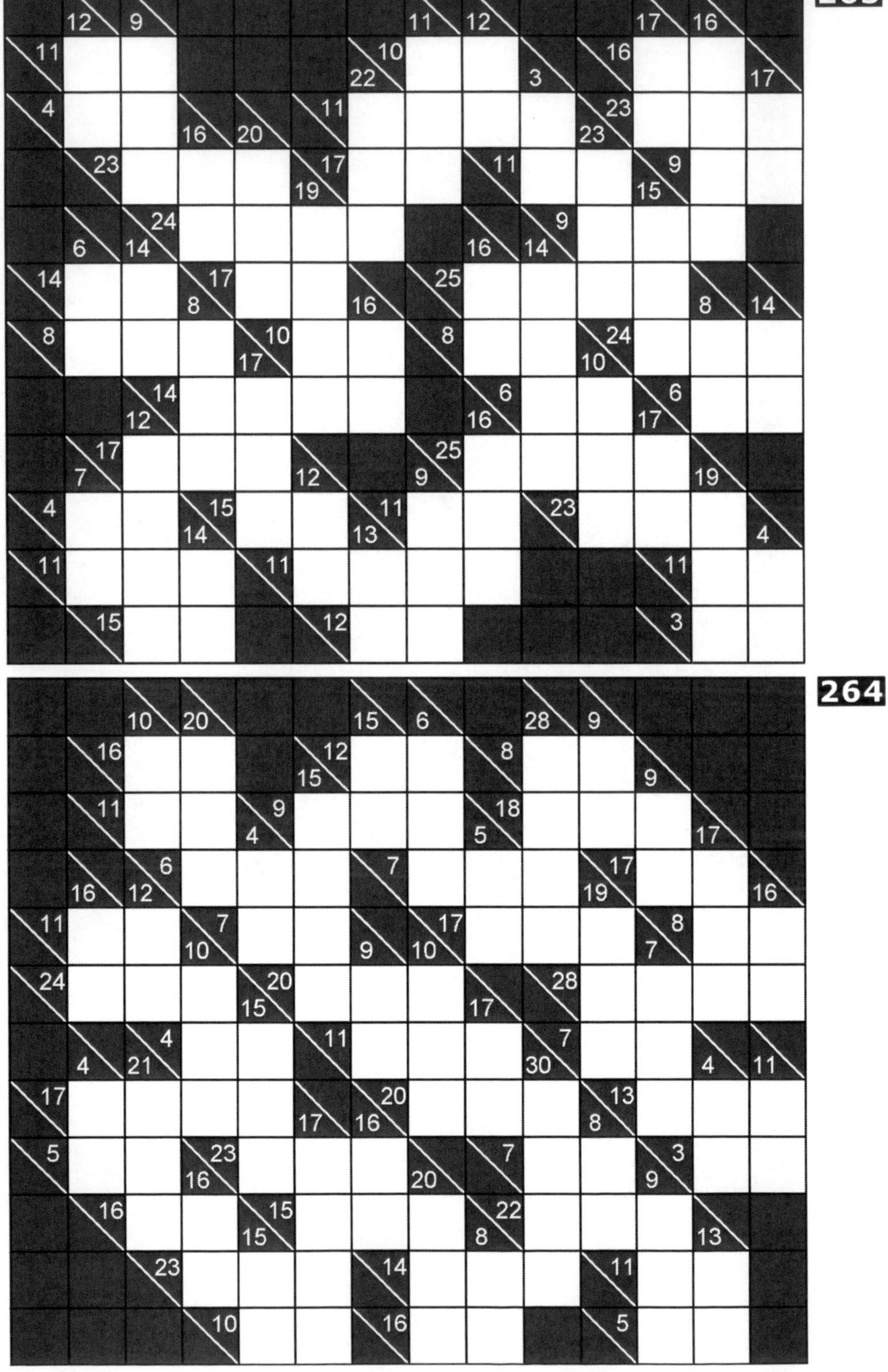
263
264

265

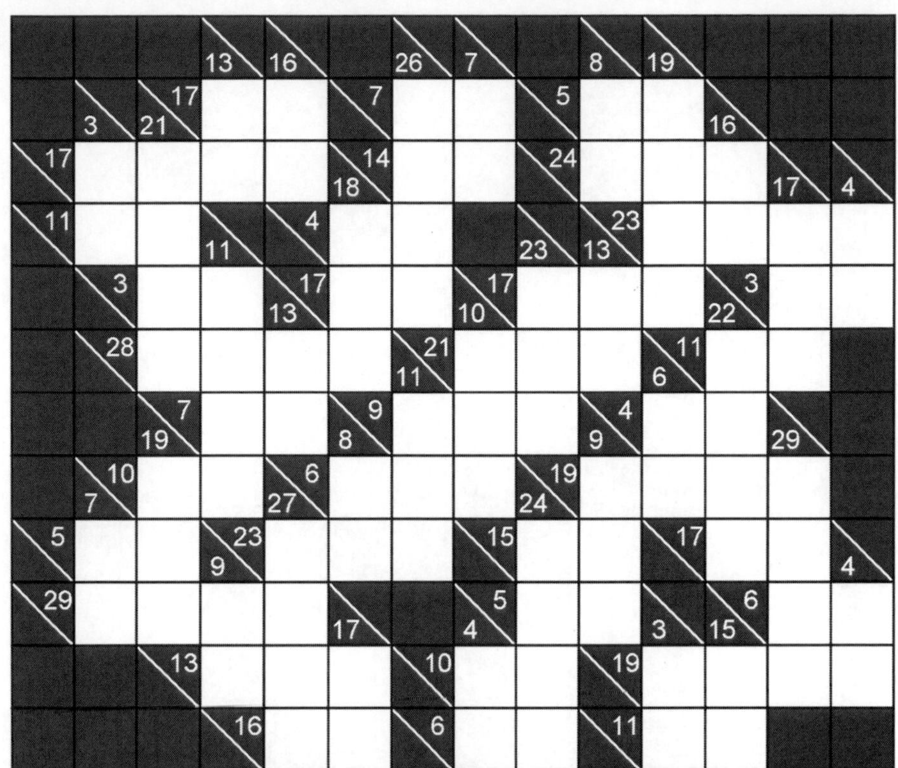

266

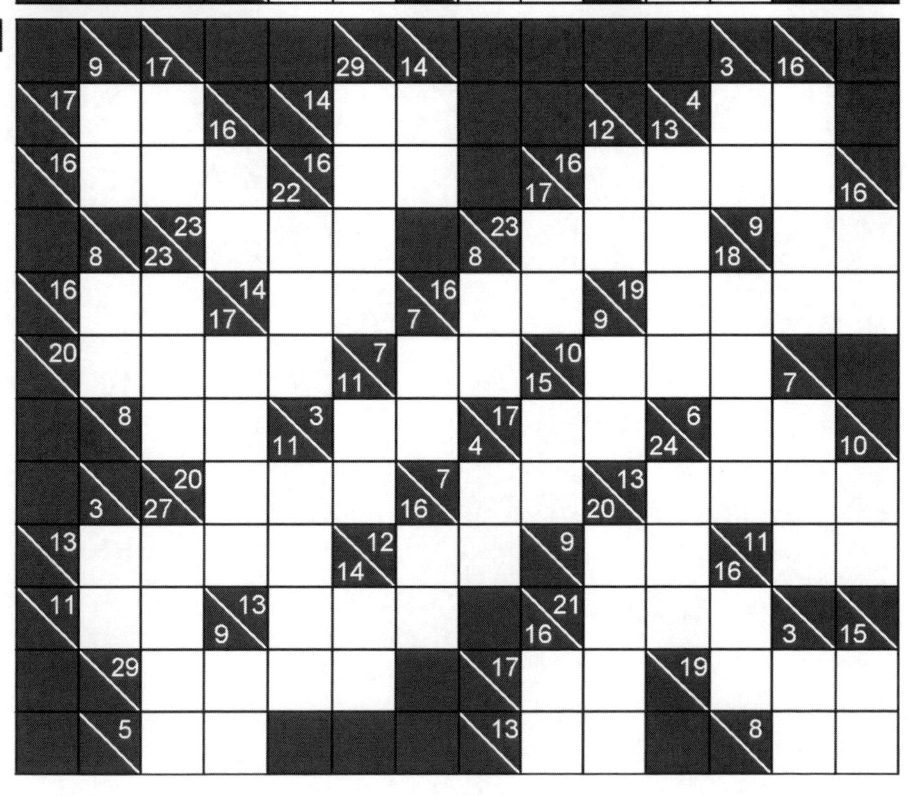

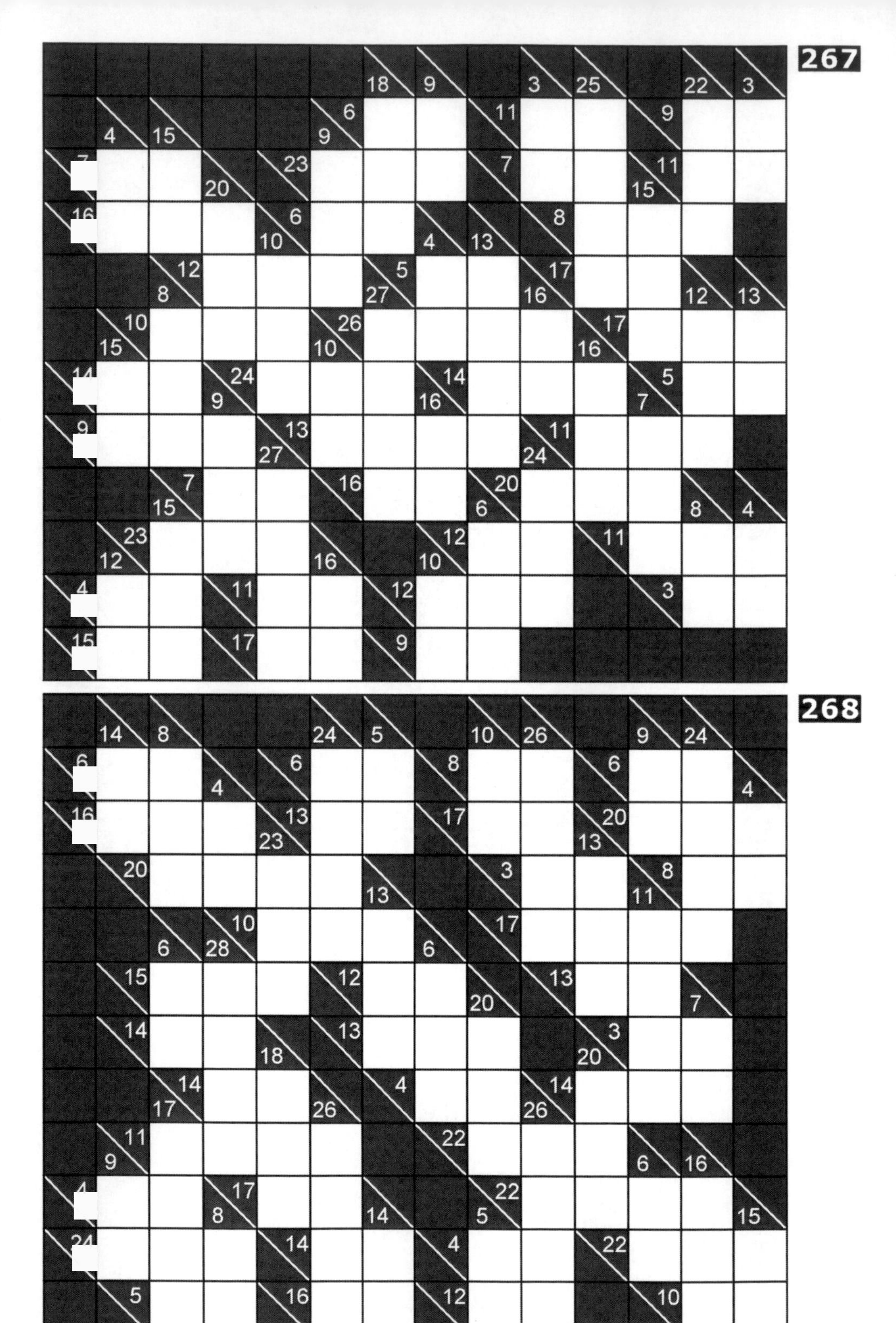
267
268

269

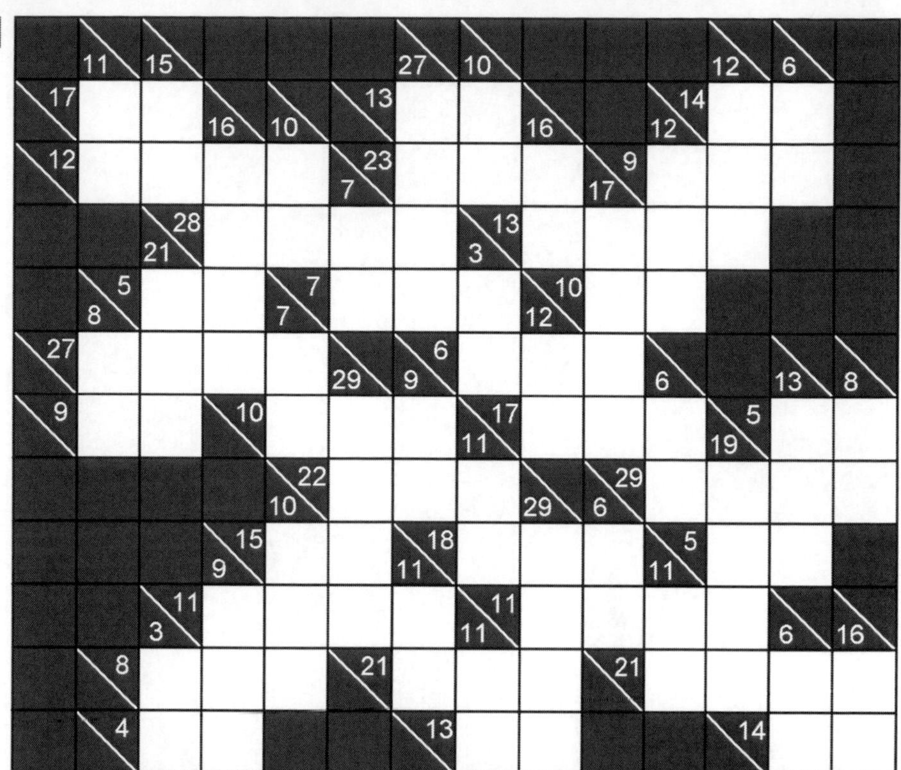

270

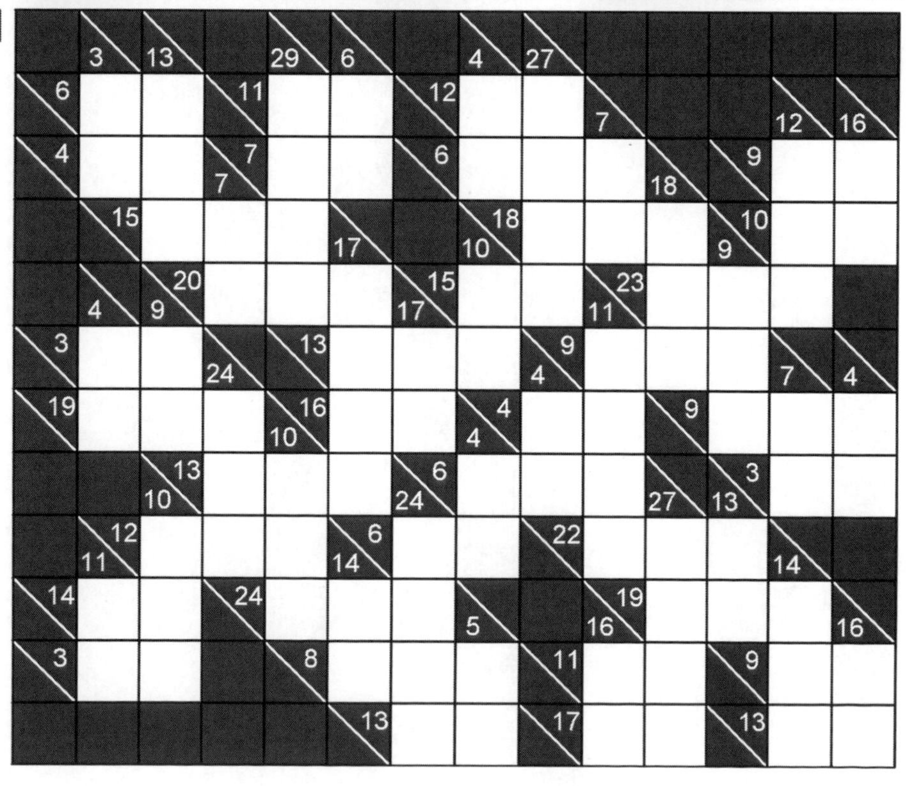

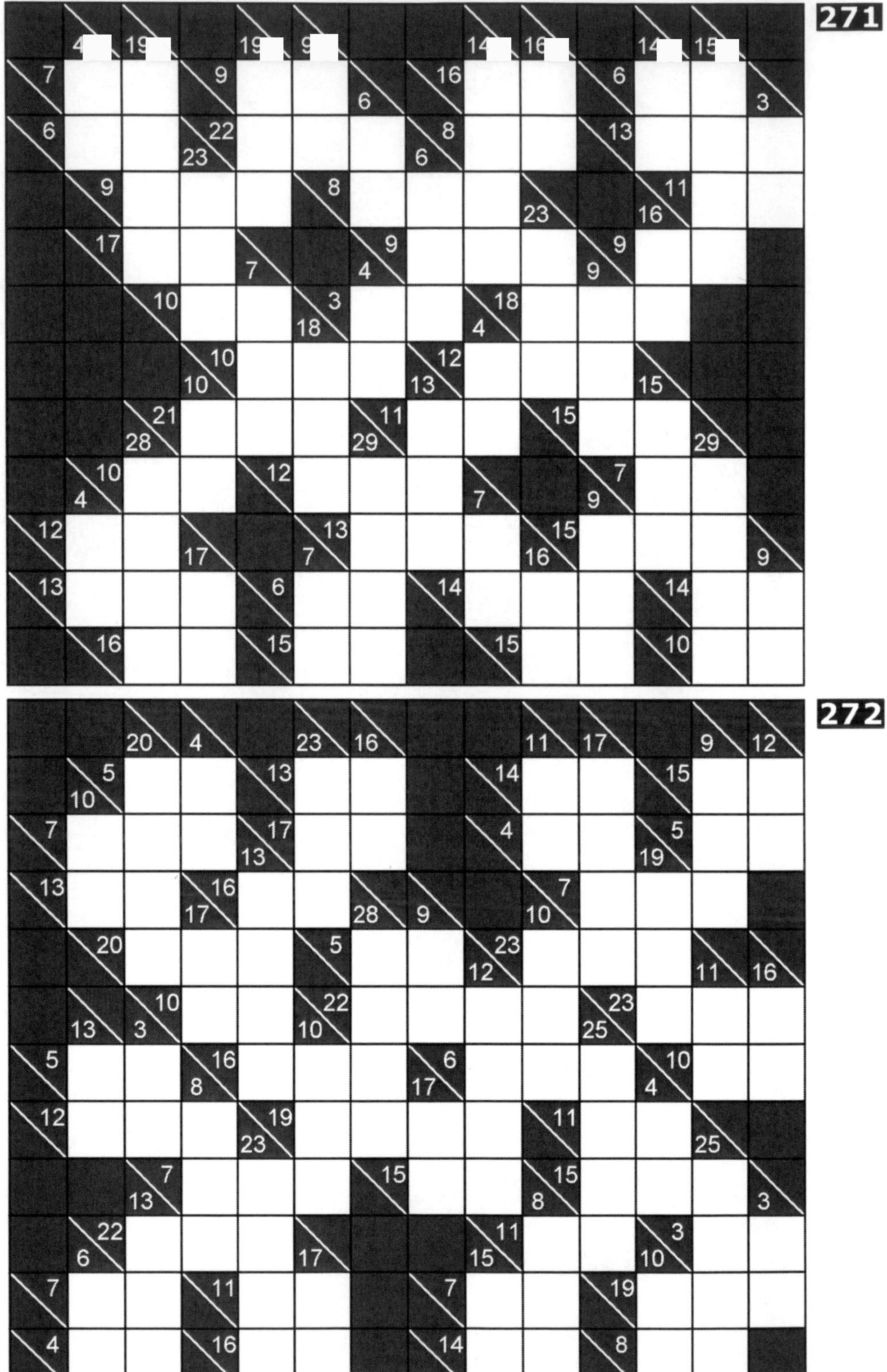
271
272

273

274

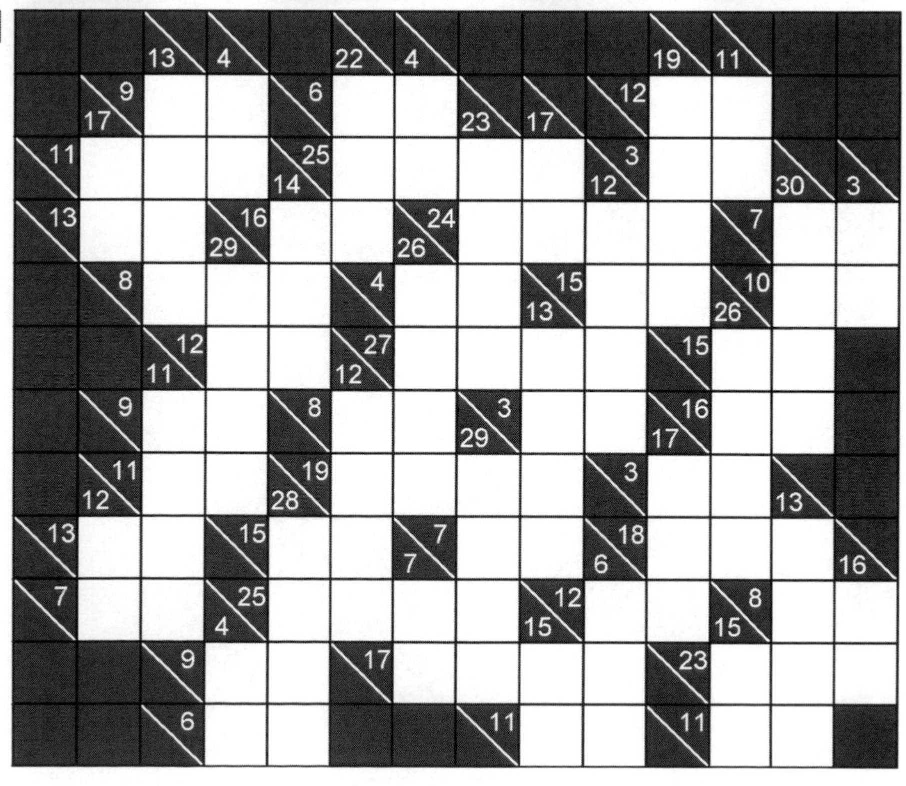

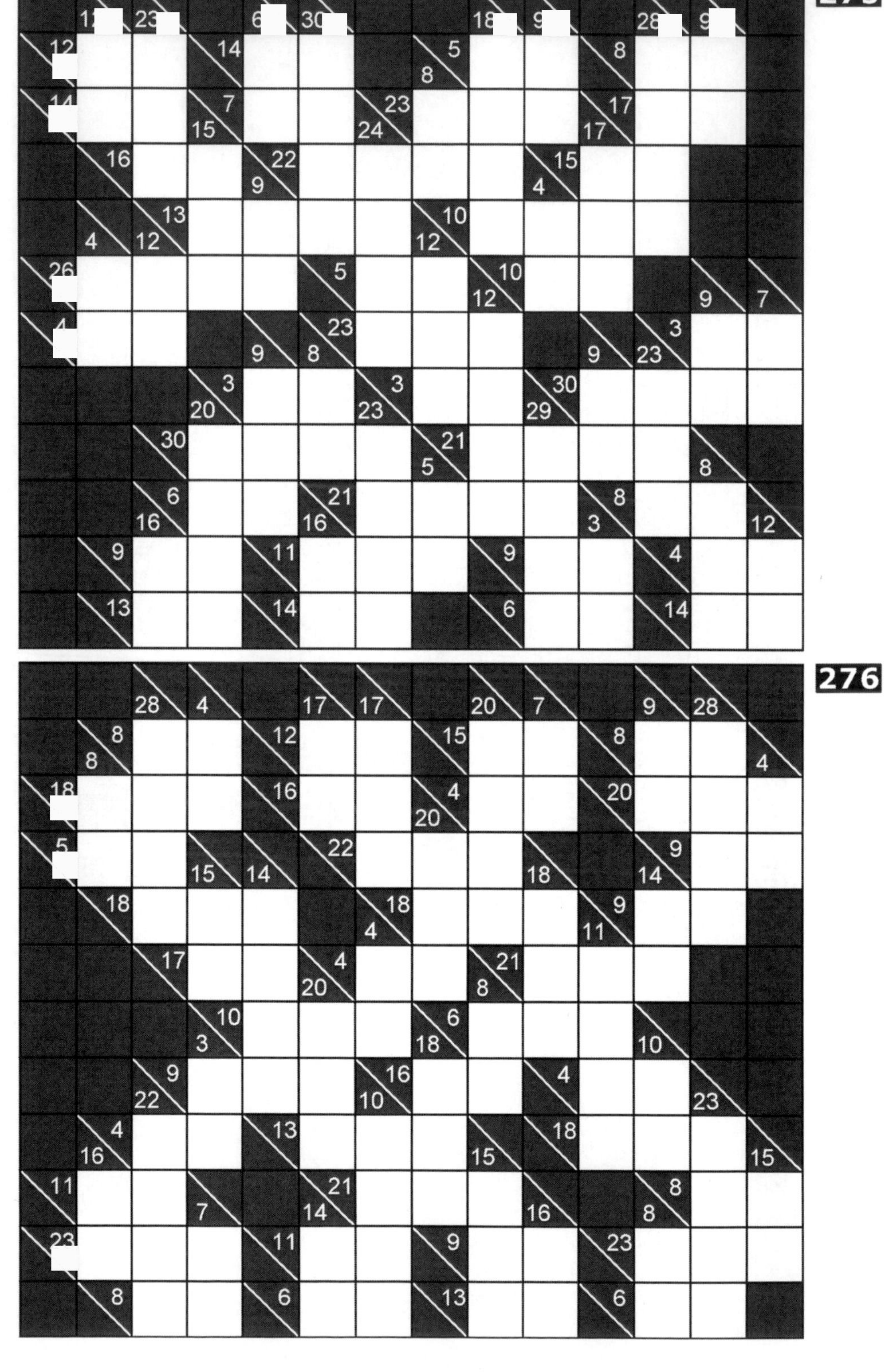

276

277

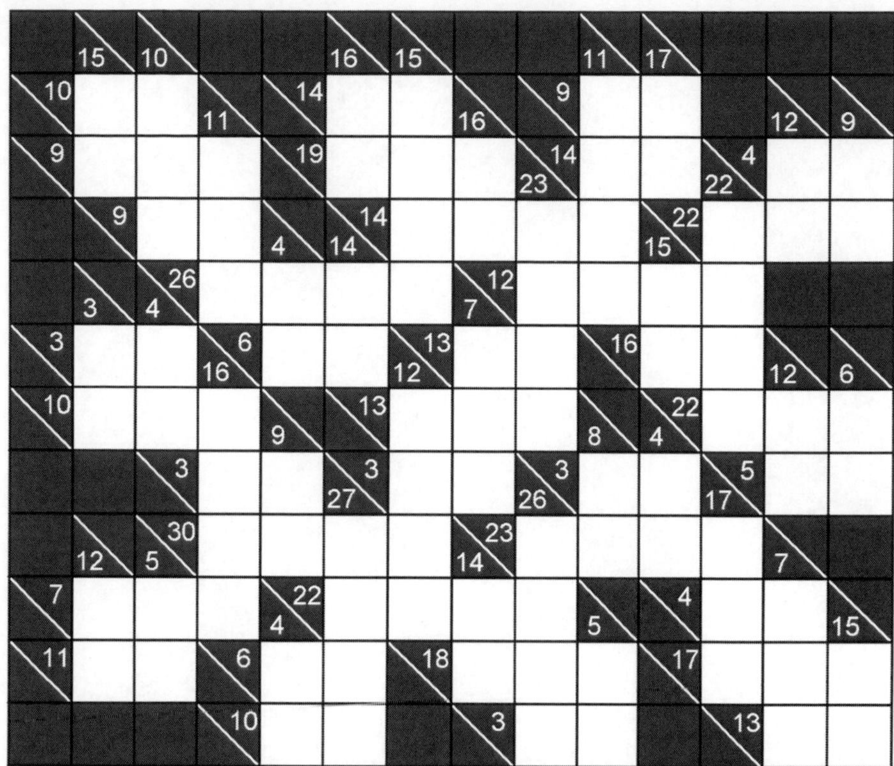

278

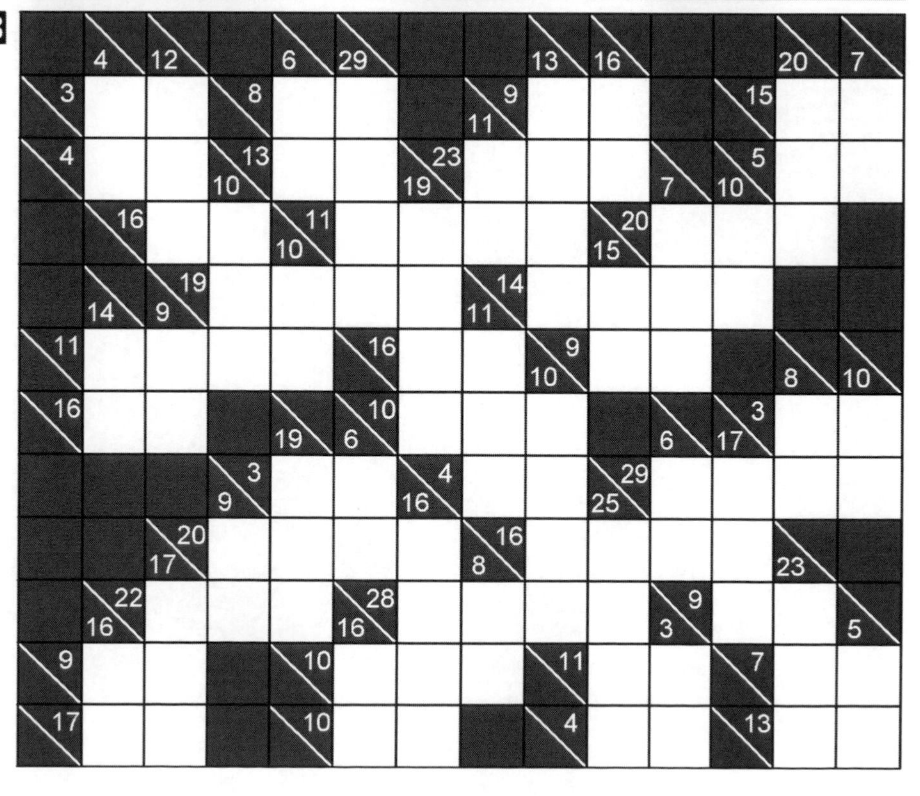

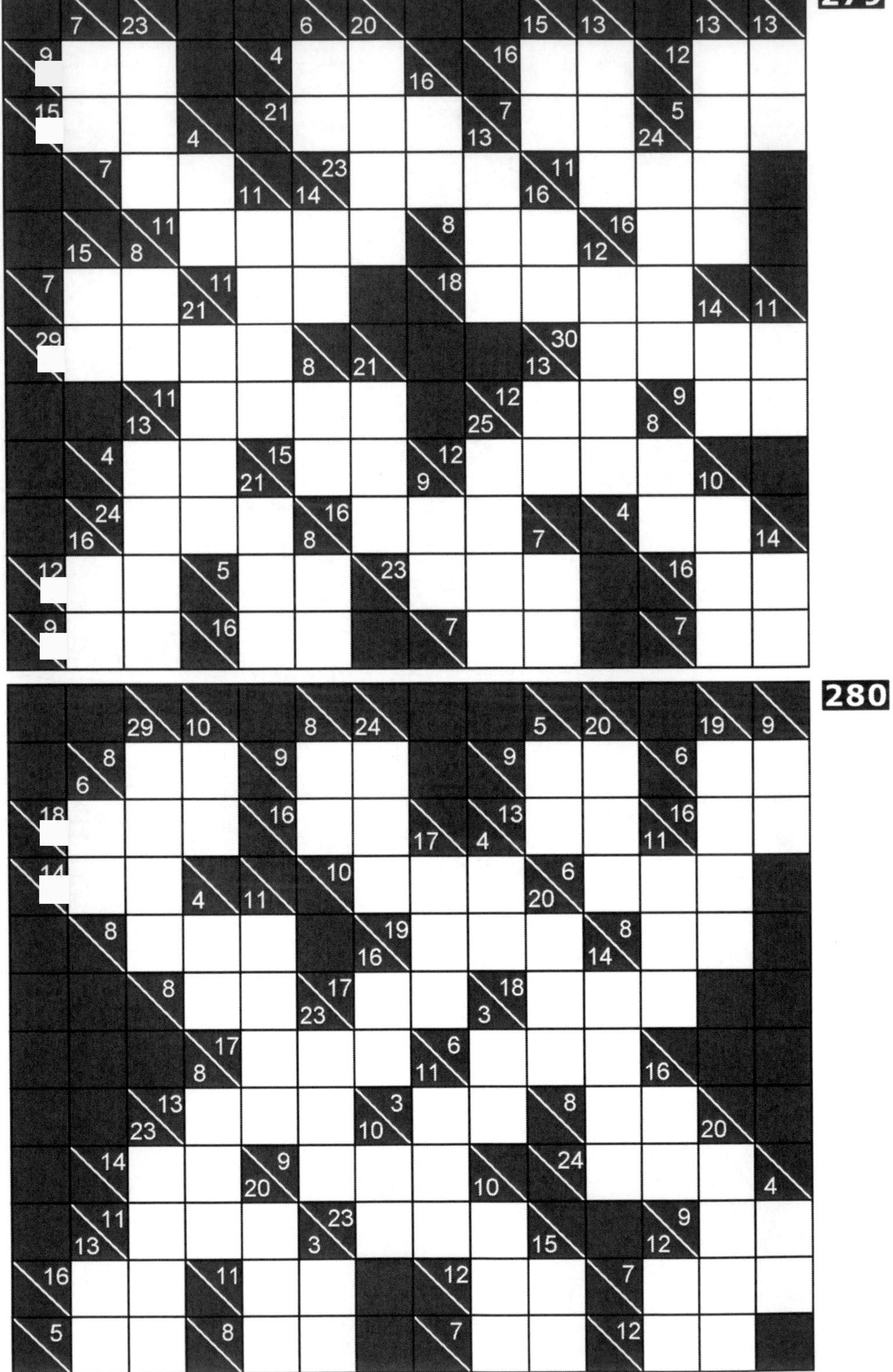
279
280

281

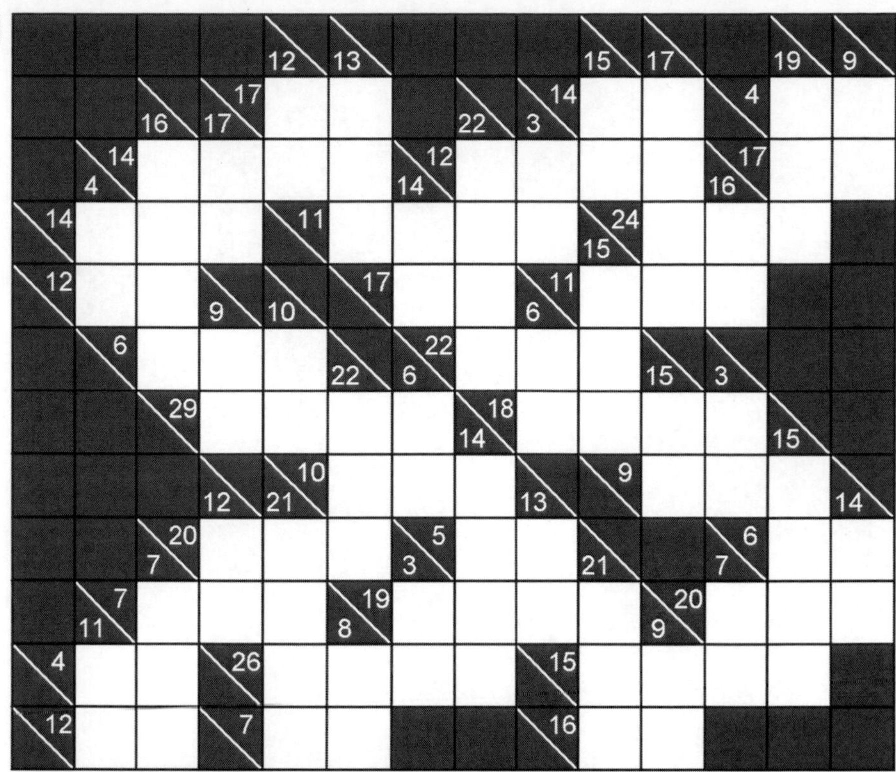

282

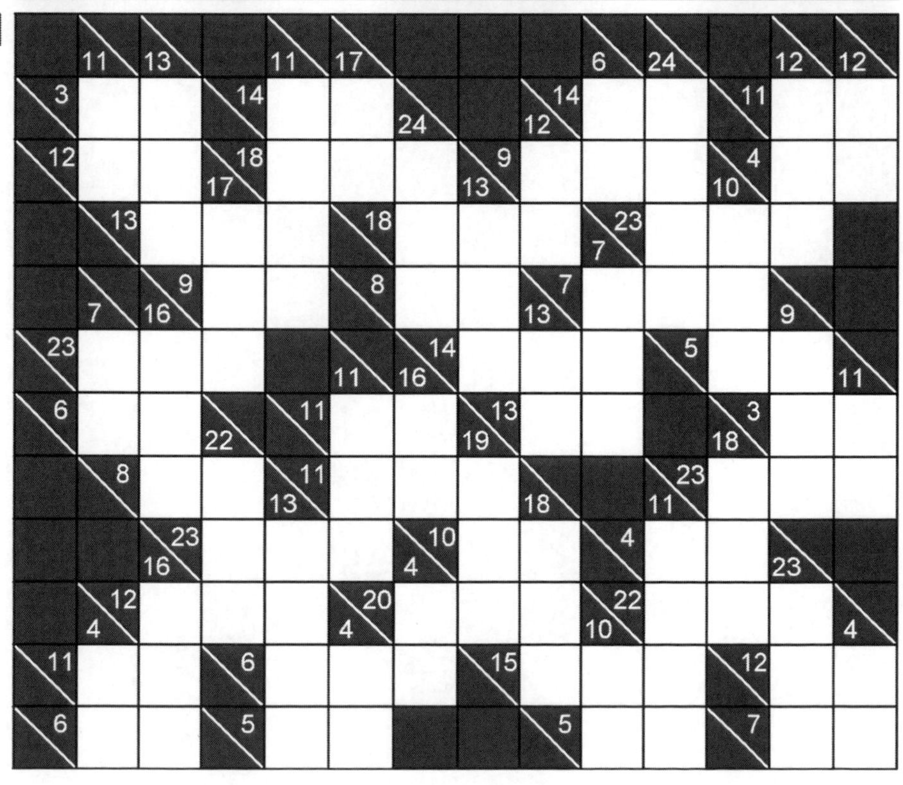

283

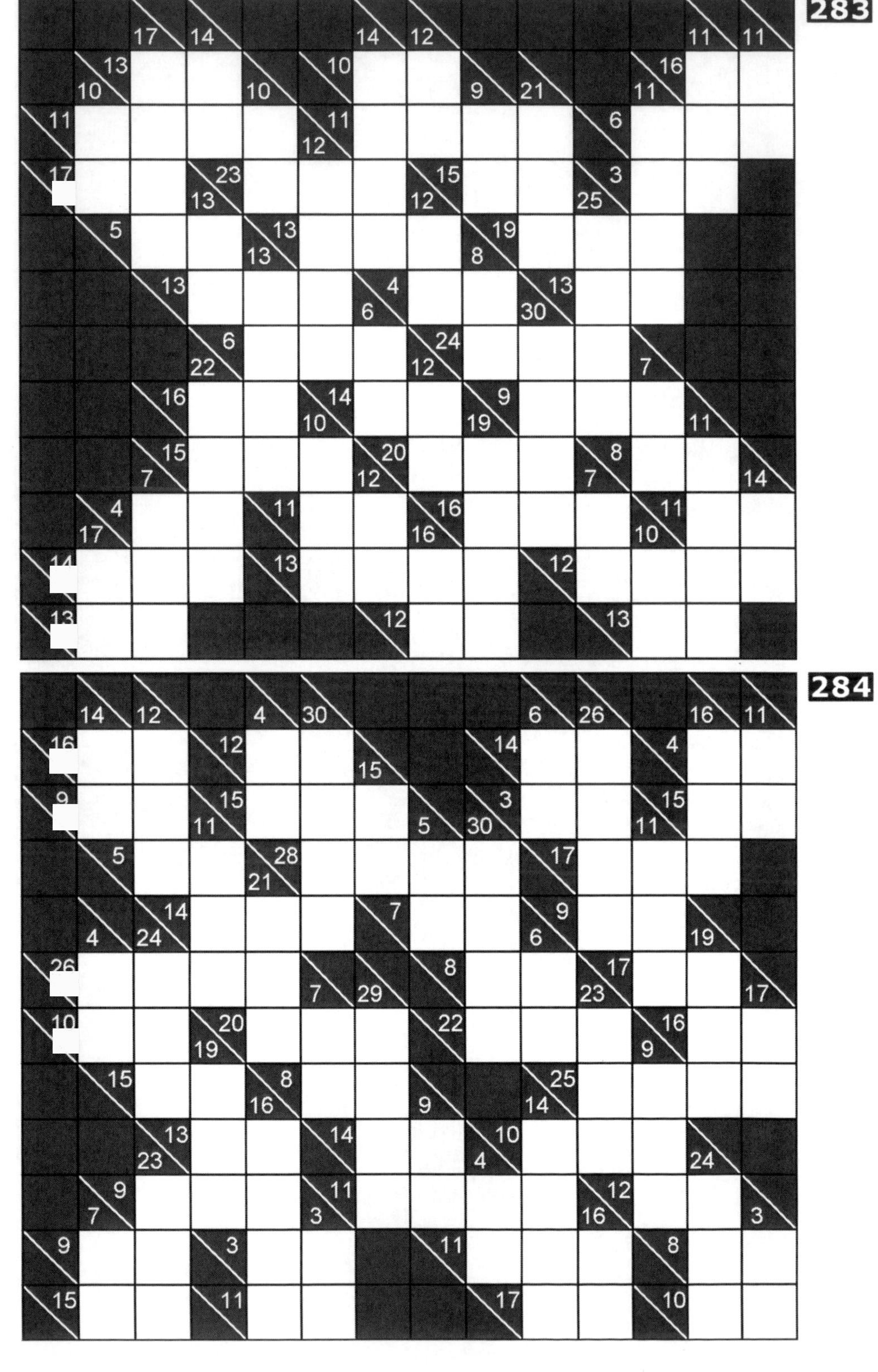
284

285

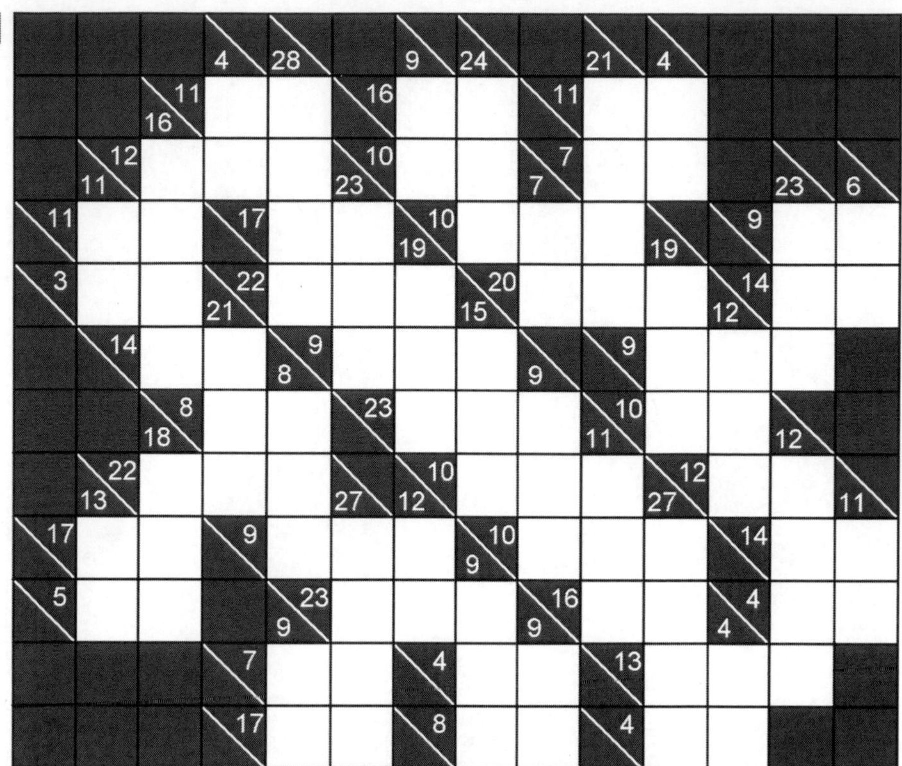

286

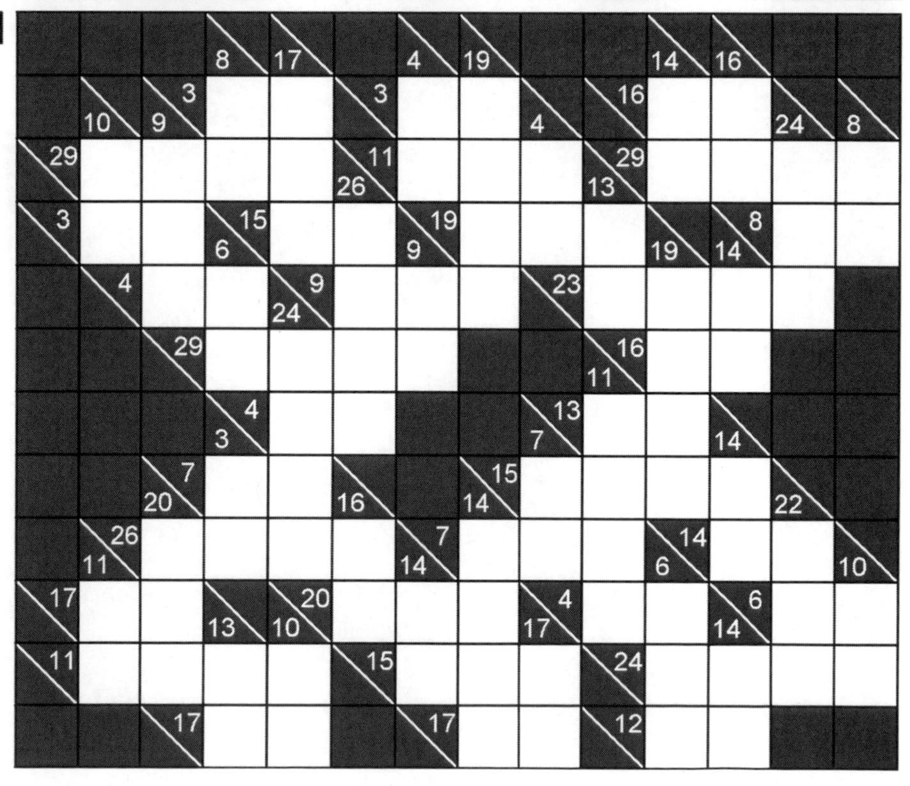

287

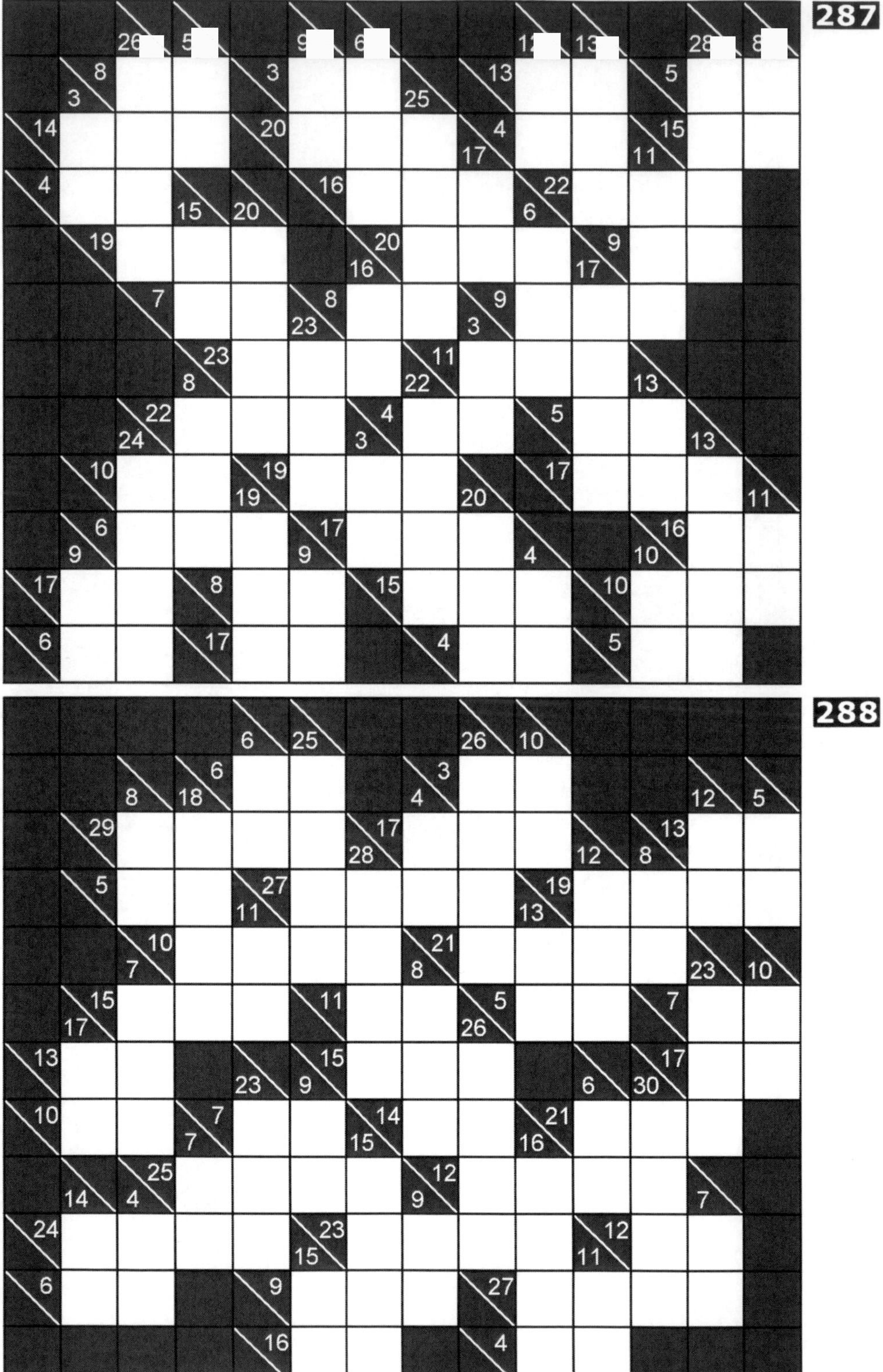
288

289

290

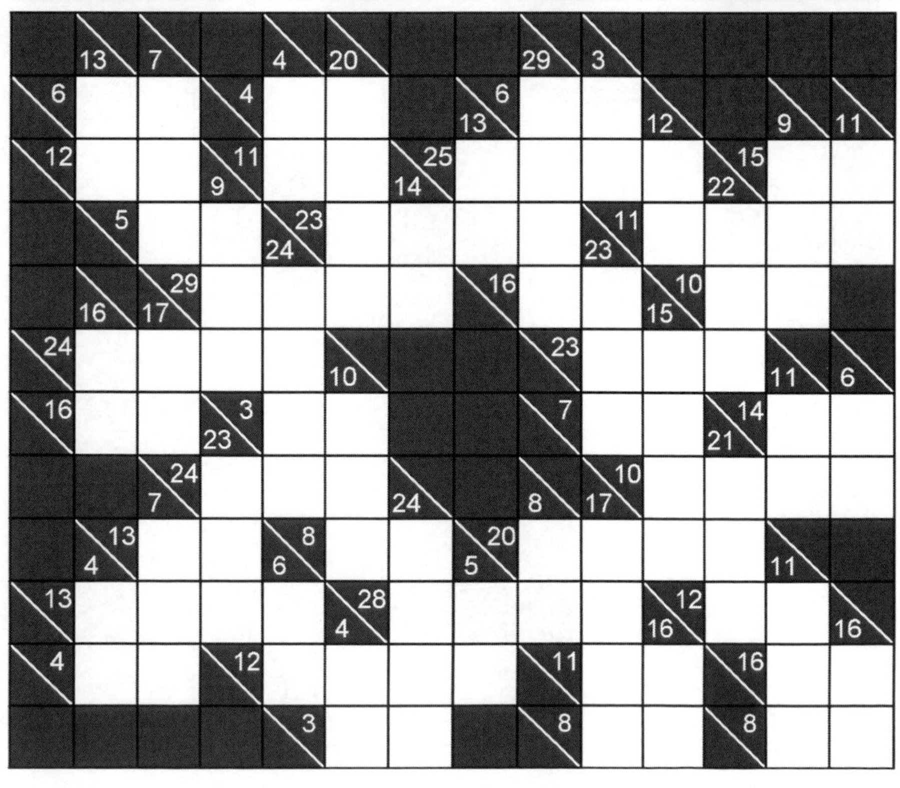

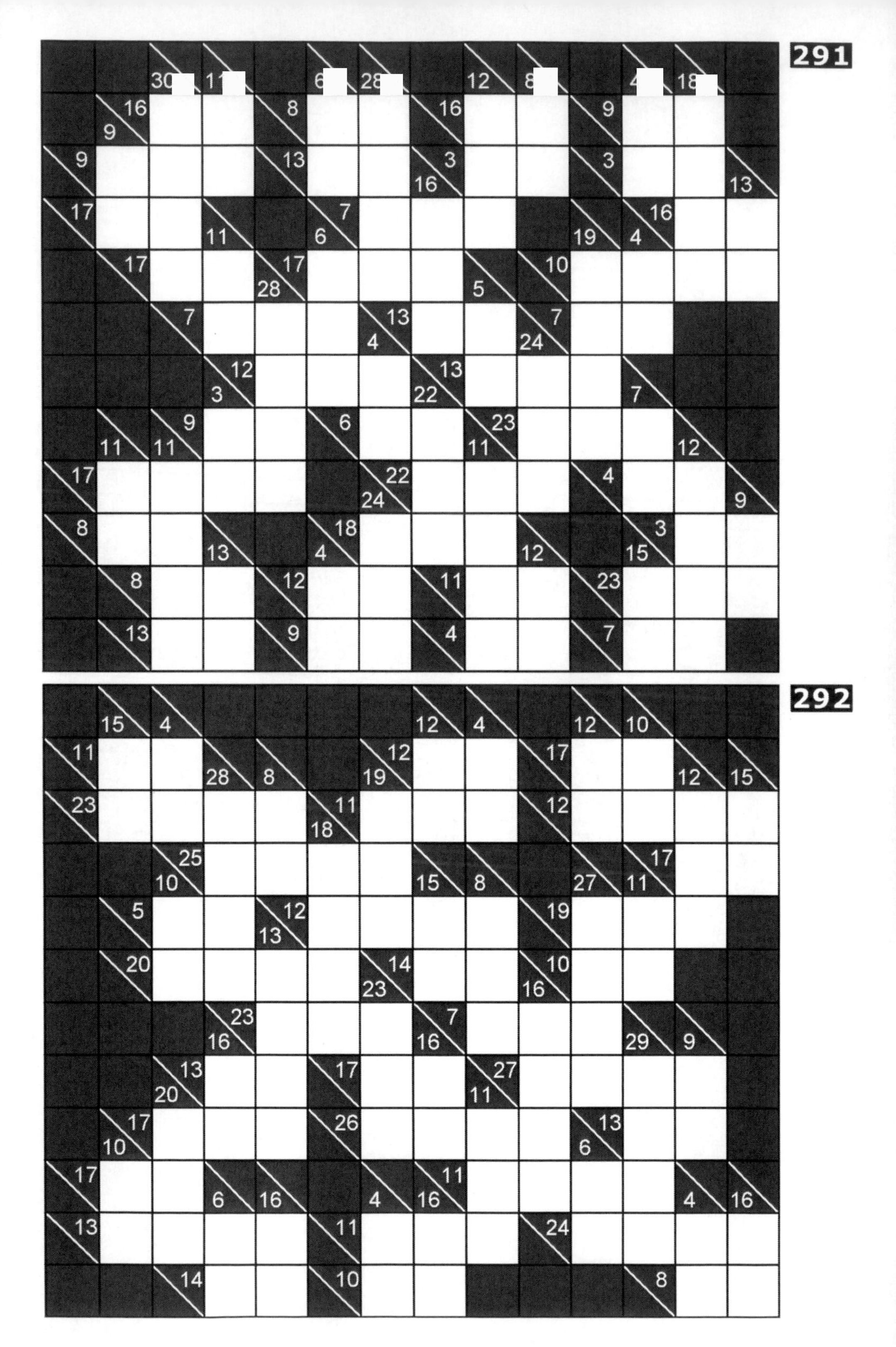

293

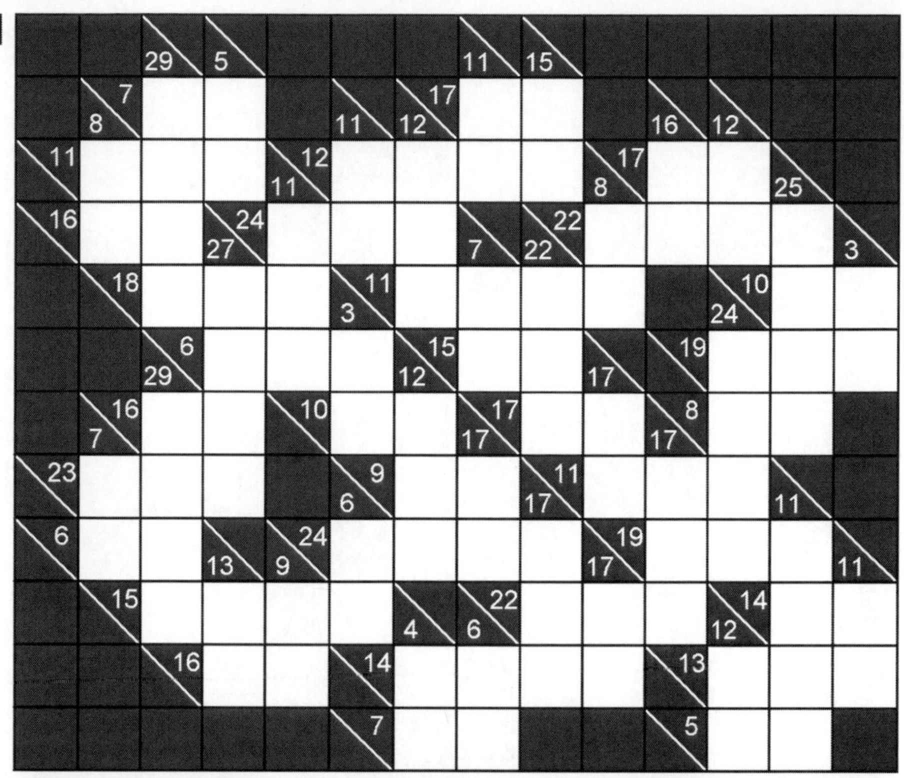

294

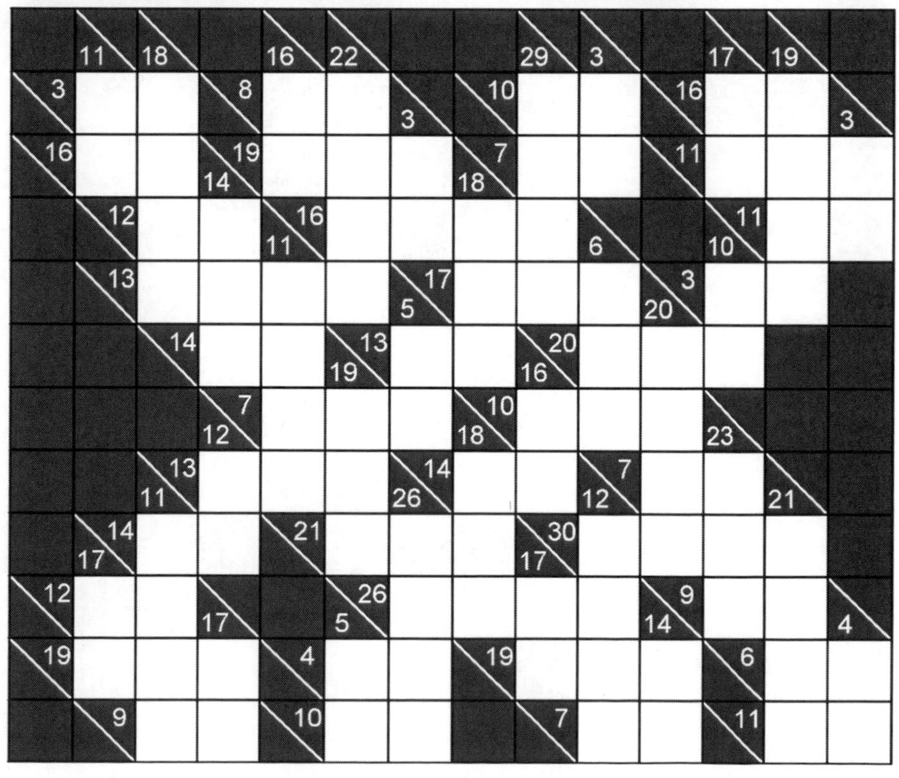

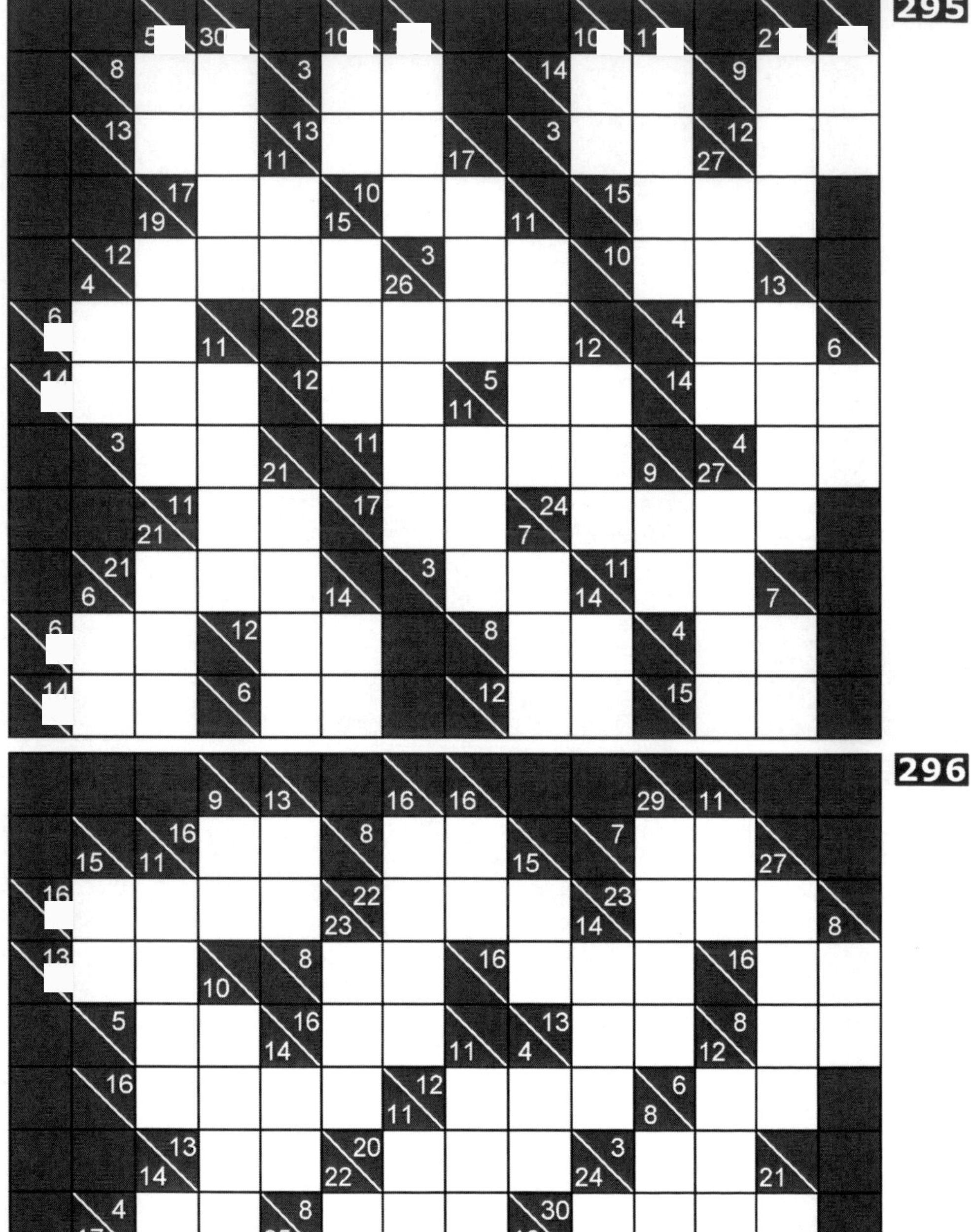

295

296

297

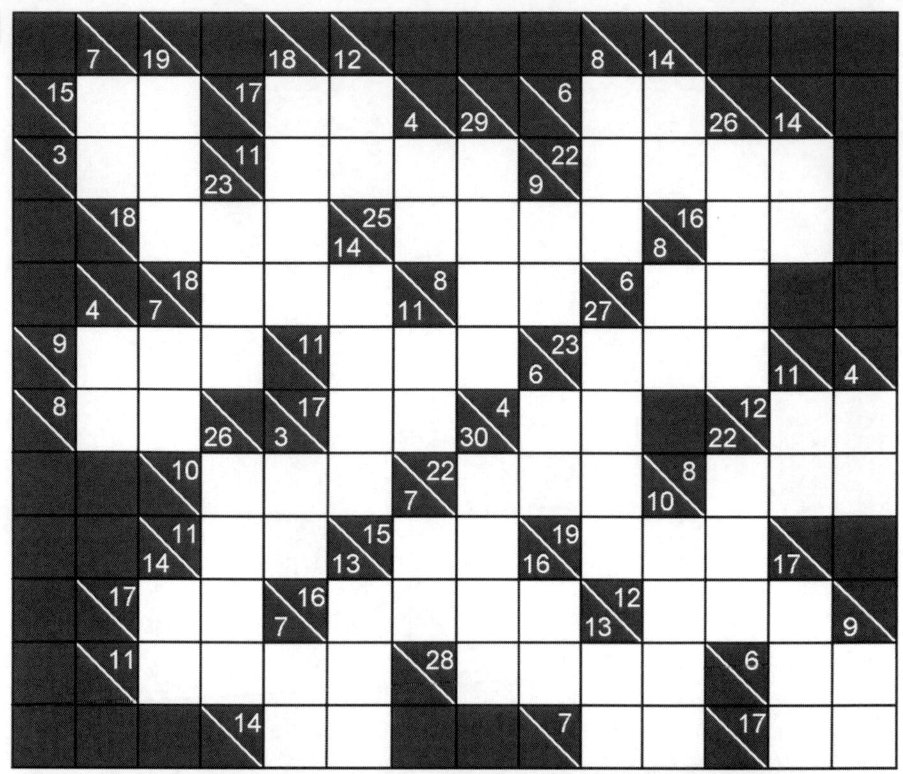

298

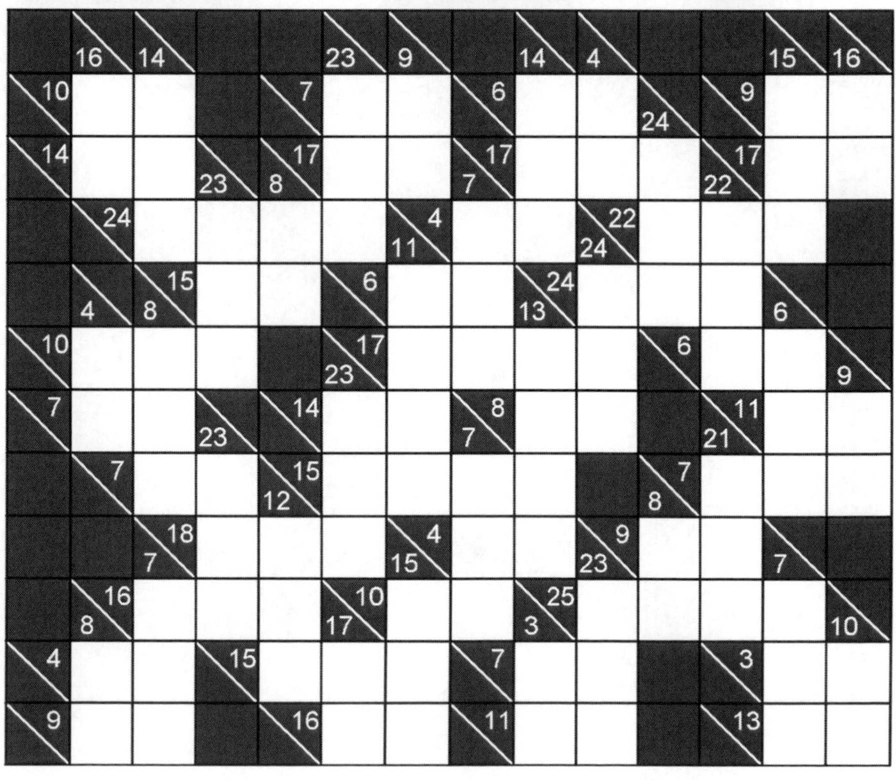

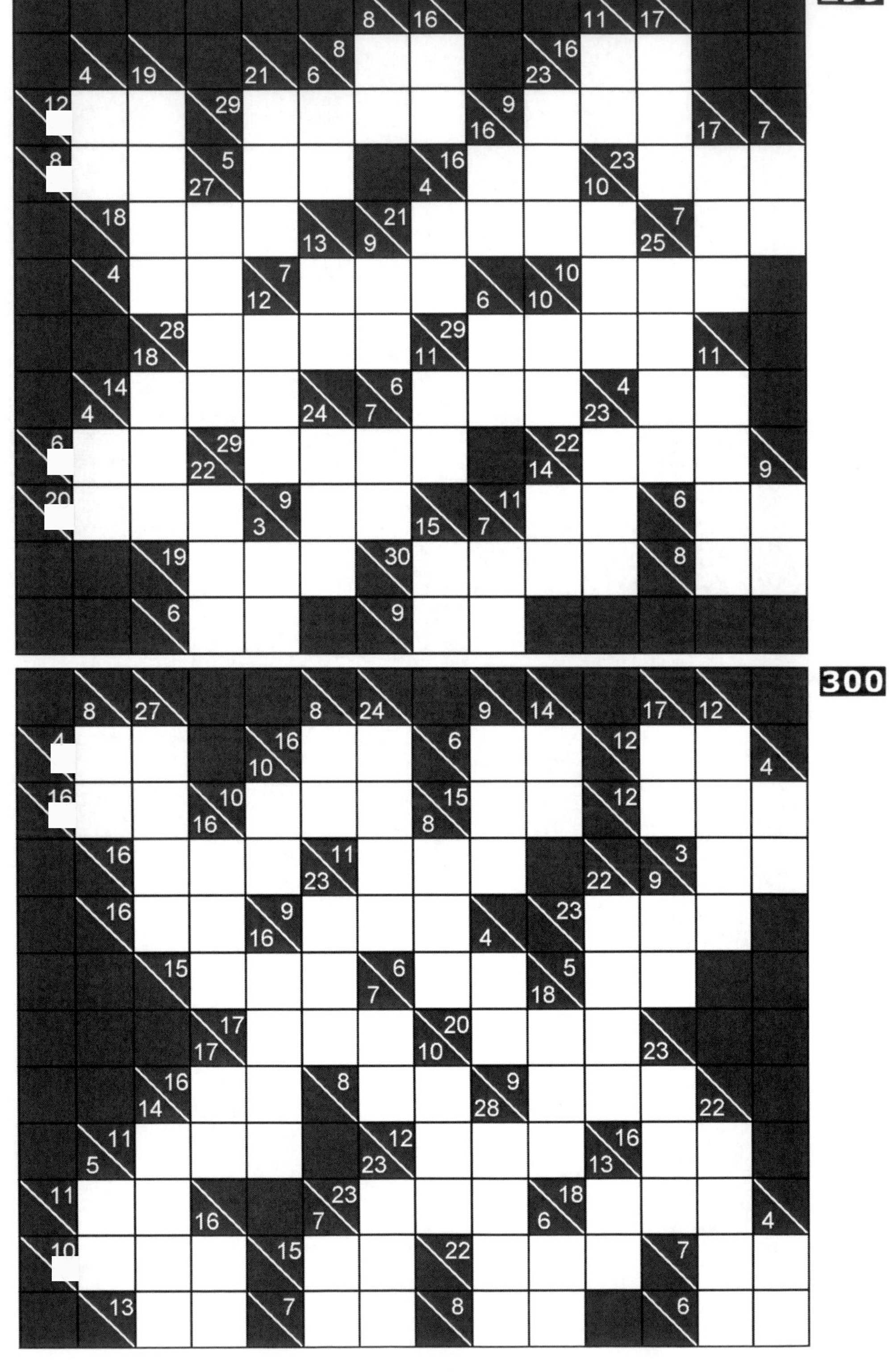

SOLUTIONS

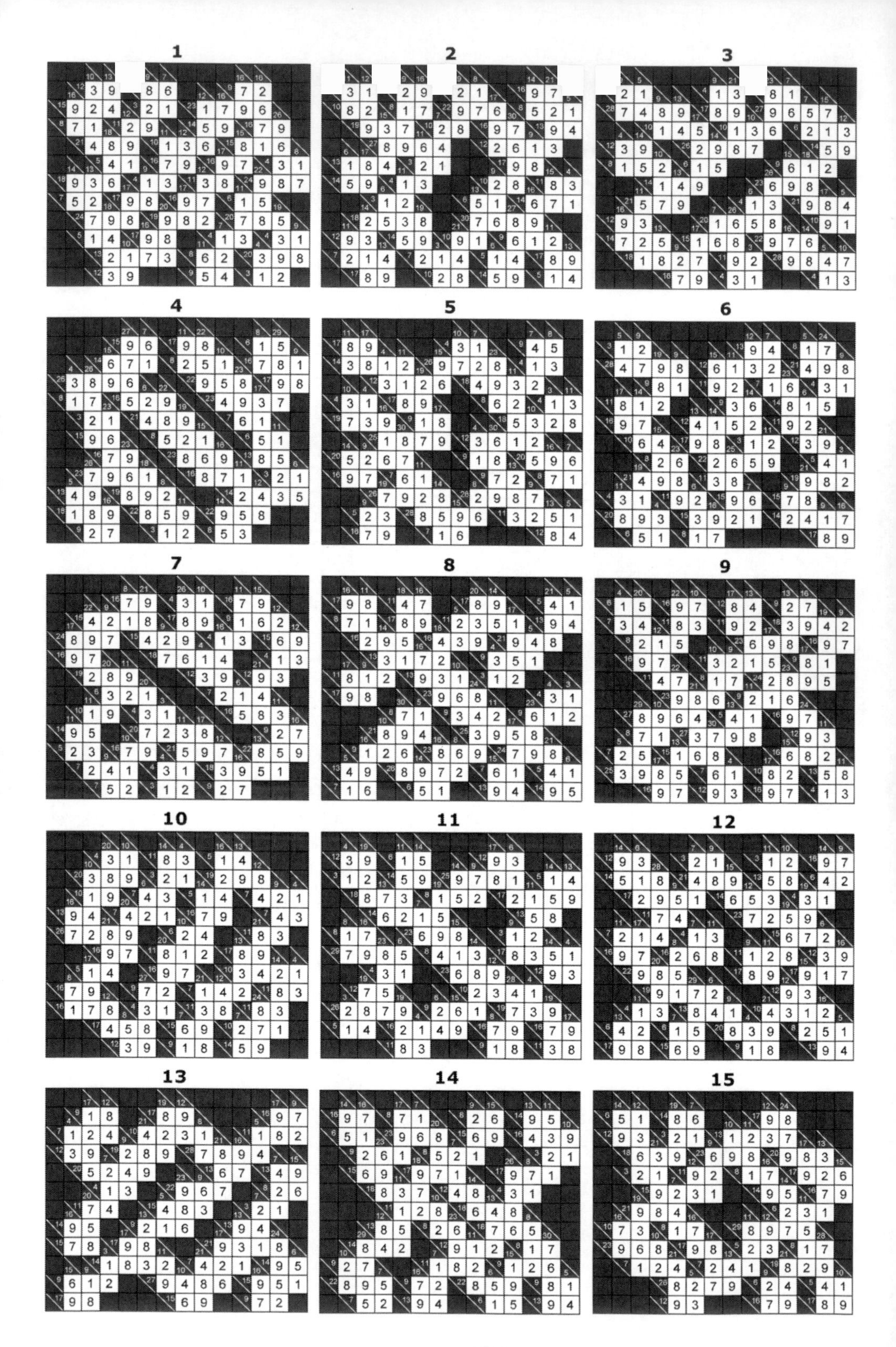

16
17
18
19
20
21
22
23
24
25
26
27
28
29
30

46
47
48
49
50
51
52
53
54
55
56
57
58
59
60

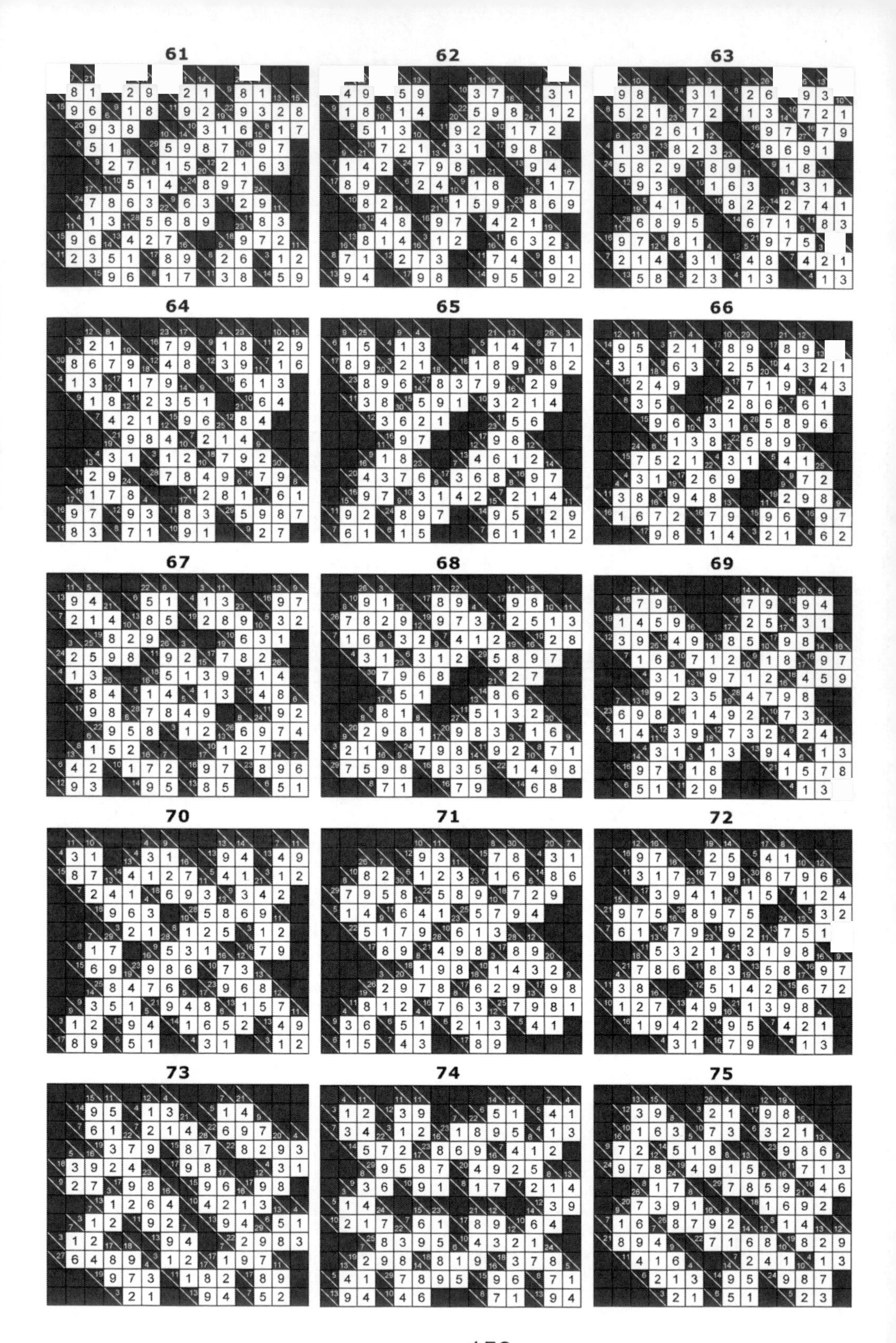

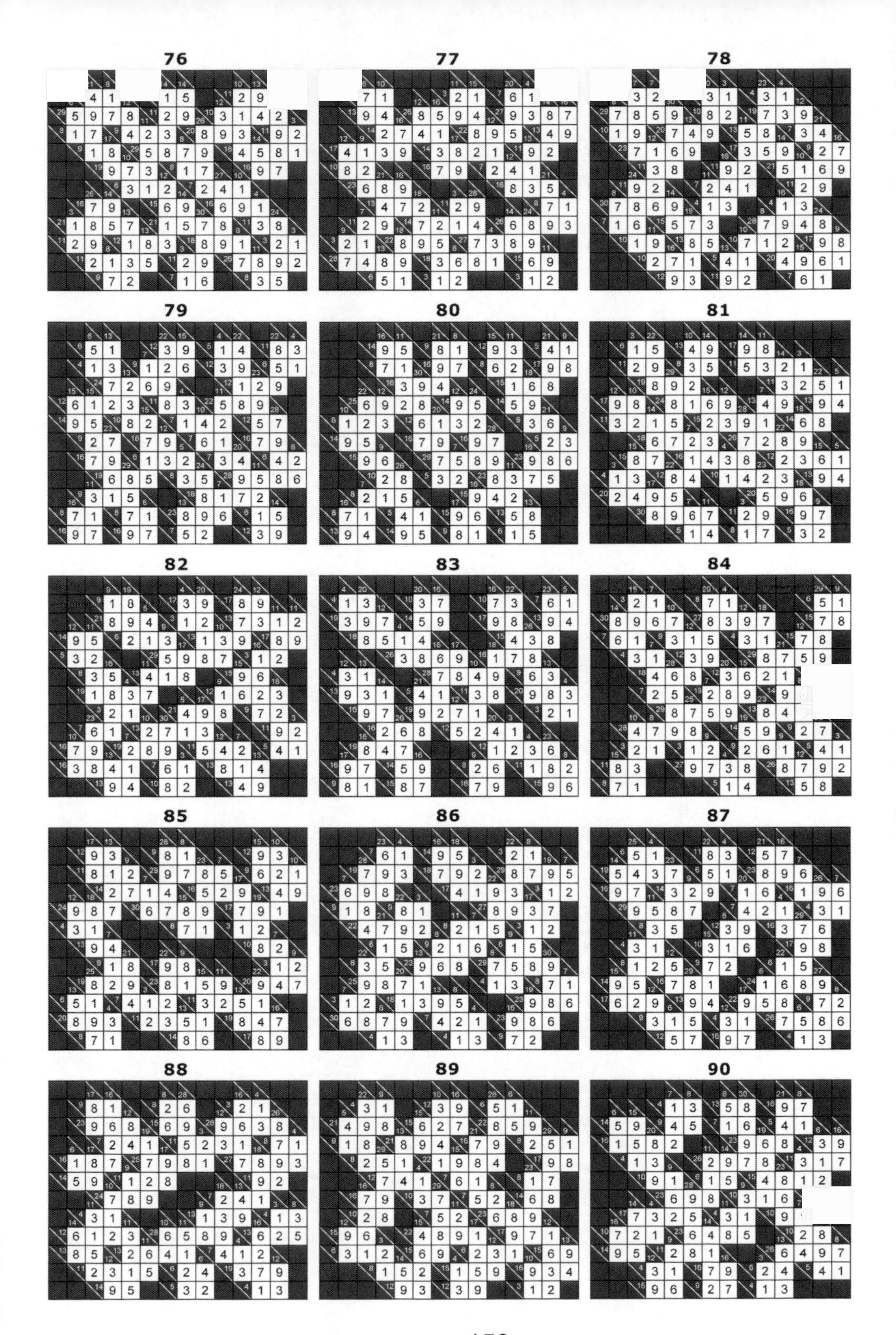
76
77
78
79
80
81
82
83
84
85
86
87
88
89
90

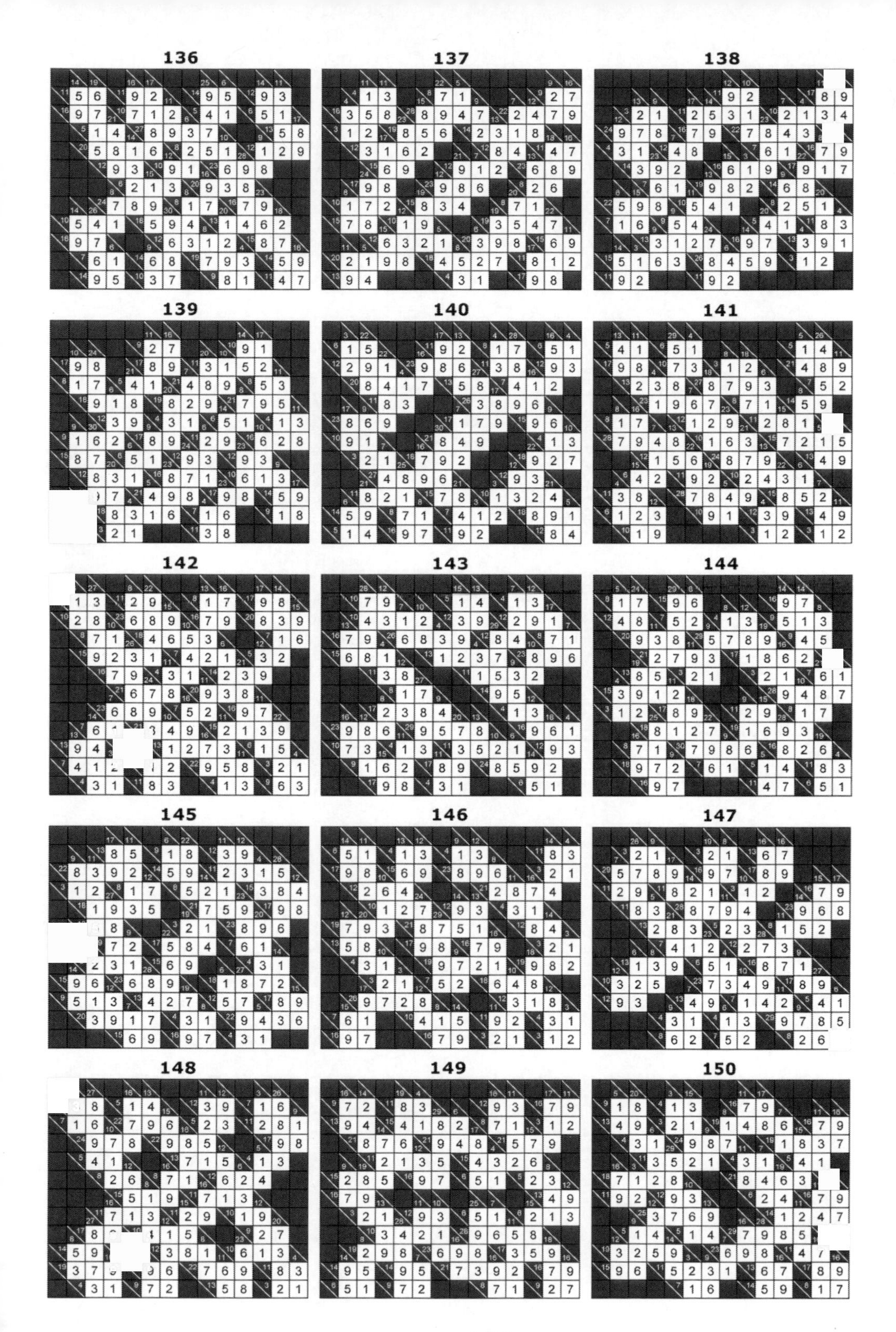

136
137
138
139
140
141
142
143
144
145
146
147
148
149
150

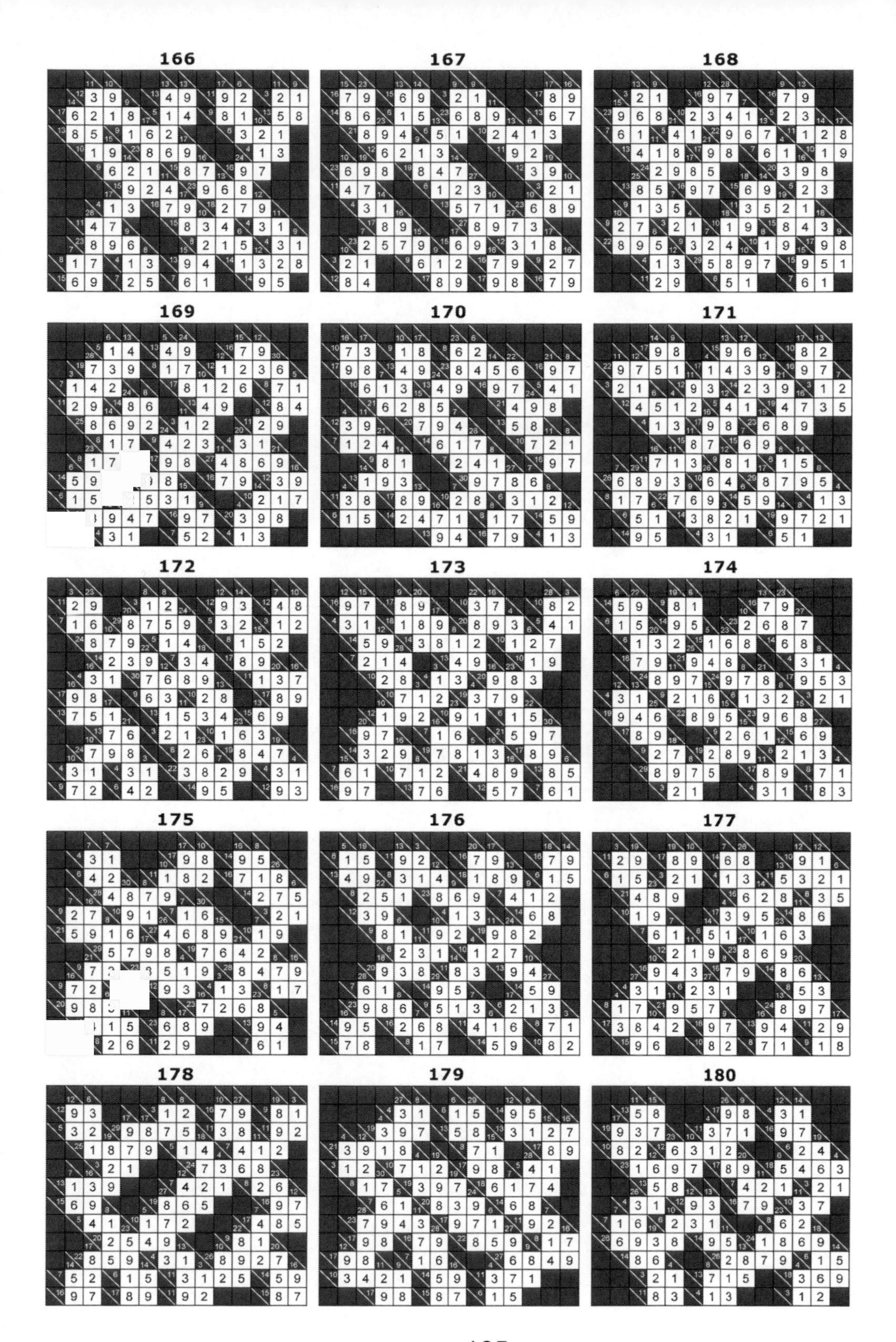

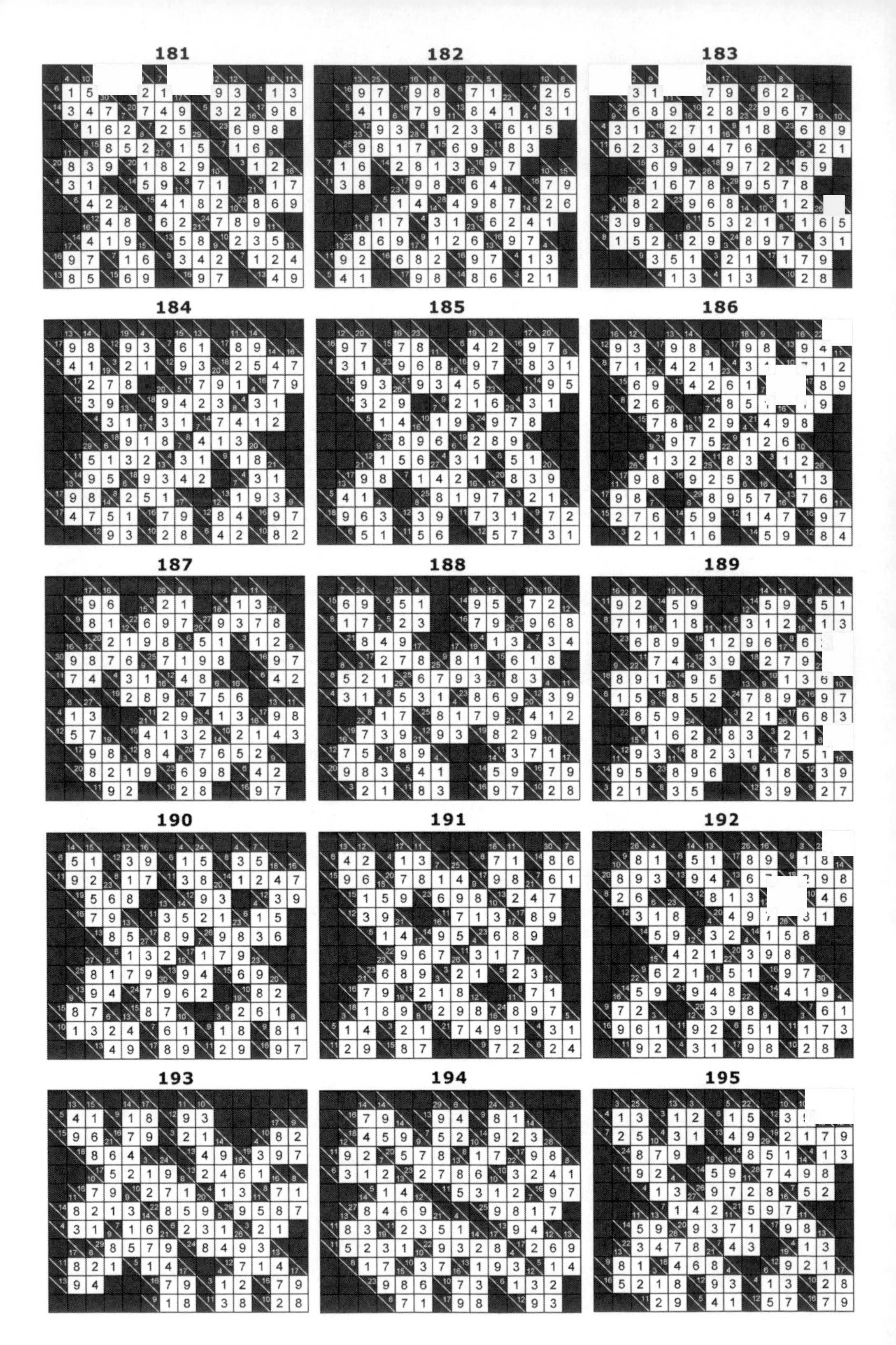

226
227
228
229
230
231
232
233
234
235
236
237
238
239
240

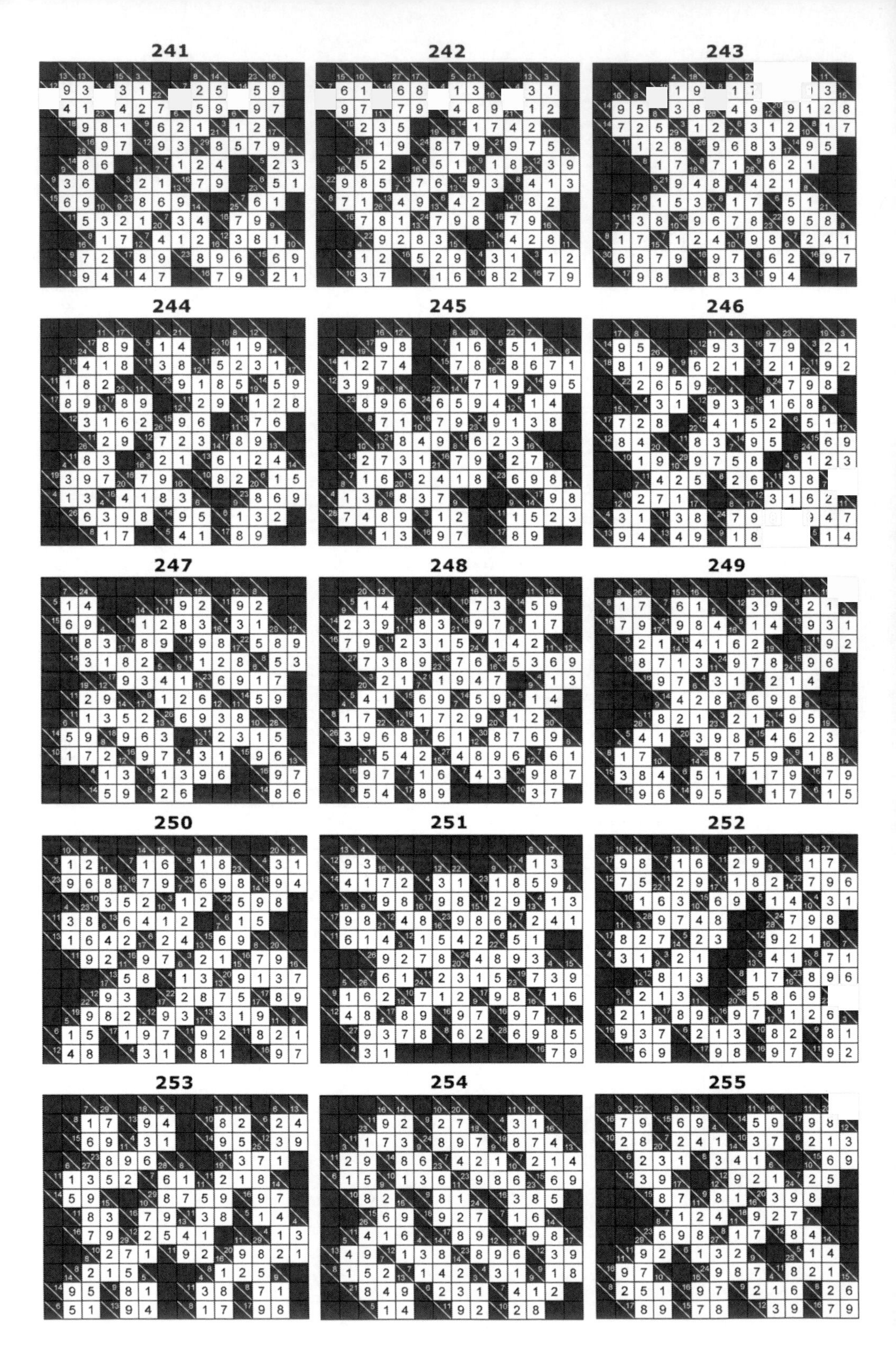

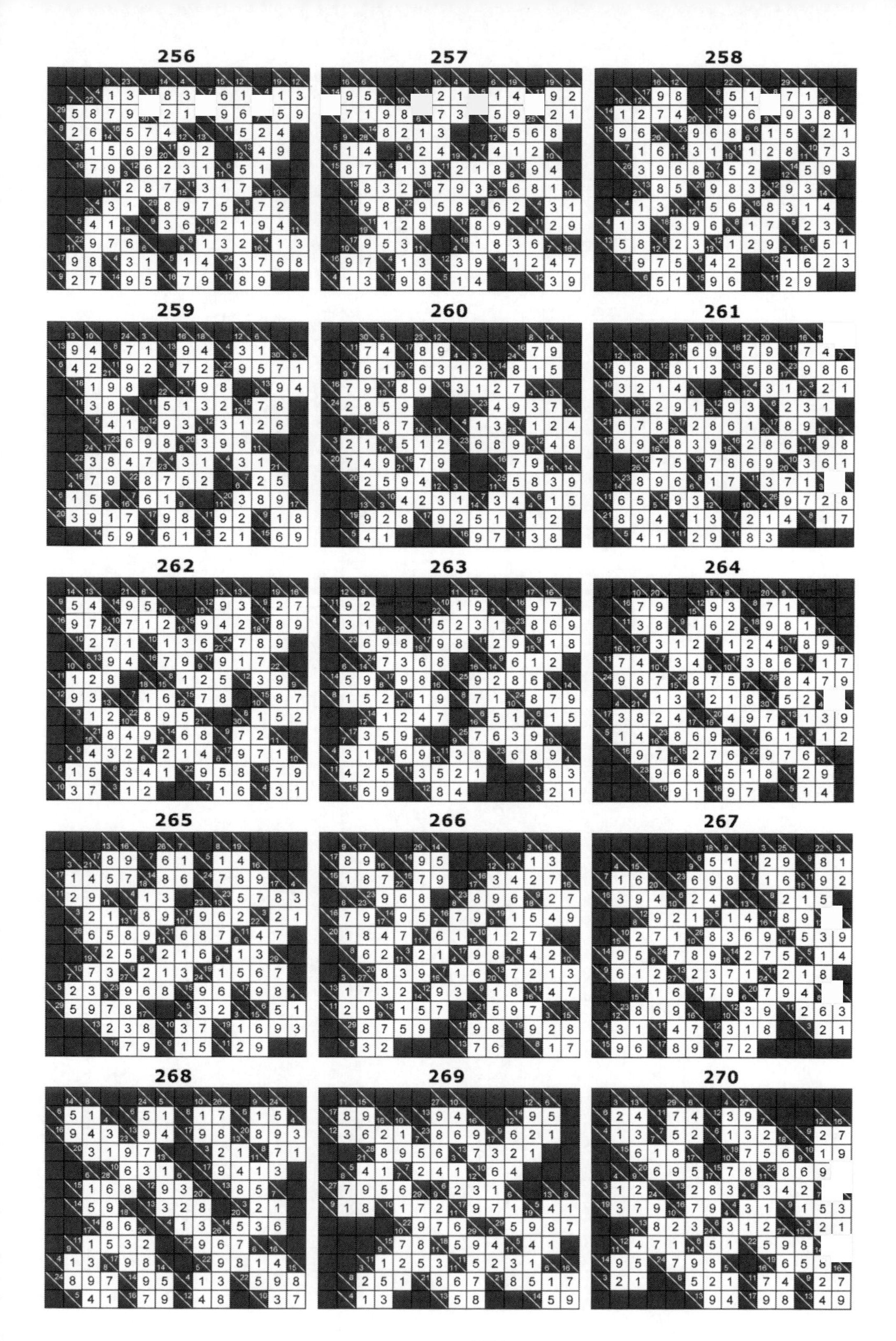

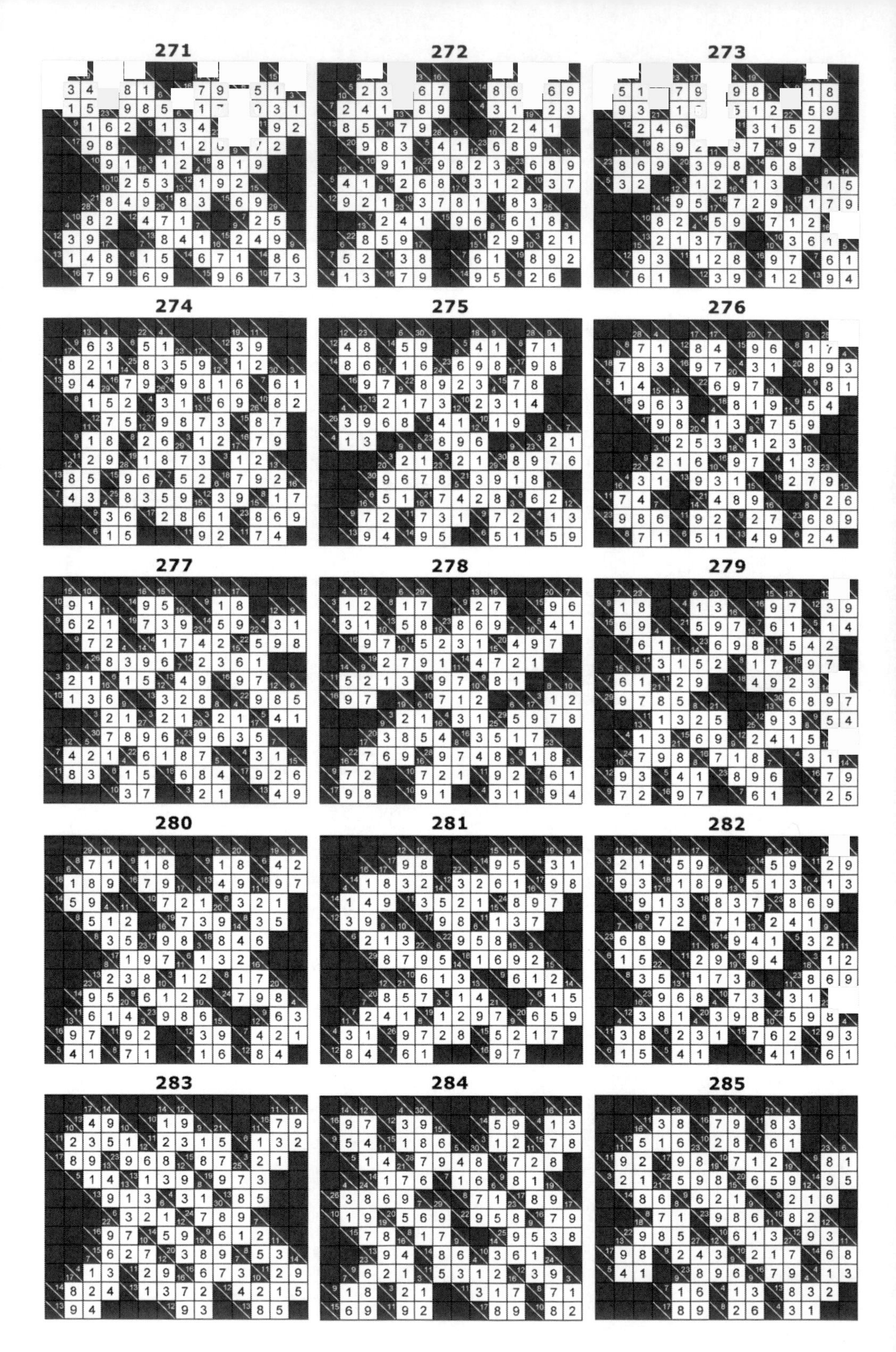

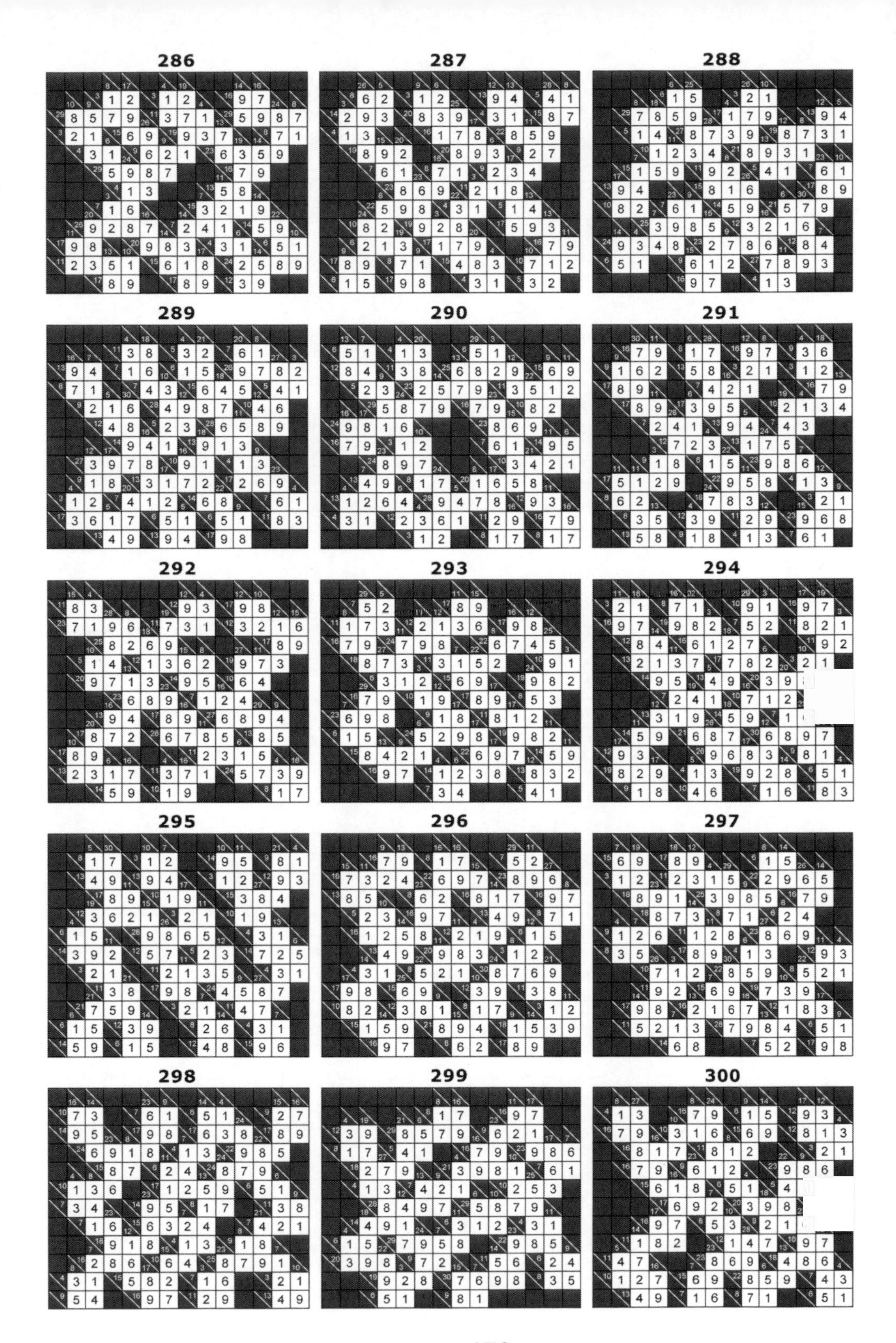
286
287
288
289
290
291
292
293
294
295
296
297
298
299
300

Target Numbers & Cells with only one Combination		
Target Number	Cells	Combination
3	2	12
4	2	13
6	3	123
7	3	124
10	4	1234
11	4	1235
15	5	12345
16	2	79
16	5	12346
17	2	89
21	6	123456
22	6	123457
23	3	689
24	3	789
28	7	1234567
29	4	5789
29	7	1234568
30	4	6789
34	5	46789
35	5	56789
38	6	356789
39	6	456789
41	7	2456789
42	7	3456789
43	8	13456789
44	8	23456789
45	9	123456789

Target Number	Cells	**All Number Combinations**
3	2	12
4	2	13
5	2	14 23
6	2	15 24
6	3	123
7	2	16 25 34
7	3	124
8	2	17 26 35
8	3	125 134
9	2	18 27 36 45
9	3	126 135 234
10	2	19 28 37 46
10	3	127 136 145 235
10	4	1234
11	2	29 38 47 56
11	3	128 137 146 236 245
11	4	1235
12	2	39 48 57
12	3	129 138 147 156 237 246 345
12	4	1236 1245
13	2	49 58 67
13	3	139 148 157 238 247 256 346
13	4	1237 1246 1345
14	2	59 68
14	3	149 158 167 239 248 257 347 356
14	4	1238 1247 1256 1346 2345
15	2	69 78
15	3	159 168 249 258 267 348 357 456
15	4	1239 1248 1257 1347 1356 2346
15	5	12345
16	2	79
16	3	169 178 259 268 349 358 367 457
16	4	1249 1258 1267 1348 1357 1456 2347 2356
16	5	12346

Target Number	Cells	**All Number Combinations**
17	3	179 269 278 359 368 458 467
17	4	1259 1268 1349 1358 1367 1457 2348 2357 2456
17	5	12347 12356
18	3	189 279 369 378 459 468 567
18	4	1269 1278 1359 1368 1458 1467 2349 2358 2367 2457 3456
18	5	12348 12357 12456
19	3	289 379 469 478 568
19	4	1279 1369 1378 1459 1468 1567 2359 2368 2458 2467 3457
19	5	12349 12358 12367 12457 13456
20	3	389 479 569 578
20	4	1289 1379 1469 1478 1568 2369 2378 2459 2468 2567 3458 3467
20	5	12359 12368 12458 12467 13457 23456
21	3	489 579 678
21	4	1389 1479 1569 1578 2379 2469 2478 2568 3459 3468 3567
21	5	12369 12378 12459 12468 12567 13458 13467 23457
21	6	123456
22	3	589 679
22	4	1489 1579 1678 2389 2479 2569 2578 3469 3478 3568 4567
22	5	12379 12469 12478 12568 13459 13468 13567 23458 23467
22	6	123457
23	3	689
23	4	1589 1679 2489 2579 2678 3479 3569 3578 4568
23	5	12389 12479 12569 12578 13469 13478 13568 14567 23459 23468 23567
23	6	123458 123467
24	3	789
24	4	1689 2589 2679 3489 3579 3678 4569 4578

Target Number	Cells	**All Number Combinations**
24	6	123459 123468 123567
25	5	12589 12679 13489 13579 13678 14569 14578 23479 23569 23578 24568 34567
25	6	123469 123478 123568 124567
26	4	2789 3689 4589 4679 5678
26	5	12689 13589 13679 14579 14678 23489 23579 23678 24569 24578 34568
26	6	123479 123569 123578 124568 134567
27	4	3789 4689 5679
27	5	12789 13689 14589 14679 15678 23589 23679 24579 24678 34569 34578
27	6	123489 123579 123678 124569 124578 134568 234567
28	4	4789 5689
28	5	13789 14689 15679 23689 24589 24679 25678 34579 34678
28	6	123589 123679 124579 124678 134569 134578 234568
28	7	1234567
29	4	5789
29	5	14789 15689 23789 24689 25679 34589 34679 35678
29	6	123689 124589 124679 125678 134579 134678 234569 234578
29	7	1234568
30	4	6789
30	5	15789 24789 25689 34689 35679 45678
30	6	123789 124689 125679 134589 134679 135678 234579 234678
30	7	1234569 1234578
31	5	16789 25789 34789 35689 45679
31	6	124789 125689 134689 135679 145678 234589 234679 235678
31	7	1234579 1234678
32	5	26789 35789 45689

Target Number	Cells	**All Number Combinations**
32	6	125789 134789 135689 145679 234689 235679 245678
32	7	1234589 1234679 1235678
33	6	126789 135789 145689 234789 235689 245679 345678
33	7	1234689 1235679 1245678
34	5	46789
34	6	136789 145789 235789 245689 345679
34	7	1234789 1235689 1245679 1345678
35	5	56789
35	6	146789 236789 245789 345689
35	7	1235789 1245689 1345679 2345678
36	6	156789 246789 345789
36	7	1236789 1245789 1345689 2345679
36	8	12345678
37	6	256789 346789
37	7	1246789 1345789 2345689
37	8	12345679
38	6	356789
38	7	1256789 1346789 2345789
38	8	12345689
39	6	456789
39	7	1356789 2346789
39	8	12345789
40	7	1456789 2356789
40	8	12346789
41	7	2456789
41	8	12356789
42	7	3456789
42	8	12456789
43	8	13456789
44	8	23456789
45	9	123456789

More Books By Christian Demarco

Easy - Volumes 1-5

Medium - Volumes 1-5

Hard - Volumes 1-5

Many more books available
Search Amazon for Christian Demarco

Amazon.com/author/christian-demarco

Easy - Volumes 1-10

Medium - Volumes 1-10

Hard - Volumes 1-10

www.christian-demarco.com